BEYOND A REASONABLE DOUBT?

BEYOND A REASONABLE DOUBT?

The Original Trial of Caryl Chessman

BY WILLIAM M. KUNSTLER

GREENWOOD PRESS, PUBLISHERS
WESTPORT, CONNECTICUT

Library of Congress Cataloging in Publication Data

Chessman, Caryl, 1921–1960, defendant.
  Beyond a reasonable doubt?

    Reprint of the ed. published by Morrow, New York.
    Proceedings in the trial of Caryl Chessman for
robbery, kidnapping, attempted rape, etc. in the
California Superior Court of Los Angeles County,
Apr. 29–May 21, 1948.
    1. Chessman, Caryl, 1921–1960. I. Kunstler,
William Moses, 1919–   ed. II. California.
Superior Court (Los Angeles Co.) III. Title.
[KF224.C4K84 1973]   345'.794'025   73–8155
ISBN 0–8371–6951–8

Originally published in 1961 by William Morrow and Company, New York

Reprinted with the permission of William Morrow and Company, Inc., Publishers

Reprinted by Greenwood Press, Inc.

First Greenwood reprinting 1973
Second Greenwood reprinting 1977

Library of Congress catalog card number 73-8155
ISBN 0-8371-6951-8

Printed in the United States of America

"A defendant in a criminal action is presumed to be innocent until the contrary is proved, and in case of a reasonable doubt whether his guilt is satisfactorily shown, he is entitled to an acquittal, but the effect of this presumption is only to place upon the State the burden of proving him guilty beyond a reasonable doubt. Reasonable doubt is defined as follows: It is not a mere possible doubt; because everything relating to human affairs, and depending on moral evidence, is open to some possible or imaginary doubt. It is that state of the case which, after the entire comparison and consideration of all the evidence, leaves the minds of the jurors in that condition that they cannot say they feel an abiding conviction, to a moral certainty, of the truth of the charge."

An excerpt from Judge Charles W. Fricke's
charge to the Chessman jury,
May 20, 1948.

TABLE OF CONTENTS

To Karin and Jane

INTRODUCTION

The Chessman case was unique in American criminal juris-
prudence. When it began on January 24, 1948, it had all the
earmarks of just another run-of-the-mine felony prosecution.
Except in Los Angeles, where it enjoyed a momentary noto-
riety, it went largely unnoticed in the nation's press. Before
it ended, more than twelve years later, the Queen of Bel-
gium, Dr. Albert Schweitzer, Pablo Casals, Aldous Huxley
and the Vatican had joined millions throughout the world
in protesting the execution of a man who had, by his literary
and legal skills, succeeded in making himself a dramatic sym-
bol in the perennial struggle against capital punishment as
an instrument of law enforcement.

Carol Whittier Chessman—he later affected the fancier
"Caryl"—was born in the front bedroom of a small frame
house in St. Joseph, Michigan, on May 27, 1921. Several
weeks after his birth, the obstetrician who had delivered the
eight-pound blond infant warned his mother that it would be
extremely dangerous for her to have another child. In the
fall, because of the precarious state of Mrs. Chessman's health,
the family migrated to Southern California, where they rented
a home on Greensward Road in Glendale.

When the boy was five years old, he almost died from a
siege of pneumonia that kept him out of school for more
than three months. A year later, he contracted bronchial

asthma and his parents moved to Pasadena in an effort to find a more sympathetic climate for their sickly son. The new neighborhood agreed with him and he began to study the piano, for which he showed an amazing aptitude, but had to give it up when an attack of encephalitis the following summer left him completely tone-deaf.

In 1929, a car in which he and his mother were riding was involved in a collision at a busy Los Angeles intersection. In addition to a fractured skull, Mrs. Chessman had two crushed vertebrae and she was permanently paralyzed from the waist down. Caryl, who had been sitting in the auto's back seat, appeared to be uninjured until X-rays revealed that he had broken both his nose and his jaw.

The resultant drain on the family finances forced the boy's father to give up the Pasadena house and rent an apartment in one of Glendale's poorer sections. After two years of living from hand to mouth, Mr. Chessman finally gave up and put his family on the relief rolls. In 1936, Caryl caught diphtheria and was sent to the county hospital from which he was finally released with a recommendation that he spend the next six months in bed.

When he recovered, he obtained an early morning paper route and began to pilfer groceries which had been delivered to the rear doors of neighborhood shops. He soon graduated to minor burglaries, forgeries and car thefts. Finally, he was caught redhanded rifling a butcher's cash register and taken to the Glendale police station, from which he escaped by leaping out of an open window. In the summer of 1937, he was picked up on a stolen car charge and sent to a county forestry camp. After running away twice, he was committed to the Preston State Industrial School at Ione in late September.

The following April, the judge who had committed him suddenly ordered his unconditional release. One month later, he stole the Pasadena postmaster's automobile, complete with gasoline credit card, and began a new career of holding up houses of prostitution in the Hollywood Hills area. Early on the morning of his seventeenth birthday, he was arrested in front of a Glendale drugstore by two radio policemen. There were jimmy marks on the druggist's front door, and the postmaster's Ford was parked at the curb. Five days later, he was recommitted to Preston for vehicle theft and forgery.

In June of 1939, with ten dollars and a ticket to Los Angeles in his pocket, he was released from the reformatory. He returned home to find that his parents now occupied a stucco home on Glendale's Larga Avenue. In its two-car garage, his father had gone into business for himself making window shades and venetian blinds. Two weeks later, the youth was arrested for stealing a gas cap and sentenced to ten days in the Los Angeles County Jail. On Friday, October 13, he was again picked up in a stolen car. He pleaded guilty and was given a six-month term on Road Camp No. 7 in the mountains overlooking Malibu Beach.

He was paroled on June 30, 1940 and, after an unsuccessful attempt to join the Army, began working for his father. Before the summer was out, he had met a girl and eloped with her to Las Vegas. The couple rented a third-floor apartment in Glendale and the brand-new husband was soon busy recruiting a small army of Preston alumni who were interested in holding up Los Angeles stores. Just after New Year's, he and two cronies were surprised by a radio car while they were parked in a stolen Buick in the Flintridge Hills. They disarmed the policemen and drove off in their patrol car. Before abandoning it on a residential street, they used it to pull two curbside robberies.

On January 16, he and a friend stole a Packard convertible in San Marino. As they drove toward Santa Monica, they noticed that they were being followed by a patrol car. After a running gun battle through the Santa Monica tunnels, the fugitives managed to escape by crippling the pursuing car with a shotgun burst. When the convertible's front wheel crumbled, they commandeered a Ford sedan in Pasadena and drove back to upper Glendale where they ditched it.

The end came suddenly. After two more weeks of daily robberies, the teen-age gang was rounded up when a prowl car surprised its members while they were holding up a Hollywood gas station. Chessman was swiftly convicted of four counts of burglary in the first degree and sentenced to multiple five-to-life terms in San Quentin. When he arrived at the prison on May 11, 1941, he was assigned to a two-man cell in the fourth tier of the South block, directly across the yard from Death Row. He soon became the chief clerk to the Supervisor of Education and, in addition to teaching classes in secretarial studies, English and bookkeeping, was anchor man on the prison's debating team. In 1942, he started writing scripts for the Mutual radio network's weekly program, "San Quentin on the Air."

A year later, he was transferred to the California Institution for Men at Chino, a new minimum-security prison just forty miles east of Los Angeles. Four months after his arrival, he escaped by slipping through the institution's rear gate to a back road where two friends were waiting for him with a car. He was quickly recaptured in Glendale and returned to San Quentin in January of 1944. Although he was scheduled to be sent to maximum-custody Folsom, his skill as a stenographer delayed his transfer. A year after his return, the Adult Authority fixed the length of his imprisonment at forty years, a term which it later reduced to twenty-eight.

On August 6, 1945, the day the first atom bomb was dropped on Hiroshima, he was sent to Folsom in Sacramento County. The following spring, his wife, at his urging, filed suit for divorce. In January of 1947, he again appeared before the Adult Authority which decided to grant him an eleven-year parole, effective the following fall. On December 8, 1947, he was driven by the Receiving and Release Sergeant to the Folsom railroad station. When he arrived back in Los Angeles, he discovered that his father, who had gone into the florist business during his absence, had lost one of his two shops and was barely making a living with the other.

He promptly bought himself a gun and began to prey on local bookmakers. At 7:40 P.M. on Friday, January 23, 1948, forty-six days after his release from Folsom, he was driving a gray Ford coupé up Hollywood's Vermont Avenue when a radio car began to follow him. He drove into a gas station and turned back on Vermont. When he noticed that the police car was still trailing him, he pressed his accelerator to the floorboards and roared down the avenue. After a harrowing five-mile chase, he was finally captured at Sixth Street and Shatto Place. Four months later, a Superior Court jury, after deliberating thirty hours, found him guilty of three counts of kidnapping for the purpose of robbery (as well as fourteen other crimes), and fixed his punishment at death.

The eleven years, eleven months and twelve days that were to elapse before its verdict was carried out, by a handful of cyanide pellets dropped into a bucket of sulphuric acid some four hundred miles to the north, were a period of incredible activity. During it, two appeals to the Superior Court of Marin County, eleven to the Supreme Court of California, seven to the United States District Court for the Northern District of California, five to the United States Court of Appeals for the Ninth Circuit, and sixteen to the United States Supreme Court originated from San Quentin's Cell 2455. In addition, starting in 1954, with the autobiographical *Cell 2455, Death Row*, which sold more than 500,-000 copies and was translated into a dozen languages, four books emitted from the reconditioned Royal portable whose eternal clacking often gave Death Row the sound of a college dormitory.

Early in 1960, when Governor Edmund G. Brown was urged to grant clemency to Cell 2455's tireless occupant, he said that he had read the transcript of his trial and that "the evidence of his guilt is overwhelming." After the execution,

Warden Fred R. Dickson told reporters that Chessman had insisted until the last moment that he had not committed the crimes of which he was convicted. From these two remarks this book was born. It has been my intention to present an objective study of Chessman's trial so that those who, for one reason or another, are interested in analyzing the evidence and deciding for themselves whether justice has been done or perverted, would have the necessary material with which to do so.

With the help of George T. Davis, Chessman's attorney-in-chief, I was able to assemble a complete trial record. This, together with certain corrections in the transcript ordered by the Superior Court in 1948 and 1957, formed the basis of my research. In addition, interviews with J. Miller Leavy, the deputy district attorney of Los Angeles County who prosecuted Chessman, and Al Matthews, the former deputy public defender who was his legal advisor, were invaluable adjuncts to the coldly impassive record. Lastly, with the assistance of Brad Williams, George T. Davis' biographer, I visited most of the significant locales mentioned during the trial.

It was never my purpose to prove or disprove Chessman's guilt. I was merely concerned with presenting as objectively as I was able the evidence as it was received by the eleven women and one man who constituted the Chessman jury. Whether the convict or the governor was right in his appraisal of guilt or innocence is, of course, wholly academic at this time. What is of lasting importance is whether the means of making that determination—the adversary method of trial—is relatively trustworthy. A reconsideration of that proposition may well be Caryl Whittier Chessman's only monument.

WILLIAM M. KUNSTLER

Nov. 14, 1960
New York, New York

BEYOND A REASONABLE DOUBT?

1

THE PRELUDE

(JANUARY 3-23, 1948)

On Saturday, January 3, 1948, Donald E. McCullough, a clerk in Carl Hoelscher's clothing store in Pasadena, reported for work at 9:30 A.M. Business was very brisk and, by early evening, he had taken in more than eight hundred dollars. Shortly before seven, he decided to take advantage of a lull and begin counting the shoes in stock. Mr. Hoelscher had scheduled the next day—Sunday—for the taking of the year-end inventory, and McCullough hoped "to get a little ahead, so it wouldn't take us so long on Sunday." He had just finished tallying one row, when he noticed two men enter the store. As he stepped forward and asked, "May I help you?", one of the men reached under his coat and pulled out a pistol. Because of his army experience, McCullough recognized the weapon as a .45 caliber automatic.

The man with the gun ordered him to open the register and put the large bills in his companion's pocket. While McCullough was complying with this request, the gunman scooped up the rest of the money in the till, leaving only the pennies behind. He then told the clerk to walk to the rear of the store. When McCullough reached a small case near the basement steps, he turned around and saw that both men had disappeared. He then ran down the stairs and informed

3

his employer, who was ticketing merchandise in the cellar, that the store had been robbed. Mr. Hoelscher told him to call the police.

Ten days later, Mrs. Rose K. Howell, a young South Pasadena housewife, parked her 1946 Ford near the northeast corner of Colorado Boulevard and Marengo Avenue. Her car, a gray club coupé, bore 1947 California license plates, number 7P5618, and was equipped with a spotlight on the driver's side. At 3:55 P.M., Mrs. Howell walked across Colorado to a supermarket, leaving her keys in the Ford's ignition. When she returned, five minutes later, the car was gone.

At eight o'clock on the night of January 17, Mrs. Mary Tarro was returning to her home at 3306 Garden Avenue in Glendale. As the car in which she was riding with her husband and daughter pulled into their driveway, she noticed the figure of a man climbing through her bedroom window. Mrs. Tarro, who was sitting in the front seat, opened the door and jumped out before her husband could bring the car to a complete stop. She yelled, "Hey you!" and ran toward the bedroom window. Just before she reached it, the intruder dropped to the ground and, with the rather rotund Mrs. Tarro at his heels, jumped the back fence and disappeared. The Tarros, who were sure that the window had been locked when they had left the house at 7:30, found that its latch had been broken.

As soon as Mrs. Tarro had satisfied herself that there was nothing missing, she called the police. When they arrived, she told them that, in the bright moonlight, she had gotten a good look at the would-be thief. He had been dressed in blue slacks and a sports coat. She thought that he weighed about 160 pounds and that he was "fair complexioned." She was sure that he had not been wearing a hat. As for his track and field abilities, she reported that "he ran like a deer."

At 4:35 the next morning, Thomas B. Bartle, an Inglewood dentist, was driving along the Pacific Coast Highway near its intersection with Sunset Boulevard. He was pleasantly occupied, chatting with his pretty passenger, a young lady by the name of Ann Plaskowitz, when a 1947 gray Ford coupé, with a flashing red light, forced him over to the side of the road. A stocky man got out of the coupé and, after announcing that he was police officer, told Bartle that he was going to "run him in." When the dentist said, "Go ahead, where is your identification?", the man walked back to his own car, with Bartle at his heels. Suddenly, the "policeman" whipped out a .45 automatic and ordered his inquisitive victim to "start shelling out."

Bartle flushed out every cent he had—he thought it had been about fifteen dollars—and handed the money to the bandit. He was then instructed to "get going." Bartle needed no second invitation. He turned down Malibu Road and stopped at the first service station he could find. He telephoned the police who arrived one hour and two calls later.

Bartle told the officers that the man who had accosted him was about 5 foot 6, weighed in the neighborhood of 150 pounds, and appeared to be around thirty years old. He had been wearing a gray felt hat with a black band and was dressed in khaki-colored clothing. The only garment he could remember distinctly was a short jacket. He thought that the gunman had "a protruding lip" and "crooked teeth in front." Miss Plaskowitz claimed that she "could not see him but I heard him talk."

Later that day, Floyd C. Ballew, a car salesman who was visiting California from Custer City, Oklahoma, asked Elaine Bushaw, one of his sister's friends, to go for a drive with him in his Mercury convertible. At 7:30 P.M., after supper at a drive-in restaurant, the couple were parked just west of the Rose Bowl in Pasadena. Suddenly, a light-colored sedan with a red spotlight near the driver's seat pulled up alongside. A man got out of this car and, after turning off the spotlight, walked over to the Mercury. Ballew, convinced that the new arrival was a policeman, lowered his window and asked him what he wanted. He was informed that "This is a stick-up and if you don't give me your money, I will kill the both of you."

As Ballew reached for his wallet, he told the gunman that "I don't want to give you my billfold. I have a lot of valuable papers in it." The man informed him that he didn't want the wallet, just the money in it. While the Oklahoman opened the wallet and extracted twenty dollars from it, the other man kept the beam of a pencil flashlight on the billfold. Out of the corner of his eye, Ballew thought he could see a revolver in the thief's right hand.

Then the man turned to Miss Bushaw. "Where's your purse, sister?" he asked her. Although her purse was lying on the Mercury's back seat, she told him that she didn't have one. When she had obeyed his command to "turn your face, sister," he slapped her with the back of his hand. The girl began to sob and said, "Now that you got your money, why don't you leave us alone?" After several moments of indecision, the man went back to his car and drove away. Ballew raced after him, with his horn blaring, but lost him when the gunman cut in front of a bus and streaked up a side street. Then the couple drove to the Pasadena police station where they reported the incident.

According to Ballew, the man who had robbed him was in the neighborhood of thirty years old and weighed about 160 pounds. In the light of a nearby street lamp, he had noticed a "sort of protruding underjaw." The gunman was wearing a dark hat and was attired in a brown, close-fitting jacket and dark trousers. In addition to the red spotlight, Ballew had observed that the bandit's car was a 1946 Ford two- or four-door sedan which had no rear license plate. Miss Bushaw recalled that her assailant had been wearing rimless glasses and that he had "a big nose." She thought that he had been about her height, "five foot nine or a little over."

At 7:30 the following evening, Jarnigan Lea, a Los Angeles woodworker, dropped in on his old friends, Harry and Regina Johnson, who lived just across the street from him in South Pasadena. Mr. Johnson, who was a retired inventor, asked Lea if he would take his wife for a drive. Widower Lea was not one to turn down a spin with an attractive woman and he readily consented. The couple drove in his 1940 Chevrolet coupé to the Flintridge Hills section of West Pasadena, just south of the Sacred Heart Academy, where there was an excellent view of the city. Mr. Lea had been in the habit of going there every Fourth of July to watch the fireworks display at the Rose Bowl.

After they had been there about ten minutes, a car came up the hill and parked directly in back of Lea's car. As soon as it stopped, Lea could see a red spotlight in his rear view mirror. He was sure that the vehicle was a police car and told Mrs. Johnson, "It is probably the cops." A man got out of the car and walked over to Lea. He was asked, "Do you have any identification?" The woodworker replied, "Lots of it," and took out his wallet. As he thumbed through the billfold, he extracted a card and said, "There is my driver's license; that is probably what you want."

When he looked up, Lea saw the muzzle of a fully cocked .45 automatic staring him in the face. The man holding it said, "This is a stick-up. Don't move or I will kill the both of you." He took Lea's wallet and told him to turn his back to him. Then he asked Mrs. Johnson whether she had a purse and, when she replied that she did, he ordered her to give it to him. After emptying the purse, he told Mrs. Johnson to get out of the car. He took the keys to Lea's car and told him that, if he didn't want to go home in a casket, he'd better wait until the thief returned from "one of those blind streets farther up the hill" with Mrs. Johnson. When Lea pleaded with him to "Show mercy, this girl has not been out of the hospital but a short while with infantile paralysis," he was told to remain where he was if he wanted to stay alive.

Mrs. Johnson was so frightened that, at first, she was unable to get out of Lea's car. Finally, her legs began to work and she managed to walk the twenty or so feet to the automobile with the spotlight. When she was in the car, the man, who, she noticed, was wearing a handkerchief over the lower part of his face, asked her to get undressed. She told him she was menstruating, but he said "he didn't want it that way, anyway." He seemed outwardly nervous, and in an apparent attempt to overcome this, added "we would both be taken away in a casket unless I did what he wanted." With obvious reluctance, she complied with the bandit's wishes. When the lights of an approaching car were seen on the Sacred Heart grounds, the man pulled the handkerchief down from his face, gave Lea's keys to Mrs. Johnson and told her to get out of his car. As she stumbled toward her friend's automobile, she saw the man's car, which she later described as "a tan, sort of grayish-tan Ford coupé," speeding down St. Catherine Street.

While she was in the coupé, the bandit had told her that he had a short-wave radio. Once, he had reached down and said, "This is equipped to pick up police calls." Mrs. Johnson heard a click and then the words "Go to . . ." He also had shown her that his gun was real by ejecting the clip. When she tried to seize the weapon, he told her that she "could be taken away in a casket if [she] did that again." In the brief instant that she had the pistol in her hand, it felt "cold or metal like." She had observed that the man used a pencil flashlight to inspect the contents of Mr. Lea's wallet. At one point, the man had asked her where she lived. She gave him a fictitious address on Mount Washington. When he asked her where Mount Washington was, she said, "You ought to know." He replied, "No, I am from New York. I don't know."

Mrs. Johnson was hysterical when she returned to Mr. Lea's car. After stopping at a filling station so that she could wash her face and neck, Lea drove her to the Sheriff's sub-station on Foothill Boulevard in Montrose. There he described the bandit's car as "a late model Ford, either tan or gray or beige, a light color." Because of the lights from the Sacred Heart Academy and the quarter moon, he had been able to get a good view of the man's face. He had been "between 5 foot 8 and 5 foot 10, approximately 160 pounds, crooked teeth, possibly stained, and a protruding lower jaw." He was "a tough-looking egg." He had been wearing a light gray hat but he didn't remember seeing any glasses. Outside of confirming the car's color, Mrs. Johnson could only add that its dashboard seemed to give off a "sort of a bluish color," and that she had felt some chrome on the inside of the door as well as leather strips on the front seat.

At midnight on January 20, Gerald Stone, a West Hollywood truck salesman, was parked on Mulholland Drive with a girl named Esther Panasuk. The couple had been watching the moon rising over Laurel Canyon when a car with a red light pulled up in front of them. A man walked over to their vehicle and asked to see Stone's identification. When the salesman pulled out his wallet, he was informed that "This is a stick-up." In the moonlight, he could see that the man had a pistol in his hand and that his face was covered by a white handkerchief. In his nervousness, the salesman dropped his wallet in the road. When the bandit bent to pick it up, the handkerchief mask slipped, giving Stone a momentary glimpse of his face. After the thief had found a dollar in the wallet, he walked around to the other side of the car and relieved Miss Panasuk of her purse. The pickings here were equally slim as it contained only a dollar bill and some loose change. With a warning to the couple to stay where they were for an hour, the man took their car keys and drove away in the direction of Cahuenga Boulevard.

When Stone reported the robbery, he told the police that he didn't get a good view of the thief's car because the red spotlight was shining in his eyes. The best he could say was that it was a tan or gray 1946 Ford standard coupé. As for the man, he had only seen enough of his face to say that he had black hair, a light complexion and "a sharp nose." He guessed that he had been in his early twenties and was possibly of Italian descent. He thought that the bandit had been about six feet tall, weighed 180 pounds, and was of medium build. About all that he had been able to observe about his clothing was that the fellow had been dressed in "a tight-fitting windbreaker jacket [and] GI pants" and wore a hat.

Frank J. Hurlbut, a student at Loyola College, had been dating eighteen-year-old Mary Alice Meza for several months. A little after midnight on January 22, the couple, who had been attending a parish dance at the Holy Spirit Church, were sitting in Hurlbut's 1940 Plymouth coupé on Mulholland Drive, about a quarter of a mile from Coldwater Canyon. They had been there for half an hour when an automobile with a red spotlight drove up the hill and stopped in front of the Plymouth. A man got out of the strange car and walked over to the right side of Hurlbut's coupé where Miss Meza was sitting. He opened the door and, pointing a gun at the couple, announced, "This is a stick-up!"

Hurlbut, who thought that the man was a police officer, had been searching for his driver's license when he heard the word "stick-up." He looked up and saw that the man's face was covered by a dark handkerchief and that his hat was pulled down over his forehead. When the man asked him to empty his pockets, Hurlbut told him that he didn't have any money. The gunman then ordered Mary Alice to leave the car. After the girl had done so, Hurlbut was told to "pull down the road and park." As he started his car, he saw that his date was now sitting in the front seat of the other vehicle.

As the student drove slowly down Mulholland Drive, he noticed that the other vehicle was following him. Hurlbut pressed his accelerator to the floor and tried to get away from the red light that he could see in his rear view mirror. The other car finally pulled up until its front bumper was parallel to the rear end of the Plymouth. The bandit then attempted to turn his car into Hurlbut's and force him off the road, but the student was too fast for him. Five minutes later, Hurlbut saw that he had outdistanced the other vehicle and he parked on the side of the road. He walked back until he found a house from which he was able to telephone to the Beverly Hills substation.

When the police arrived, he told them that Mary Alice had been kidnapped by the gunman. He described the man's car as "a 1946 or 1947 dark Ford, either a club coupé, coupé, or sedan." He had not seen any license plates on its front end. He was sure that the red spotlight had been located on the passenger side of the car. As for Mary Alice's abductor, he had been "between the height of 5 foot 9 to 5-11 or 5-10 . . . maybe 6 feet." He might have weighed "anywhere from 150 to 180." He had been wearing a knee-length overcoat which was either "salt and pepper or checkered."

As the bandit's car raced down Mulholland Drive after Hurlbut, Mary Alice Meza sat petrified on her half of its split front seat. The man next to her said, "Shall I kill him, or do you want me to take you?" When she told him to "take me," he made a U-turn and drove off in the opposite direction. As they roared along, she noticed that two of the instruments on the dashboard panel gave off a reddish glow.

After twenty minutes of driving, the man turned left at a crossroads onto a dirt road. He stopped the auto in a "sort of ravine [that] was kind of a crevice in the mountain." As they sat there in the darkness, Mary Alice asked the man what he was planning to do to her. When he said "You know," she began to cry. "Why do you do this to me? I never did anything to you," she sobbed. While she was pleading with him, she kept watching his face. She saw that he had "a hooked nose, a curved nose" and that it was "a large nose, a long nose." She couldn't see the lower part of his face because of the "white" handkerchief which covered it.

After some ten minutes of listening to the crying girl, the bandit had had enough. As Mary Alice later recalled it, "He told me he would kill me, strangle me, if I didn't, so I did." After several minutes of oral copulation, he ordered her to take off her clothes and get in the car's back seat. She obediently did as she was ordered. After taking a moment to disrobe himself, the man then climbed into the rear of the vehicle with her. He told her to lie on her stomach and, when she complied, he hurled himself on top of her. After five or ten minutes, he stood up, threw her clothes at her, and instructed her to go behind the car and get dressed. As she began to put on her clothes, she noticed "a sticky substance" between her legs.

Before the couple left the ravine, the man, using a small flashlight, did something to the spotlight. Mary Alice heard "the sound of tools . . . like some kind of metal he was jangling together." Because he told her to turn her head away, she was unable to see what he was doing but she was sure that, before he walked over to the spotlight, he had taken something out of the glove compartment. When he returned to the car, she saw him put an unidentifiable object under the back seat.

On the way to the ravine, the man had asked her where she lived and Mary Alice informed him that her address was 1568 Sierra Bonita Avenue in West Hollywood. After she had dressed herself and returned to the car, he told her that he was going to take her home. He asked her to direct him because he said that he was from New York and was not familiar with Los Angeles. As they drove toward Hollywood, she asked him why "he did things like this," and he told her that it was because his wife had been unfaithful to him while he was in the Navy. At one point during the drive, they noticed a police car on Wilshire Boulevard and the man avoided it by going up a side street. At 4:00 A.M., he let Mary Alice off a block away from her home, warning her not to look back at the car as he drove away.

During the ride home, she had asked her captor whether he was Italian and he had said, "Yes." She had gotten a good look at him in the ravine because he had put the dome light on while they were undressing. He had "sort of brown hair and light brown skin . . . and brown eyes." As for his height, he was "shorter than the usual man." In fact, she was about 5 foot 5 and he had been just "a little bit taller." She had noticed a "fine . . . very short, fine line scar" extending from his right eyebrow. He had been wearing gloves, a slate-colored coat, and a gray hat.

The next day—January 23—at 6:30 P.M., Melvin Waisler, the owner of Town Clothiers, a men's furnishings store in Redondo Beach, an ocean-front community some three miles south of the Los Angeles city limits, watched what he thought were two new customers walk into his emporium. Joe Lescher, his salesman, soon had them in tow and, before Waisler left the floor to go into his office, he heard one of the men say, "I want a gabardine coat." When Lescher told him that the store didn't sell gabardine coats, the man answered, "That is the only kind I want." But he was willing to try on some other types although he kept reiterating that gabardine was his first choice.

Waisler remained in his office a minute or two before returning to the floor. As he walked toward Lescher and the two men, he heard one of the latter say, "Stick them up!" He noticed that each man had a gun in his hand. The taller of the two men ordered Waisler and Lescher to "get in the back room." They obeyed at once and remained in the room with their hands above their heads for about five minutes. At one point, Lescher was escorted to the selling area where he was asked to open the register. He was then returned to the back room.

A few minutes later, both captives were ordered to "throw out your wallets." Waisler didn't carry a billfold but Lescher tossed his through the door of the store room. The bandits kept warning them to keep their heads turned to the wall. When Waisler tried to sneak a look at them, one of the gunmen clubbed him over the head with the butt of his revolver. After the men had left the store, Waisler told Lescher to call the police while he flagged a cab and tried to chase the "gray Ford or Mercury coupé" in which he had seen the bandits leave. However, by the time he managed to locate a taxi, the gray car had disappeared down Pacific Avenue.

Because of his head wound, Waisler was taken immediately home, but Lescher remained in the store to check the register. He discovered that $214.00 was missing, some of which had consisted of coins still wrapped in their paper bankjackets. The following Monday, Waisler and Lescher counted their stock and found that some five hundred dollars' worth of coats and slacks were missing.

An hour before the robbery at Town Clothiers, Colin C. Forbes and A. W. Hubka, Los Angeles police officers attached to the Hollywood Detective Bureau, had finished bulletinizing the information received from Floyd Ballew, Elaine Bushaw, Thomas Bartle, Jarnigan Lea, Regina Johnson, Gerald Stone, Frank Hurlbut and Mary Alice Meza. The copy was sent to the Hollywood Record Bureau and was aired as an all-points-broadcast shortly after 6:00 P.M. At 7:37 P.M. it was sent by teletype to all stations. It read as follows:

APB SUPPLEMENTING LOS APF OF 1-22-48: FOLLOWING IS ADDITIONAL DESCRIPTION OF VEHICLE AND SUSPECT WANTED FOR KIDNAPPING, ATTEMPT RAPE

AND ROBBERY THIS CITY: MALE, CAUCASIAN, POS-
SIBLY ITALIAN, SWARTHY COMPLEXION, 23-35 YEARS,
5'6" TO 5'10", 150 TO 170 POUNDS, THIN TO MEDIUM
BUILD, DARK BROWN WAVY HAIR, CLOSE CUT, DARK
BROWN EYES, CROOKED TEETH, NARROW NOSE WITH
SLIGHT HUMP ON BRIDGE OF NOSE, SHARP CHIN, POS-
SIBLE SCAR OVER RIGHT EYEBROW. ARMED WITH .45
OLD LOOKING BLACK AUTOMATIC. PUTS ON WHITE
HANDKERCHIEF WHEN TALKING TO VICTIMS. USES
SMALL PEN TYPE FLASHLIGHT. BELIEVED TO BE DRIV-
ING EARLY MODEL 1947 OR LATE 1946 LIGHT GRAY OR
BEIGE CLUB COUPÉ, BACK OF FRONT SEAT IS SPLIT
TO FACILITATE GETTING INTO BACK SEAT, DASH
BOARD HAS RED AND WHITE NUMERALS ON SPEED-
OMETER AND CLOCK WHICH REFLECTS A RED CAST ON
DASH BOARD WHEN LIGHTED. POSSIBLE ALL OF DASH
BOARD IS PAINTED RED. FOUR INCHES BENEATH EACH
FRONT HEADLIGHT THERE IS A CIRCLE PARKING
LIGHT. ON BODY ABOVE LICENSE PLATE IS A PLAIN
CHROME BAR WITH "FORD" IN CENTER OF BAR. A RED
SPOTLIGHT HAS BEEN SEEN ON LEFT AND RIGHT SIDE
OF CAR. BELIEVE THIS TO BE A PORTABLE SPOTLIGHT
WITH RED LENS: POSSIBLE RADIO WHICH RECEIVES
POLICE CALLS WITH SWITCH UNDER DASH BOARD. NO
ANTENNA ON CAR. BELIEVE SUSPECT WHEN OPERAT-
ING KEEPS LICENSE PLATES IN BAGGAGE COMPART-
MENT IN REAR OF CAR AND AFTER LEAVING SCENE
OF CRIME REPLACES LICENSE ON AUTO. CLOTHES
WORN BY SUSPECT VARY FROM BROWN OR DARK
SLACKS WITH TWEED COATS, BROWN LEATHER, GRAY
CHECKED OVERCOAT, LIGHT GRAY HAT. INTERRO-
GATE ANY AND ALL OCCUPANTS USING ABOVE DE-
SCRIBED VEHICLE. CHECK REAR COMPARTMENT FOR
SPOTLIGHT AND LICENSE PLATES. USE CAUTION AS
SUSPECT MAY BE ARMED.

2

THE CHASE

(JANUARY 23, 1948)

Shortly after 7 P.M. on Friday, January 23, 1948, Robert J. May and John D. Reardon, two ex-servicemen assigned to the Accident Investigation Division of the Los Angeles Police Department, were cruising North Hollywood in Traffic Car Number 16-T. Their black-and-white sedan sported an electric siren on its right front fender and a red light mounted over the driver's seat. Three hours into their four-to-midnight shift, Reardon was at the wheel while May sat next to him on the vehicle's front seat.

An hour earlier, they had received the Forbes-Hubka APB from Central Broadcast Bureau. By 7:50 P.M. they had seen only two cars that resembled the vehicle described in the APB. They had checked them both out when they spotted a gray Ford coupé going north on Vermont, some five hundred feet south of Hollywood Boulevard. The police car, which had been headed south on Vermont, made a U-turn and began to tail the coupé. At the junction of Hollywood and Vermont, the Ford turned right into a Richfield service station on the southeast corner. By this time, May and Reardon were close enough to see that it contained two men.

The gray car continued through the service station and

16

emerged back on Vermont, driving south. Reardon followed suit and, as soon as he was on the avenue, turned on his red light. A few moments later, he pressed the siren button. The Ford, which had been traveling very slowly, immediately picked up speed and began to race down Vermont. When it crossed Sunset Boulevard, it was doing better than fifty miles an hour and it was obvious to both officers that it was going to take more than a siren and a flashing red light to stop it.

By the time the Ford crossed Lexington Avenue, it was some two hundred feet ahead of its pursuers and pulling away rapidly. Just before it reached Santa Monica, the light changed to red and it was forced to broadside across the intersection, losing most of its advantage in the process. When both cars spun sideways through the crossing, the police car had pulled up to within fifty feet of the coupé.

As the two vehicles careened past Los Angeles City College, May leaned out of his right-hand window and began firing at the speeding car in front of him. As soon as the shooting started, the occupants of the Ford crouched low in their seats, and only the tops of their heads could be seen by the pursuing policemen. May emptied his own revolver and, rather than waste time reloading, grabbed his partner's weapon and fired two more shots. Reardon saw one of the bullets shatter the coupé's rear window.

Traffic became fairly heavy south of Melrose Avenue and both automobiles had to weave from one side of the six-lane avenue to the other. The Ford began to open up the gap between it and the police car, and Reardon attempted to obtain better acceleration by shifting into second gear. The speed of his vehicle made this maneuver impossible and he could do nothing but press his gas pedal to the floor.

Just before the Beverly Boulevard intersection, Reardon saw another police car approaching on Vermont. Its driver turned it directly in the path of the fleeing coupé which just managed to career around it by mounting the sidewalk. In between taking pot shots at the Ford, May was relaying his progress back to headquarters by radio. The two officers could see two or three red lights blinking on Vermont as other prowl cars flocked to the area.

One of these cars—Number 14-T—was occupied by Officers Cremins and Childers. Just before eight o'clock, they had picked up May's running broadcast which was being relayed to all cars by Central Mike. At the time, 14-T was southbound on Hillhurst Avenue, just two blocks east of Vermont. After crossing Sunset, the two patrolmen proceeded south on Virgil, following the pursuit which was running parallel to them. When they heard that the gray coupé had turned left on Sixth, Childers, who was driving, spun his car to the right. As the two officers continued west on Sixth, they found that 16-T had collided with the fleeing Ford and that both vehicles had come to a halt on Shatto Place.

When Reardon saw the car in front of him turn left into Sixth Street, he spun his vehicle around the corner. After going one block to the east, the Ford's driver turned north at Shatto Place in what looked like an attempt to make a U-turn and double back on Sixth Street. Reardon promptly rammed his car into the left side of the coupé which ground to a halt against the intersection's northeast curb. Its passengers clambered out of the right-hand door and ran across the street to the northwest corner of Shatto Place. As the two men jumped to the ground, May thought he heard "a metallic sound on the street."

One of the fugitives surrendered when he reached the grass strip between the street and the sidewalk. The other man, who had been driving, disregarded all shouts to halt, and, with May and Reardon at his heels, raced down the driveway of a private house on the west side of Shatto Place. May, with Reardon's pistol still in his hand, fired two shots at the fleeing man. His target appeared to stumble as he skirted some shrubbery that lined the driveway. He quickly recovered his balance and raced down the macadam pavement toward a row of garages. May lost his footing in the shrubbery but got up in time to join Reardon in tackling their quarry near a small fence at the end of the building lot. E. D. Phillips, another traffic officer, who had been following Reardon and May down Vermont, arrived in time to help subdue the Ford's driver by hitting him on the head with a three-cell flashlight.

After handcuffing the still struggling man, the policemen dragged him back to the rammed car where they found his companion in the custody of Cremins and Childers. They noticed that the gray Ford had only one license plate—California 8Y1280—hanging from its rear bumper. Under its back seat, they found two additional California plates bearing registration number 7P5618. A loaded .45 caliber automatic was discovered lying on the ground a few feet from the coupé's right running board. In the glove compartment, Reardon saw a toy pistol and a pen-type flashlight.

On the car's rear seat, the officers found a topcoat, a leather jacket, two or three suits, some slacks and a number of hats. All of the clothing bore price tags and the cuffs of the trousers had not been turned. A man's wallet was lying on the front seat while a small piece of red ribbon, a pair of gloves and a hair rat were scattered on the car's floor. Before turning the vehicle over to Officers Cremin and Childers, Reardon removed the lens and lens rim from the car's spotlight. He noticed, he subsequently claimed, that the bolt to tighten the rim over the lens was missing. Later that evening, he turned everything he had found in the coupé over to the desk officer at the Hollywood Division Police Station.

May's shooting had been more effective than he had realized. In addition to the rear window, he had hit both rear fenders and a tail light. The car was in no condition to be driven and, some fifteen minutes after the collision, it was towed away to the police garage on South Figueroa Street.

After handcuffing their prisoner, May and Reardon frisked him for weapons. As Reardon ran his hands over the man's body, he noticed that he was wearing a tan gabardine top-coat under which he had on a brown tweed sport coat and a pair of slacks. His hands were covered by brown leather gloves. The policeman also observed the edge of a large book-type wallet protruding from the man's rear trouser pocket. Finding no guns on his person, the officers ordered him to get into the rear seat of the prowl car with his erstwhile passenger.

May, accompanied by Officers Snyder and Morrow of the Accident Investigation Division, then drove both captives to the Hollywood Police Station on North Wilcox, leaving Reardon to stay with the coupé and await the tow truck. During the short trip, the officer, exhibiting a fine sense of professional curiosity, asked the Ford's driver, "Why didn't you shoot back?" The prisoner contented himself with looking out of the side window and resisted every effort to draw him into conversation. At the station house, he was booked as Caryl W. Chessman, of 3280 Larga Avenue, in Glendale. His companion gave his name as David Hugh Knowles.

Thirty minutes later, Chessman was taken upstairs to the Detective Bureau where he was thoroughly searched by May. In the suspect's right front trouser pocket, the officer later said, he found a small nut through which a piece of wire had been twisted. He also uncovered $150 in bills and some small change. An Eversharp pen and pencil set, a wallet and some miscellaneous papers completed the list. May turned this property over to the Hollywood Division's desk sergeant.

3

THE PRELIMINARIES

(JANUARY 23—APRIL 29, 1948)

The Hollywood Police Station was a very busy place that night. Bruce R. Doebler, a reporter for the *Hollywood Citizen-News,* who had heard May's running broadcast at the Sheriff's sub-station, arrived at the second-floor Detective Bureau a few minutes after nine o'clock. In the southernmost room of the L-shaped floor he found Chessman, who was handcuffed to a chair, surrounded by Officers E. M. Goosen, Colin C. Forbes, and A. W. Hubka, as well as Reardon and May. The small room was filled to overflowing with reporters and photographers and the popping of flashbulbs made conversation all but impossible. Doebler noticed a small scratch on the right side of Chessman's head.

Joe Ledlie of the *Los Angeles Daily News* had been in the City Hall Press Room when he first heard the pursuit on Vermont being broadcast. He immediately called his city editor, who told him to go to the Hollywood police station as there was a good possibility that the "Red Light Bandit" had been captured. When he arrived, shortly after 8:30, Chessman was being searched and the contents of his pockets were lying on a small table in the squad room. Ledlie saw that one of the items on the table was a small nut. He heard Sergeant Hubka remark that it was extremely unusual

21

to find such an object in a suspect's pocket. "I think he said that . . . it might involve a spotlight, or might fit a spotlight, automobile spotlight, which they also thought to be involved in this case."

Some time after ten o'clock that night, Hubka and Goosen unlocked Chessman's handcuffs and accompanied him to the desk on the first floor of the station house. Billy B. Alley, the desk sergeant, remembered fingerprinting and booking him between 10:45 and 11:00 P.M. After Alley saw the prisoner taken through the door that led to the detention cells, he finished recording Chessman's personal effects and the property that had been found by Reardon and May in the gray coupé. Because of the extent of this material, he did not finish checking it in until well after midnight.

Sergeant Forbes arrived at the Hollywood police station at eight the next morning. Accompanied by Hubka and Goosen, he took Chessman and Knowles from their cells to the station lobby where Otis E. Phillips, Jr., a photographer from the *Los Angeles Herald & Express,* took a picture of both suspects. Then Chessman was returned to his cell while the police officers questioned Knowles in the Detective Bureau. When they had finished interrogating Knowles, they started in on Chessman. After an hour or so, the detectives decided that it was about time to show him to Mary Alice Meza.

Forbes called the Meza house and spoke to the girl's mother who told him that her daughter was still in bed suffering from a severe nervous shock and an inflammation of the chin. Mrs. Meza did not think that Mary Alice would be able to leave the house for at least three more days. At eleven o'clock, Forbes and Goosen took Chessman to Sierra Bonita Avenue and parked on the street directly in front of the Meza home. Forbes went into the house and asked Mrs. Meza to bring her daughter to a downstairs window so that she could get a good look at the suspect.

Miss Meza's bedroom was on the second floor of her house

and Forbes had to wait about four minutes for her to come down to the living room. "When she came down, I told her I had a suspect for her to look at." Chessman was standing on the sidewalk next to Goosen who was dressed in plain-clothes. A uniformed patrolman, who had been following the detectives' car as a precautionary measure, was standing guard across the street, some thirty or forty feet away. The moment Mary Alice looked out of the window, she said, "That's him." When Forbes asked her, "Which one?" she replied, "The man with the crooked nose."

When they returned from Sierra Bonita Avenue, Forbes and Goosen took Chessman across the street to a restaurant where the three men had some T-bone steaks. After lunch, they sat around the squad room. When Goosen asked Chess-man, "How about those jobs where the girls were assaulted?" he was told that "it was a guy named Terranova who was pulling some spotlight jobs." Hubka had entered the squad room just as Chessman described Terranova as being "an Italian, 5 foot 8, 25 years old, curly hair, a fast talker." The detective thought that Chessman's description fitted a man named Tuzzolino and, when he showed the suspect a picture of the latter, he said, "Yes, I think that could be him. It looks like him. He hangs around Bradley's on Hollywood Boul-evard."

After they had returned Chessman to his cell, the three policemen tried, without success, to locate Tuzzolino. When they returned to the station house, they spent most of the afternoon talking to Knowles. Earlier, Jarnigan Lea and Regina Johnson, who had been asked to come to the station house, had been sitting in the lobby when they happened to see Chessman in an adjoining room. Lea turned to his companion and said, "There is the man right there." When Mrs. Johnson looked into the room, she cried out, "It's you. What did you do those things to me for?"

The next day—Sunday—at 2:30 P.M., Dr. Paul J. De River, a psychiatrist for the Los Angeles Police Department, examined Chessman in the second-floor squad room. In the presence of several officers, Dr. De River asked the prisoner to strip and then gave him a physical examination. He observed a recent scar on Chessman's face, "a slight scar on the right side near the hair line." Then, after asking Hubka & Company to leave the room, he proceeded to question the suspect "for maybe two or three minutes."

On Monday, the twenty-sixth, Forbes and Hubka took Chessman and Knowles to the mug room in the basement of the Central Police Station on First Street. Mug shots of both were taken by Howard C. Gibbs, a police photographer. He took two pictures of Chessman—a full length shot and one showing just the head and shoulders. As Hubka recalled it, the photographs were taken between 6:30 and 7:00 P.M. During the ride downtown, Chessman told the police officers that he had read in the newspapers that a suspect named Jetton would have been convicted of murder if the fatal gun hadn't been found on another man. Cops were always making mistakes, he reminded them.

On the ninth floor of the Hall of Justice Building on Broadway, a temporary show-up room had been constructed. At one end of the room was a platform raised some eighteen inches off the floor. On the wall in back of the platform height marks, graduated from 5'6" to 6'6", were printed in black figures. A row of floodlights attached to steel bars were regulated so that their beams would be directed on anyone who was standing on the raised platform. On January 26, T. V. Rawson, who was in charge of the show-up room, had some fifty-eight suspects to parade before the interested spectators who sat on hard-backed chairs behind the spotlights. Chessman was given number 49 and Knowles 50.

At the end of the show-up, six suspects, including number 49, were ordered to remain on the platform. Rawson, who had difficulty in identifying persons sitting in the audience because of the strong lights, heard someone ask him to place a handkerchief over Chessman's face. Another person wanted the prisoner's hat pulled down lower on his fore-head. When the policeman started to comply with these requests, Chessman told him that he "had it wrong" and pro-ceeded to adjust his hat and arrange a handkerchief over his face. Regina Johnson's husband, who was sitting out front with his wife, thought he heard Chessman tell Rawson, "Don't bother. I know how I wore it."

After announcing that the suspect was Caryl W. Chessman, of 3280 Larga Avenue, Glendale, who was suspected of armed robbery, Rawson began to ask him a variety of ques-tions. "I think I asked you . . . as to guns, because through the teletype it told of your gun, the gun was possibly in your room, in your car, in some place. I also knew that a car was involved, and the questions asked you were probably a little more than the other suspects because of some of the answers I received." Chessman admitted that he had been arrested with Knowles and that a gun had been found at the time. Mary Tarro, Don McCullough, Regina Johnson and Jarni-gan Lea, who were sitting in the front row at the show-up, told Rawson that Chessman was the man who had victim-ized them.

After the show-up, Chessman and Knowles were taken up-stairs to cell block 10A2, the so-called High Power Tank of the Los Angeles County Jail, an area reserved for prisoners accused of crimes of violence. There, Chessman was put into a cell next to one occupied by a Howard Gibson. He was informed that his case would be called in the Munici-pal Court for a preliminary examination as soon as possible. Under California law, it was not necessary to proceed by a grand jury indictment; the Municipal Court judge could hold him for trial by finding that there was "sufficient cause" to believe that he was guilty of the crimes charged against him.

The opening salvos in The People of the State of California vs. Caryl Chessman began before Judge Arthur S. Guerin in Division No. 2 of the Municipal Court at 10:05 A.M. on Wednesday, February 4. Guerin, a stocky man in his late forties with bushy eyebrows, a thick shock of hair and intense eyes, read the charges aloud. In Complaint No. 84719, the prisoner was accused of one count of burglary, five counts of robbery, one count of attempted robbery, two counts of kidnapping for the purpose of robbery, one count of sodomy, and one count of attempted rape, all felonies. Chessman appeared *in propria persona,* a latinism that meant that he had elected to defend himself. His father had contacted one attorney whose $1500 retainer was much too rich for the family's blood and the suspect had summarily rejected the free services of the Public Defender.*

Simon L. Rose, the deputy district· attorney, had nine witnesses and two exhibits to get into the record. Dr. Bartle had convinced him that he was going to lose half his practice unless he got back to his office promptly, and the dentist was the first of the People's witnesses to take the stand. After he had told of being forced to the side of the road on the Pacific Coast Highway, on January 18, by a man in a car with a flashing red light, he identified Exhibit A, a photograph of a Ford coupé, as being a true, correct and fair representation of the automobile which had pulled alongside of him. When Rose showed him Exhibit B, a black .45 caliber automatic, Bartle said that the pistol which the bandit had pointed at him that day "was a gun very similar to that, if not the same gun." As to whether he could recognize anyone in the courtroom "as being the person who pointed that gun at you that you testified to," the dentist was quite definite. Without a moment's hesitation, he looked over at Chessman, who was sitting at the counsel table, and said, "I do; that man right there."

Gerald Stone was next. He was scheduled to leave for

* He apparently lost his aversion to lawyers because, before his case ended on May 2, 1960, he was represented, in one way or another, by Rosalie S. Ascher, Melvin Belli, George T. Davis, Jerome A. Duffy, J. W. Ehrlich, W. L. Ferguson, Ed Gritz, William Roy Ives, Morris Lavine, Al Matthews, Fred Okrand, Paul M. Posner, Berwyn A. Rice and A. L. Wirin.

Honolulu that afternoon and Rose called him out of turn. The truck salesman and his date, Esther Panasuk, had been robbed on Mulholland Drive at midnight on January 20. Exhibits A and B looked familiar to him, and he "would suspect" that Chessman was the man who had held him up. When Guerin reminded him that "we can't rely upon suspicion," the witness retorted that "due to the fact that he wore a handkerchief over his face, I can't be certain." No, he couldn't say positively that Chessman was the man but he was pretty certain that Exhibit C, a pencil flashlight, was the one that had been used by the bandit to examine his wallet's contents.

Mary Tarro, a heavy-set, gum-chewing matron, had known Chessman's parents for many years but had never seen their son before. She was sure that he was the man whom she had observed crawling out of her bedroom window on January 17. When Rose asked her whether she had given Chessman permission to enter her house that evening, she replied, "No, with a big N." She had seen his picture in the newspaper after his capture but she had not made up her mind until she had seen him in the lineup. "No, siree; I wouldn't say a newspaper photograph would say anything," she asserted.

The clerk then called out the name of Floyd C. Ballew, the Custer City car salesman, who had run into more than he bargained for when he parked his Mercury convertible near the Rose Bowl on January 18. When Rose shoved People's Exhibit B under his nose, the witness was positive that the gun which he had seen under the Pasadena moon "had this kind of barrel." As for Exhibit C, "it was some flashlight that looked like it." But Ballew insisted that the bandit's car had been "either a two-door or a four-door sedan. It was not a coupé or a five-passenger coupé car." The best he could say about the photograph Rose showed him was that "it was the same color car." He recognized Chessman as the man who had taken his money and slapped his girl.

Jarnigan Lea was a tall, thin, wiry man in his late forties

who had served several hitches in the Navy's submarine service. A carpenter, he was employed by Western Sash and Door in Rosemead, California. When his old friend, Harry Johnson, had "told me to get Regina out of the house, that she was tired, cross and nervous, she had been working all day," he had driven her in his old Chevy to St. Catherine Street in the Flintridge Hills between La Cañada and Glendale. When the man who had taken his money had driven by after releasing Mrs. Johnson, Lea had seen "the rear of his car." As far as he was concerned, he was prepared to say that it was "the exact model car" as the one depicted in Exhibit A.

He had only been able to see the lens portion of the bandit's flashlight during the holdup. He had reported to the police that it was "probably a $\frac{5}{16}$ lens." When Rose showed him Exhibit C, he was able to say only that "this portion . . . is the exact size of the light portion that I saw, the lens." The pistol he now saw in the courtroom was the "exact model and the same appearance exactly" as the one he had last seen on St. Catherine Street. He believed that Chessman was the man who had taken his money and abducted Mrs. Johnson.

When Regina Johnson, an attractive woman in her middle thirties, was called to the stand, Judge Guerin thought that it was time to clear the courtroom because "the nature of the charge in this complaint is one in which the testimony produced would be very embarrassing to any person required to listen to it." He ordered everyone "who is not a police officer or a lawyer" to retire. The reporters who filed out of the room obviously did not share his opinion about their sensibilities.

Mrs. Johnson had just begun to describe what had happened after Mr. Lea had parked his car off St. Catherine Street, when her eyes filled with tears and she could not continue. Rose marked time while Judge Guerin did his best to calm a witness who was close to hysteria. "You will have

THE PRELIMINARIES / 29

to compose yourself," he told her. "You recognize the need for testifying. I understand, as I said before, that this must be very embarrassing but, nevertheless, it is necessary that you testify and go through this ordeal in the interest of justice. Now, please compose yourself and speak right up and tell us what happened." Mrs. Johnson, whose eyes never wavered from Guerin's face, pulled herself together and started again.

When she had accompanied the man who had robbed her escort back to his car, he had sat beside her on the front seat, exposed himself, and said, "You know what I want." When she told him that "I don't know what you mean," he ordered her to "get busy." She protested that she was menstruating but he assured her that "I don't want it that way." As she told Guerin that "he made me use my mouth," she broke down again, sobbing "Oh, I hate him, please take him away!"

With Guerin's help, she completed her testimony. Chessman was the man who had forced her to "use my mouth on his privates." She described the car as "'47 or a '46 Ford . . . a club sedan." She thought Exhibit B was the gun with which she and Lea had been intimidated. When Rose excused her, her husband and Jarnigan Lea rushed her out of the courtroom as Guerin ordered the bailiff to let the chagrined reporters back in.

Frank Hurlbut, who lived just a few blocks from where Chessman and Knowles had been captured, was the Loyola student who had squired Mary Alice Meza to the Holy Spirit Church dance on the evening of January 22. While he hadn't gotten a good look at the man who had kidnapped his date because "it was dark and he had a handkerchief over his face," he thought that the defendant looked "similar." He had seen enough of the man's gun to say that it was "similar in appearance" to Exhibit B. The car which had chased him down Mulholland Drive that night was "a '47 or '46 Ford, either a sedan, coupé, or club coupé . . . dark in color." Apparently, Rose thought that Hurlbut's identification of the car was less than definite and he did not ask him to comment on Exhibit A.

As Hurlbut left the witness chair, the clock at the rear of the courtroom was striking twelve noon. At this convenient reminder, Guerin adjourned for lunch. The first witness of the afternoon session was Miss Meza, a slight brunette, who was just two months shy of her eighteenth birthday. A City College physiology student, she was a pretty but far from voluptuous girl who spoke in such a low voice that Mack M. Racklin, the official reporter, moved his chair a little closer to the witness stand in order to hear her.

As soon as the testimony got around to what Miss Meza, with just a hint of some pre-trial coaching, called "attempted rape," Judge Guerin asked, "Are you embarrassed, little lady?" When she replied that she certainly was, he again ordered the courtroom cleared of everybody but "the officers and the lawyers." After the disgruntled reporters had once more taken up their stations in the corridor, Mary Alice told her story of back seat sex. When Rose asked her if she saw the man in the courtroom who had assaulted her, she pointed at Chessman and said, "He looks like him, yes, he is the one." Because she had been ordered to keep her head turned, she hadn't even noticed if the car had a spotlight or not. She only knew that it was a "neutral color Ford club coupé." But she had seen the pistol, that Rose held up for her, in Chessman's hand when he made her get into his car.

Mary Alice was the last of the victims to testify. Judge Guerin told Rose that he was satisfied that "the record is amply sufficient" about all the counts in the complaint except that involving the Gerald Stone robbery. Since Stone had not been able to identify Chessman as the man who had held him up, Guerin suggested that, if the district attorney had anything like a confession or an admission to buttress this count, now was the time to trot it out. This was too broad a hint for Rose to miss and he promptly called Colin Forbes. The police officer remembered a conversation which he and three other detectives had had with the defendant in the Hollywood Detective Bureau late in the afternoon of Sunday, January 25. Chessman had admitted that he was responsible for the robbery "involving the couple on Mulholland Drive at midnight where you didn't get much money." As Forbes recalled it, the accused had said, "Yes, I remember that one" and then proceeded to describe it in detail.

That was enough for Judge Guerin. He was convinced, he said, that all of the crimes mentioned in the complaint had taken place within the borders of Los Angeles County "and that there is sufficient cause to believe the within named defendant, guilty thereof." He set bail at $25,000 and ordered the defendant "committed to the custody of the Sheriff of Los Angeles County until he gives such bail."

After a ten-minutes recess, the clerk called Complaint No. 84720 against both Chessman and Knowles. Although he expressed grave doubts about his ability to defend himself, the latter informed Guerin that, like Chessman, he was going to be his own lawyer. However, this decision proved to be predicated mainly on the low state of his finances and, when the judge informed him that the good State of California was prepared to provide an attorney for him without cost, Knowles quickly accepted the offer. H. F. Mead, a deputy public defender, was appointed, and Rose started things off by calling Donald McCullough to the stand.

McCullough identified Chessman as the man who had ordered him to open the cash register in Carl Hoelscher's Pasadena store back on January 3. He wasn't quite so sure about his co-defendant because "I didn't get a good look at his face." However, the sport coat Knowles was wearing in court looked very much like the garment worn by the second thief during the robbery. He knew this because he had waited on the man just before the holdup. The .45 automatic that Rose showed him was "the same type gun" as the one he had seen in Knowles' hand.

Melvin Waisler was sure that both Knowles and Chessman were the men who had held up his Redondo Beach store just before they were captured by May and Reardon. He recognized Knowles as the man who had hit him over the head with People's Exhibit A when he was standing with his face to the wall in the back room of his store. When Rose showed him a toy gun with a black muzzle and a white handle, he said that it looked like the pistol Chessman had pointed at him. Before he stepped down, he identified a brown tweed sport coat with a Biltmore label as being part of the merchandise which had been stolen from his racks.

After Rose Howell said that she had seen her car for the first time following its theft in the police garage on Figueroa Street, Officer May identified Knowles and Chessman as the men he had arrested at Shatto Place and Sixth Street on the night of January 23. He claimed that he had found the .45 automatic "lying on the pavement right by the front door of the car." He recognized seven rounds of live ammunition with Reardon's initials on them which he said his partner had taken from the automatic.

Reardon stated that he had searched the Ford coupé after the collision on Sixth Street. In it, he had found "a penlike flashlight in the glove compartment, along with a toy pistol, which was dark metal with a white handle. There were about three or four suits on hangers in the back seat. There was a leather jacket, and brand-new clothing still on hangers. There was also a tweed overcoat or topcoat on the back seat, and in the pockets of this tweed coat there were coins rolled in paper. There were also two license plates under the rear seat of the car." When he had picked up the .45 in the street, "it was in a half-cocked position with one cartridge in the chamber and the rest in the clip." Lastly, he had found a wallet with a social security and other identification cards in the name of Joe Lescher on the Ford's front seat.

After Guerin decided to hold Chessman on all the counts in the two complaints, he dropped the Hoelscher robbery charge against Knowles. Then he asked Rose whether he had brought each man's record into court. The deputy district attorney had. Would he kindly hand them up, to the bench? He would. Guerin took one look at Chessman's dossier and, with the caustic observation that "the judges put them in, and they let them out," proceeded to damn all parole boards for keeping "our crime records as high as they are in this jurisdiction." Knowles' curriculum vitae was hardly any better and Guerin set $25,000 bail for each defendant. Their arraignment was scheduled for 9:00 A.M. on February 20 in Department 42 of the Superior Court.

On February 18, Informations 117963 and 117964 were filed by District Attorney William E. Simpson with Earl Lippold, Clerk of the Superior Court of Los Angeles County. In them, Chessman was accused of the following crimes:

Information 117963

Count I   Robbery for taking checks and money from Donald E. McCullough on January 3, 1948.

Count II   Robbery for taking clothes valued at $500.00 and $214.00 in cash from Melvin Waisler on January 23, 1948.

Count III   Robbery for taking a wallet worth $5.00 and $38.00 (later raised to $43.00) in cash from Joe Lescher on January 23, 1948.

Count IV   Kidnapping Melvin Waisler for the purpose of robbery on January 23, 1948.

Count V   Kidnapping Joe Lescher for the purpose of robbery on January 23, 1948.

Count VI   Grand Theft for stealing Rose K. Howell's car on January 13, 1948.

Information 117964

Count I	Burglary for entering Mary Tarro's house on January 17, 1948.
Count II	Robbery for taking $15.00 from Dr. Thomas B. Bartle on January 18, 1948.
Count III	Robbery for taking $20.00 from Floyd C. Ballew on January 18, 1948.
Count IV	Robbery for taking $45.00 from Jarnigan Lea on January 19, 1948.
Count V	Violation of Section 288a of the California Penal Code for forcing Regina Johnson to copulate his penis with her mouth on January 19, 1948.
Count VI	Robbery for taking $6.00 from Regina Johnson on January 19, 1948.
Count VII	Kidnapping Regina Johnson for the purpose of robbery on January 19, 1948.
Count VIII	Robbery for taking $2.00 from Gerald Stone on January 20, 1948.
Count IX	Attempted Robbery against Frank J. Hurlbut on January 22, 1948.
Count X	Kidnapping Mary Alice Meza for the purpose of robbery on January 22, 1948.
Count XI	Attempted Rape on Mary Alice Meza on January 22, 1948.
Count XII	Violation of Section 288a of the California Penal Code for forcing Mary Alice Meza to copulate his penis with her mouth on January 22, 1948.

Under California law, all the kidnapping counts carried the death penalty, provided the jury found that the victims had "suffered bodily harm."

However, it wasn't until the middle of March, after he had run through four adjournments and two lawyers, that Chessman got around to pleading not guilty to all the charges. The Public Defender had made a valiant effort to provide legal representation but gave it up as a bad job on

March 12, when he announced that "we have been relieved, Your Honor." As far as the defendant was concerned, after discharging two private attorneys who had appeared briefly for him, he informed Judge Thomas L. Ambrose that "I wish to represent myself." When the judge inquired, "Are you a good lawyer?" Chessman assured him that he thought he was "a good enough lawyer." At long last, Ambrose decided that he meant what he said, and the case, which, at Chessman's request, had been severed from Knowles', was assigned for trial on April 29, in Department 43 before its eminent high priest, Judge Charles W. Fricke, who was referred to in some quarters as "the hanging judge." In view of the fact that California had given up the rope in favor of cyanide pellets in 1941, the title was somewhat inaccurate but hardly susceptible of misinterpretation by capital defendants.

Round One was over.

4

THE TRIAL—THE FIRST DAY

(APRIL 29, 1948)

The Hall of Justice is an impressive fourteen-story edifice that sits securely on the southeast corner of Broadway and Temple Street in downtown Los Angeles. With the exception of the rows of Doric columns that extend from the ninth to the twelfth floor on all of its four sides, and which give it the appearance of one building erected on top of another, it is very much like the hundreds of granite block government offices that were erected in the twenties and thirties. Its sixteen courtrooms have long since become inadequate for a county that has more than doubled in population since they were built, and two new courthouses have just been completed several blocks away.

Department 43 (now 102), is on the Hall's eighth floor. A small, cluttered courtroom, it seems a wholly unimpressive forum in which to weigh the issue of life and death. One enters the rear of the room through two large doors which open on an aisle that threads its way through two blocks of uncomfortable folding chairs which are anchored to the floor. A rail with the traditional swinging gate divides the room in half. On the far side of this rail are two long cater-cornered conference tables flanked by hard-backed chairs, reserved for opposing counsel.

The judge's bench resembles the desk in the Hollywood facsimile of a metropolitan police station. At the extreme left is a water cooler whose curved spiggot reaches almost to the top of the mahogany paneling that extends some five feet up the wall, until it runs into the faintly yellow plaster walls. The judge's leather-covered revolving chair stands in front of beige drapes that reach almost to the ceiling. The court stenographer sits at a little table directly before the bench with the witness chair, half-hidden behind a waist-high partition, directly to his left and slightly behind him.

A limp American flag stands in the room's right hand corner while the California Bear standard is at the judge's left elbow where it shares space with two brown filing cabinets, on top of the first of which is a large electric fan, a poignant relic of the days when air conditioners were not standard courtroom equipment. The jury box starts at the base of the American flag and extends past several windows that skirt the right side of the room, all furnished with pull drapes which, at one time, must have been the same color as those which hang behind the bench. Since the courtroom is on the west side of the building, the drapes are always closed during the afternoon.

Just to the right of the water cooler, a paneled door leads into the prisoner's detention room. Through it, at three o'clock on the afternoon of Thursday, April 29, Caryl Whittier Chessman, accompanied by a burly deputy sheriff, was led into Judge Fricke's domain. Dressed in the clothes in which he had been captured, the prisoner was led to the counsel table where he was told to sit down. Judge Fricke, observing that both the defendant and the People, the latter represented by J. Miller Leavy, a short, stocky deputy district attorney, were present, promptly called the case for trial.

J. (for Julius) Miller Leavy, a native of Los Angeles, graduated from UCLA in 1927 and from the University of Michigan Law School three years later. In 1932, he joined the

District Attorney's office where, after a routine apprentice period, he began to specialize in the trial of murder cases, many of which were of the sensational variety. After the Chessman case, he would go on to prosecute Barbara Graham for the murder of a Burbank bookmaker; Betty Ferreri for the fatal stabbing of her husband; Fred Stroble for the slaying of a child, and L. Ewing Scott for the suspicious disappearance of his wife. At the time of this writing, he is rounding out his professional career as the deputy in charge of the District Attorney's branch in suburban Inglewood, an area of operations in which he is unlikely to be involved in any more highly publicized cases.

Before instructing Deputy Clerk Cecil J. Luskin to call a jury, Fricke, a thorough man, decided to establish some ground rules. He reminded the defendant that "when a man acts as his own attorney, he does not have any greater rights than any attorneys would have in trying a case." In other words, things would run much more smoothly if Chessman limited his questions to those areas "which are proper to the general conduct of the trial, and in accordance with the provisions of law." But, he assured him, the court would give him all the help it could "to appraise you of what the law is, and from time to time assist you in presenting your defense."

At the time of the Chessman trial, Fricke, who had been sitting in Superior Court for more than two decades, was sixty-six years old and a recognized authority on California criminal law. Born in Milwaukee, he had graduated from the New York University Law School in 1902 and wandered west some thirteen years later. In 1917, he was appointed a deputy district attorney for Los Angeles County and, in ten years, had worked himself up to chief deputy. Originally appointed to the bench by Governor Young in 1927, he was elected to the office a year later.

Noted for a marked predilection for flamboyant ties and baggy double-breasted suits, he was a thin-faced wispy sort of man who looked like a cross between Chic Sale and a Welsh terrier. But he was far from a comic character to the defendants whose cases were assigned to Department 43. They soon learned that the little man with the rimless glasses and the biggest ears in Southern California had a sharp tongue, little mercy and no scruples against capital punishment. To one lady who asked him to go easy on her husband because he was the father of five children, he replied in his surprisingly deep voice, "Madam, jail is not for bachelors only," and proceeded to sentence the luckless defendant to ten years at Folsom.

The fireworks began early. The defendant, who had apparently made up his mind to lose no time in impressing Fricke with his spirit of enterprise, moved for the return of his case to the Master Calendar for reassignment. The reason —he challenged his qualifications to act as his own attorney "on the grounds that I may be legally insane." He asked the court to appoint three psychiatrists "to determine my sanity and report their findings before further proceedings are had in this matter." Fricke, who hadn't "the slightest doubt as to the sanity of the defendant," promptly denied the motion.

Then Chessman took the tack that he was entitled to a continuance because the officials at the county keep were not cooperating with him insofar as his legal defense was concerned. They weren't supplying him with books, subpoenas or any of the other paraphernalia which he considered necessary if he was going to have half a chance with a jury. Things had come to such a pass, he said, that he had written a letter of complaint to Fricke and asked Deputy Carl Linderman to deliver it. The jail censor, however, had intervened and the letter had been returned to him with the comment that "no inmate may correspond with the court."

If that wasn't bad enough, *The Equalizer,* a Los Angeles monthly, whose circulation was confined to Civic Center, had been publishing such inflammatory articles about him that it was highly unlikely that he could obtain a fair trial anywhere in the county. Besides, since the district attorney was certain to parade his prior convictions before the jury, he had instituted proceedings in Department 42 to vacate one of these judgments and a hearing on his motion was scheduled for the next day. Furthermore, he wanted to petition the court to "permit me to be given the lie-detector test, provided the prosecution will agree that the findings may be presented in court as evidence."

Fricke told him that the reason for all his troubles was that he had refused to have a lawyer. For the sake of the record, Leavy decided to introduce transcripts of the proceedings before Judge Ambrose in which the defendant had been urged to retain counsel, and he offered the notes of Goldie Cree, the Department 42 stenographer, to that effect. Then he called Al Matthews, a deputy public defender, who said that Chessman had refused his offer of help when he had visited him in the county jail "some time during the middle of March." All that time, he had been "ready, willing and able to represent this defendant."

Fricke denied all of the defendant's motions and was about to bring in the jury panel, when Chessman decided to thrash out the question of his rights as his own attorney. Was it the judge's position that "you lose certain rights when you appear for yourself?" Not at all. "I didn't say that, Mr. Chessman," Fricke replied. "Don't misquote me. I said there are certain rights which an attorney has, which a man who is acting in propria persona does not have. When you are in jail there are certain limitations on your freedom of locomotion, movement, which are incident of being in jail. That is one big reason why the court, undoubtedly, sent Mr. Matthews, to afford you such opportunity of doing things which you might not, as a prisoner, be able to do. In other words, Mr. Matthews could have taken care of the matter of subpoenas, the service of notices, make notice of motions, make motions and so forth. You have a perfect right to refuse that, but you cannot come into court afterward and complain that you were not afforded the opportunity, when the court furnished you with that machinery."

The defendant subsided, but only momentarily. A minute later, he was on his feet again with a request that his father be permitted to bring him some new clothes. "I intend to enter the clothes I am wearing as evidence," he informed Fricke. The judge saw no objection and ordered Bailiff Paul Nester to see that Chessman Senior was allowed to bring his son a new suit. Fricke looked relieved as the defendant sat down once more, and, for the third time, asked that the talesmen be brought in so that a jury could be chosen.

His respite was only temporary. Chessman stood up once more and wanted to know the correct procedure for making motions. This was the last straw. Fricke thundered, "Mr. Chessman, this court is not engaged in conducting a law school . . . I have been in this business for pretty nearly forty-five years, practicing law, and if I found myself in the position in which you are now, I would hire a good lawyer." When Leavy reminded him that Judge Ambrose had said much the same thing at the arraignment, Fricke looked at his watch and announced that he was going to recess the court until 9:30 the next morning, jury or no jury. Chessman was grinning broadly as he was escorted upstairs.

5

THE TRIAL—THE JURY AND THE OPENING

(APRIL 30–MAY 4, 1948)

At 9:30 the next morning, Fricke hopefully asked Luskin to "draw a jury." For a brief instant, it looked as if that would be the first order of business. But, as the clerk began to call the names of the prospective jurors, Chessman reminded the judge that he was supposed to be in Department 42 at 10:30 to argue that one of his prior convictions was invalid. Fricke disposed of this one with unassailable logic. "You cannot be in two places at the same time," he told him, "and you are here now."

The defendant shifted course immediately. There was something else he wanted the judge to know. He had given very serious consideration to the court's suggestion and he was now prepared to "accept the Public Defender as legal advisor, and in that capacity only." Fricke was happy to oblige and promptly appointed Al Matthews as "legal advisor for the defendant during the course of the trial."

A stocky, medium-sized man wih a scraggly mustache, Al Matthews was forty-one years old when he was named as the defendant's legal advisor. In his capacity as a deputy public defender, he was destined to cross swords with Leavy again in the Fred Stroble and Barbara Graham murder trials. Today, he practices law in Los Angeles where he was elected president of the Criminal Courts Bar Association in 1960. Several years ago, he purchased the Gas House, an off-beat café in nearby Venice, "because I'm trying to establish a new cultural center in Los Angeles."

Twelve prospective jurors had filed into the jury box when Matthews rose and announced that "the defendant has indicated to me he wants to make a motion for a change of venue." Before hearing the motion, Fricke swore in the waiting talesmen and then asked Chessman, Matthews and Leavy to come to the bench. It was the defendant's contention that the stories in the *Equalizer* had made a fair trial in Los Angeles County impossible. Furthermore, there had been crimes committed by a person using a red spotlight prior to the time he had been released from Folsom.* Fricke took ten seconds to deny the motion and then, with a silent prayer, asked both sides to get about the business of filling twelve waiting jury seats.

It took fifty-six veniremen before twelve were able to be sworn as trial jurors. The fact that thirty-eight were women didn't seem to faze the defendant who questioned them all with the same deadpan expression on his face. In the main, he wanted to know whether they had seen copies of the *Equalizer*, if they believed in capital punishment, if they thought there was such a thing as a criminal type, and if they considered the word of a police officer entitled to more weight than that of a defendant. As far as the women were concerned, he was interested in discovering if they had young daughters. Leavy contented himself mainly with asking each venireman whether he or she would be willing to

---

* Although hardly relevant to his motion, Chessman's contention that similar crimes had been committed in Los Angeles while he was in prison was correct. On July 21, 1946, Sam Garbo, who was parked in the Ascot Hills with a woman, was robbed by an armed Negro bandit who then raped his companion. On August 31, 1947, motorist Walter Haselbuch was flagged down by two men with a red flashlight who relieved him of $168 in cash, a $1700 ring and a $150 watch.

apply the death penalty to other crimes than murder if that was the law of California.

Dorothy C. Vamos was the first juror seated. A middle-aged housewife, she had never seen any issues of *The Equalizer,* and had no relatives on the police force. She had certain fixed ideas about criminal insanity, but was willing to vote for a conviction if the judge told her that the defendant was presumed to be sane at the time the crimes were committed. She firmly believed that persons of superior intelligence were more stable than other people.

She was followed by Caroline C. Shreves, the wife of a retired accountant, who had several grown daughters. Like Mrs. Vamos, she had never read anything about the "Red Light Bandit" before the trial. Stella Watkins, a cashier, who very emphatically stated that she was as yet unmarried, was equally oblivious of the incidents elaborated in the charges, but admitted that her father had once been a constable in an unidentified "small town."

Just before court adjourned for the weekend, Chessman, through Matthews, asked for "the same privilege as the district attorney has had to stand in front of the jury box at the time the jurors are questioned." Fricke tugged at his ear for a moment or two, and then announced that "the defendant may stand if he desires, but he will stand at the counsel table." This, he said, would be standard operating procedure for the duration of the trial.

On Monday morning, the selection of jurors continued. Jessie Wakefield, whose husband was a machinist, was not one to be influenced by the fact that the defendant was representing himself and insisted that she could hold her own with any man in the jury room if the subject of sex crimes came up. Laura Fouch would vote for a conviction only "if I am convinced he was guilty." The number of witnesses on either side would be of no decisive importance to Nanna L. Bull. She would cast her vote as her conscience dictated.

Dorothy King, a dental ceramist, was the mother of a grown son and daughter. She would need "a lot of evidence before I could form an opinion." Grace Dennis, who had a son in the Los Angeles police department, was sure that she would not "identify" with the women witnesses who might appear for the prosecution. Mary E. Graves ran a motel and had two grown daughters, a son, and a grandson. "If I was convinced you was innocent," she told Chessman, "I would vote innocent."

Sofia Thompson, the wife of a painter and decorator, and the mother of two married daughters, promised that she would listen to the evidence and be guided by it alone. Clarence R. Harte, a childless Sears Roebuck shipping clerk, passed muster when he said he would have no difficulty discussing "the sex phases of this case . . . with women jurors." Jean M. Tomkins, who had a twenty-one-year-old son, affirmed that she had no prejudice against a defendant who represented himself and would not be influenced by such trifles. At 3:40 P.M. on May third, after swearing in Grace M. Barber, Nell C. Keller and Agnes K. Carlton as alternates, Fricke, at long last, had his jury. Out of deference to the myth of male superiority, he appointed Harte as its foreman.

Before adjourning, the good judge delivered his standard pre-trial speech. He told Harte and his fourteen ladies that the jurors had the right to ask questions of the various witnesses provided they first applied to him for permission. The law allowed them to keep a notebook and, in view of the probability that the trial would be a long one, he urged them to do so. He had found that such a "memory-refresher" sometimes came in very handy in the jury room. They were not to discuss the case with any one or read or listen to anything about it. If they heard it mentioned on the radio, they were to "entirely disregard it." The best advice he could give them was to "shut the radio off or listen to some other program. There are hundreds of good ones on the air." With this realistic bit of counsel, he told them to go home, get a good night's sleep, and come back the next morning at 9:30.

When court opened on May 4, it was immediately apparent that Chessman's father had passed safely through the lines, because the defendant was nattily attired in a double-breasted blue, pin stripe suit. Leavy, in tweed, began his case by a brief dissertation on the nature of the charges and how he hoped to prove them. He assured the jurors that the case was far more simple than the two days of interrogation it had taken to select them would have suggested. "I think you will find the evidence relatively simple," he told them "[but] even though it is not complicated, I am going to just give you a brief résumé of what we expect to prove here."

He would show them that the defendant was guilty of a number of charges of robbery, some of which involved a kidnapping of the victims. In addition, he was accused of attempted rape and burglary. Lastly, he had violated 288a of the Penal Code, "which is the copulation of the mouth of one person with the sexual organ of another." Several ladies of the jury colored at that one.

He agreed with Judge Fricke that notes were a good thing. But he warned them against writing down all the exhibits since they would have these in the jury room when the case was submitted to them. And, above all, he cautioned, don't get so engrossed in note-taking that you miss some of the evidence. He would try to put in his proof in chronological order but, in some instances, he might have to "skip around" a little. All he asked of them was to "listen to . . . and examine all of this testimony very clearly." Without sparing a moment to let this advice sink in, he turned his head to the rear of the room and intoned: "Mrs. Johnson, come forward." The countdown had begun.

6

THE TRIAL—SEVEN VICTIMS AND A COP

(MAY 4, 1948)

As Regina E. Johnson picked her way down the middle aisle of Department 43, Chessman had two requests to make of the court. First of all, he wanted Ernest R. Perry, the official stenographer, to furnish him with a daily transcript free of charge. Secondly, he asked that all prospective witnesses be excluded from the courtroom until they were called on to testify. Despite the fact that such motions are ordinarily granted, particularly in capital cases, Fricke arbitrarily denied them both and ordered Leavy to get on with Mrs. Johnson who, by this time, was sitting, nervously expectant, in the witness chair.

The wife of a retired inventor some twenty-five years her senior, Mrs. Johnson was an attractive honey-blonde in her middle thirties. As Al Matthews put it, "she looked like a suburban matron who had managed to keep her shape." Stricken with infantile paralysis in 1945, she exhibited no traces of the disease, and her 130 pounds were rather decoratively distributed over a sturdy frame. During her two-hour stint on the stand, when she wasn't staring at a handkerchief which she kept twisting in her fingers, she was looking toward the rear of the courtroom, where her husband Harry sat.

From the moment she answered Leavy's first *pro forma* questions, it was obvious that no one but Fricke and the first four jurors would be able to hear her. By the time the district attorney had ascertained that she was a housewife who lived with her husband at 6068 La Prada Park, Mrs. Johnson's voice had become inaudible, and Fricke ordered Bailiff Nester to turn on the public address system. The loudspeaker, however, proved to be, as the judge sadly observed, "absolutely dead," and, with the admonition to the witness to "talk about twice as loud as you think is necessary," he told Leavy to start in again.

Early on the evening of January 19, she had gone for a drive with Jarnigan Lea, who lived across the street from the Johnsons at 6065 La Prada Park. A woodworker for a Rosemead sash door company, he had moved into the neighborhood some eleven or twelve years back with his mother and father, and the two families had become very close. Leavy wanted his comely witness to pinpoint the extent of this camaraderie.

Q. Are you and your husband very good friends with Mr. Lea?

A. Very good.

Q. I believe he lives there with his aged mother, is that right?

A. That is right.

Q. His wife is deceased, is that right?

A. That is right.

Q. How long have you been friends with Mr. Lea?

A. Around eleven or twelve years.

Q. I believe his sister is your best friend, is that correct?

A. That is right.

If there was any doubt in the jury's mind that the couple's evening ride to the Flintridge Hills section of Pasadena was anything more than the natural excursion of two old friends, the Assistant D.A. was determined to dispel it posthaste.

The rest of Mrs. Johnson's story was old hat. After stopping the car in front of the Sacred Heart Academy grounds, Lea had switched off the lights and the couple sat and watched the neon beauty of the City of Angels. Some ten minutes after they had arrived, an automobile with a red spotlight parked behind Lea's Chevy. A man left this car, which looked like a tan Ford to Mrs. Johnson, and, after asking Lea for some identification, suddenly announced that "This is a stick-up." While the bandit was going through her companion's wallet, Mrs. Johnson slipped off her rings and dropped them to the floor of the car. When the man ordered her to hand him her purse, she did so.

He then forced her to accompany him to his car, which was parked some twenty-two feet away from Lea's. After they had both gotten in the front seat, he promptly threatened to kill her and her escort unless she committed an act of oral copulation. "He told me we would both be taken away in a casket," she whispered, "the both of us, unless I did what he wanted." Because he was holding a gun to her head, a gun that looked very much like the one Leavy showed her, she complied. After he had had an orgasm, he gave her a handkerchief with which to clean her face.

She was certain that the man who had made her do these things to him was Chessman. Even though "he had a handkerchief, a white handkerchief, tied around his neck, and sort of pulled up" when he announced that "This is a stick-up," she had seen his face clearly when he first approached Lea's car. It was a face she would never forget. When she saw him in the Hollywood Police Station on January 24, she had recognized him at once. Why, even Jarnigan Lea, who had not watched him as closely as she had, had said, "There is the man right there," when he accidentally saw the defendant in the precinct lobby. As for the car, she had seen one in the police garage on Figueroa Street that looked very much like the coupé that had parked behind Lea's five days earlier.

When Chessman took over the witness, he was obviously as nervous as she was. His voice was pitched so low that even Mrs. Johnson had difficulty in hearing his first few questions. Finally Fricke, who had struggled through Mrs. Johnson's direct examination only by leaning in her direction with his hand cupped over his right ear, decided that two mumblers would be too much to take. "Keep your voice up, Mr. Chessman," he warned him. "We can hardly hear you." The defendant's "yes" was several decibles higher and the judge appeared satisfied.

Mrs. Johnson had told the police at the Sheriff's substation in Montrose that her assailant had been wearing "a sports jacket, sort of herringbone, dark trousers and a light hat." He had been "about five foot 8 or 9" but she could not say how much he weighed. No, she wasn't sure that the gun or the pencil flashlight Leavy had shown her were the ones she had seen that night but they certainly were "similar in appearance."

> Q. Were there any identifying marks on this flashlight that would assist you in identifying the actual flashlight?
> A. That is so silly—I didn't even have it in my hand. How could I tell?
> Q. Were there any identifying marks on the gun that would assist you in actually identifying the gun?
> A. The gun looked rusty.

Up to this point, both Chessman and Mrs. Johnson had referred to the bandit as "this person." The witness, however, grew steadily bolder as the cross-examination continued and finally decided to bring the matter down to a more personal level. When Chessman asked her whether Lea had tried to prevent "this person" from taking her to his car, she retorted: "He told you to have mercy, that I had been ill. You told him to shut up or you would let him have it, he would be taken away in a casket, and you said, 'She is going with me.' "

During the last fifteen minutes of her stint, she never missed an opportunity to tell Foreman Harte and his fourteen apostles that her interrogator had been the man who had assaulted her.

Q. Did this person, at the time he took you out of this car, state what his intention in taking you back to the other car was?

A. No, you didn't tell me until after I had gotten in your car.

Q. How long were you in this Ford?

A. In your car?

Q. How long were you in the Ford?

A. In the car with you? Is that what you mean?

This was too much for Chessman. He objected to her last answer, claiming that it was not responsive to his question. When Fricke proved wholly unsympathetic, Chessman reminded him that "the defense maintains its innocence."

THE COURT: I don't care what the defense maintains. The objection is overruled.

THE DEFENDANT: Well, I wasn't there, so I don't know what she means.

THE COURT: I don't know whether you were there or not. This is the question we are here to decide. I do not want any more arguments after I have ruled. Ask your next question. You would get along very much better if you respect the court's rulings.

But Chessman had had enough and, after a few desultory questions as to whether the gun Mrs. Johnson saw had been at half or full cock, he was only too happy to let her go. When she walked back to the seat alongside her husband, she was smiling broadly. Perhaps she had expected her inquisitor to ask some probing questions as to why a married woman was parked with a male friend in one of Los Angeles' favorite trysting spots.

Jarnigan P. Lea followed her to the stand. A thin, rangy man in his late forties, who was destined to be crushed to death between two cars a few years later, he quite openly relished his moment in the sun. It had been Mrs. Johnson's husband who had suggested that he take her for a ride that unfortunate evening. "He told me get Regina out of the house, that she was tired, cross and nervous, she had been working all day, and he wanted to read," he said. With a highly developed sense of Scotch frugality, he had decided to take her to see the beautiful (and free) sight of Los Angeles at night from the Flintridge Hills. He knew the area well, having gone there to watch the Fourth of July fireworks emanating from the Rose Bowl.

He remembered that it had been a beautiful moonlit night. An old navy navigator, he always made it a point to look at the moon. "It wasn't a full moon," he stated, "but it was a bright moon and practically overhead."

Q. It was by reason of that illumination you were able to look at the defendant's face?

A. Yes.

Q. You looked at him so you would know him if you saw him again?

A. Definitely.

He looked over at Chessman, who was listening intently with his head cradled in the palm of his right hand, and said, "That is the man."

Lea was not one for monosyllabic answers and Leavy decided to give him his head. As the witness described the scene on the Sacred Heart grounds that evening, he was playing to a jury whose members were eating up every word. After the defendant had brusquely ordered Mrs. Johnson to get out of his car, "She said, 'My legs will not move.' He said, 'Get out of the car.' She then got out of my car. He was standing alongside of her; I don't remember whether toward his car or alongside of her. I was about so far from the curb, and she said, 'I am going to faint. Will you please give me a drink of water.' He said, 'I haven't any water.' He said, 'Get going.' So, then, I didn't turn around; I had been told not to turn around, and I was very much afraid of her life, because she was under the point of a cocked gun, and I was positive it was loaded. So I could hear her get in the car, or a door slam, rather, and I heard another door slam, and I could hear him say, from where I sat in the car, 'Well, you know what I want.' She said, 'No, I don't.' She was crying; she was rather hysterical, naturally. And so, then, there was some low talk, and I could hear her pleading, 'Please don't do this, don't do that.' I could hear her pleading with him; I could hear him say that he would kill her. It seems like he just repeated, repeated and repeated, 'I will kill you! I will kill you! I will kill you! They will carry you away in a casket; they will carry you away in a coffin.' I just sat there. I never felt so helpless in my life. I would have gladly parted with both arms right then and there to have been able to have done something. I have never been so helpless in my life as I was at that time, because I was fearing for her life.''

Lea estimated that ten minutes had elapsed before Mrs. Johnson returned to his car.

Q. Have you told us all that you know, as best you can remember of overhearing from the other car?

A. I heard him make one statement, rather loud. He said, "Suck it."

Q. Did Mrs. Johnson return to your car?

A. Yes. There was a car that came under the overpass at the Sacred Heart Academy, with the lights on, of course, that turned as this car came up, and it makes —just blinded me for about three seconds, from where I was sitting in my car, and then the car came around and immediately passed us, and it seemed

like it wasn't but one or two seconds before Mrs.
Johnson came back and got in the right side of my
car, alone, and immediately she was in the car, I
started rolling immediately this car passed us—

Q. Which is "this car"? The third car?

A. The car coming up the hill, yes.

Q. In other words, let us refer to the defendant's car
as the second car, and this car coming up the hill
as the third car. What did the third car do?

A. He came up the hill, and as he passed my car the
defendant's car pulled out around me, without lights,
and took off down the hill with everything possible,
it seemed like.

The witness thought that Mrs. Johnson was "the most piti-
ful sight I have ever witnessed." She sat on the front seat
of his car sobbing hysterically as she told him what had happened to her in the tan car. As he listened to her, he noticed
that the lapel of her coat was soiled.

Q. Soiled in what manner, so far as you could possibly
describe at this time?

A. Well, I actually know what it was. It was semen, of
course.

Q. It appeared to you to be semen?

A. Yes.

Before reporting the incident to the Sheriff's substation on
Foothill Boulevard, he drove her to the first filling station
he could find where she washed her face and neck.

After a hurried consultation with legal advisor Matthews,
Chessman decided that the ex-submariner was better off the
stand than on, and announced, "No cross-examination." Just
before Lea left the courtroom, he stopped to say something
to the Johnsons, who were sitting in the last row. Harry
Johnson patted him once on the shoulder and smiled wanly,

before a court attendant, with a nervous glance at Fricke, managed to steer the talkative woodworker into the corridor.

Elaine Bushaw lived with her parents in Pasadena. When Floyd C. Ballew of Custer City, Oklahoma, the brother of one of her best friends, came to La Cañada for a four-month visit in the Fall of 1947, it was only natural that she would spend some time with him. On January 18, she and Floyd had passed the afternoon at the beach. After dinner at a drive-in, the couple had driven in Ballew's convertible to West Drive overlooking the Rose Bowl. Five minutes later, a car with a red spotlight pulled up alongside.

Q. What were the lighting conditions there when these things occurred?
A. We were parked under a street light.
Q. Did the street light shine on this man's face?
A. Yes, it did.
Q. Did you get a look at this face?
A. Yes, I did.
Q. Is that man in the courtroom?
A. He is sitting right there.
Q. You are pointing to whom?
A. Mr. Chessman.

The defendant, who had not been wearing a mask, had walked over to Ballew's car and told its occupants that "This is a stick-up. If you don't give me your money, I will kill the both of you." Miss Bushaw noticed that he was carrying a gun that looked very much like Leavy's Exhibit 1. "Mr. Ballew said he didn't want to give him his wallet because it had important papers in it. He said, 'All right, I will take your money.' Then he stood there a few minutes, and he said, 'Where is you purse, sister.' Of course, I said I didn't have a purse—I didn't answer. Mr. Ballew said, 'She hasn't got a purse.' My purse was lying in the back seat of the car, and I was sitting there looking at him, and he said, 'Turn your face, sister.' " When she obeyed, Chessman had slapped her on the face with the back of his hand. That would teach her, he had muttered, to play games with him.

After the bandit had returned to his car, which she thought was a light-colored 1946 Ford, and driven down the hill, Floyd had started his engine and raced after him. He told his date to "try and get his license number, the number off his car," but Miss Bushaw had informed him that she could see no rear plate. As the two cars hurtled down the incline into Pasadena, Chessman had suddenly turned right in front of an oncoming bus and his pursuers lost him in the gloom of a side street.

When Chessman took over, he was much more self-possessed than he had been with Mrs. Johnson. He turned first to the matter of the car.

Q. What type of car was this with respect to a two-door sedan or a four-door sedan?

A. It was either a two-door or four-door.

Q. You are positive of that?

A. Yes, I am.

Q. It wasn't a coupé?

A. No, it wasn't.

Q. It was not a club coupé?

A. No.

She insisted that it had been a 1946 model and that she was perfectly capable of telling the difference between 1945, 1946 and 1947 cars. When the defendant pressed her for some of the differences, the witness admitted that she didn't know them but claimed that she was sure that it had been a 1946 Ford because "Mr. Ballew sold cars and knows cars."

Like Mrs. Johnson, Miss Bushaw was content to play Chessman's game and refer to the man who had slapped her as "he" and not "you." *He* had a brown leather jacket on, *he* wore rimless glasses. Suddenly, in the middle of a question, she became aware of the anomaly of her answers.

Q. You say this person was not masked?

A. No, he was not. No, you were not.

But she was no Regina Johnson. Five minutes later, Chessman had regained his faith in the power of suggestion.

Q. How tall did you report this person was, to the police?

A. Oh, about my height.

Q. How tall are you?

A. About 5 foot 9 or a little over.

Q. How much did this person weigh?

A. I don't know.

Q. Did you report to the police what you thought he weighed?

A. I didn't put down how much he weighed, because I am not very good judging of weight. Mr. Ballew did.

It was his long nose, she said, that made it so easy for her to identify him. It was one of the longest and thickest noses she had ever seen, with a sort of bump on the bridge. As she described this unusual proboscis, the defendant kept running his finger over his nose, "It almost seemed," one of his jurors later said, "as if he was trying to rub it smaller."

She had been very upset when she saw him standing in the show-up in the county jail. But that hadn't interfered with her identification. "I would know you if I passed you on the street. I would know you—as I said, I was looking at you, and you slapped my face." You were wearing rimless glasses, she told him, glasses just like those worn by the man with the red tie in the second row. Chessman wondered whether the gentleman in the second row could bring his glasses to the front of the room, but Fricke didn't think that "there is any occasion for it."

THE DEFENDANT: I would like to show that those glasses are not rimless glasses. The witness has identified—

THE COURT: The witness has said they were the same, just as any other, merely at this distance. Obviously, those glasses are not connected with this case in any way.

As always, when Fricke ruled against him, Chessman appeared crushed.

After lunch, Leavy called Frances C. Lynch of the District Attorney's office and Deputy Sheriff R. W. Becker. Mrs. Lynch, a pleasant-faced woman, whose job it was to make sure that all criminal informations contained references to any prior convictions, had written to Folsom Prison on February 6, 1948, for Chessman's records and had received them ten days later. They were swiftly admitted into evidence as People's Exhibit 7. Becker, a short, husky, hairy man, who worked in the record division of the Sheriff's office, had rolled Chessman's fingerprints and compared them with those in Exhibit 7.

Q. They are the same prints?

A. They are the same.

Rose K. Howell lived with her accountant husband George at 311 Fairview in South Pasadena. At 3:35 P.M. on January 13, 1948, she had parked the young couple's car, a gray 1946 Ford Club coupé, on the northeast corner of Colorado and Marengo in Pasadena. She had been shopping all afternoon and had about ten dollars worth of groceries in a carton on the rear seat. She left the key in the ignition while she popped into a market on Marengo. When she returned five minutes later, the car was gone. She was not to see it again until Sunday, January 25, when she and her husband identified it at the police garage on South Figueroa Street.

The coupé's license number was 7P5618, and Leavy wrote it in large numbers on a blackboard which stood opposite the jury box. When she had seen the car on January 25, the plates had been removed and they were lying on the floor in front of the rear seat. No, she didn't know the defendant and she most certainly hadn't given him or anyone else permission to drive her car on January 13.

Mrs. Howell told Chessman that the car had been "in perfect condition" when she had left it at Marengo and Colorado. When she saw it in the police garage on the twenty-fifth, "there was a bullet hole through the back glass, and the windshield was broken; there were bullet holes in the back—two back of the front fenders and one through the dash, and, as I recall, all the fenders were damaged to some degree." The vehicle's spotlight, which roosted on the driver's side, was intact except for the fact that its lens had been removed and was lying on the front seat. The coupé had been repaired by the insurance company and she had driven to court in it that very day.

While George Howell made his way to the front of the courtroom to take his wife's place in the witness chair, Leavy returned to his table and picked up a small white envelope, a pair of pliers wrapped in cellophane, and an automobile spotlight. Howell quickly identified the latter as the one that had been on his Ford on the day it was stolen.

Q. Do you recognize it as the same spotlight?
A. I certainly do.
Q. Is that the color your car was?
A. Yes.
Q. In other words, the spotlight, as it appears here, was painted the same color as the car, rather than some chrome color?
A. That is correct.
Q. Did you ever have your spotlight apart?
A. No.

He thought that the pliers were "very similar" to the pair he had usually carried in his glove compartment. With a perfunctory "You may examine," the district attorney returned to his seat.

For some reason, Leavy had never gotten around to the

missing lens on the spotlight. Chessman, who wasn't con-
stitutionally able to let well enough alone, obligingly reminded him of it during his cross-examination of Howell.

Q. At the time you first saw this car on January 25, was
there a red spotlight on the car?

A. Was there what?

Q. A red spotlight on the car.

A. No, there wasn't.

Q. Was the glass at that time white?

A. The lens had been removed.

On redirect, a grateful prosecutor went one step further.
Howell told him that he had found the lens on the front
seat of the Ford when he had inspected it on January 25.
Now, Leavy opened the white envelope he had been holding
in his hand ever since Howell mounted the witness chair,
and showed its contents to him. In the envelope was a small
vial containing what looked like a metal nut suspended on
a paper clip. Howell, who had cleaned the car just before it
was stolen, was sure that a similar nut had been on the
spotlight and that the one Leavy was showing him "looks
exactly like it, because it looks like the gray paint on this
Ford." Leavy was almost purring when he sat down.

Since afterthoughts seemed to be the order of the day,
he was on his feet two seconds later to recall Mrs. Johnson.
When she was seated, he showed her a light tan felt hat and
a pair of gloves. She was sure that the hat that the defendant
had been wearing on January 18 "was this shape and same
color." Elaine Bushaw encored after Mrs. Johnson but could
not identify another hat that Leavy shoved under her nose
as the one she had seen on Chessman's head on West Drive
the night of January 19. "I couldn't say it is the same hat or
not, but it was a dark brown hat." But Chessman couldn't
stop playing lawyer long enough to salvage even this small
victory. With two questions, he promptly lost the slight
ground he had gained.

Q. Is it, roughly, the same style of hat?

A. Yes.

Q. Does it look like the hat?

A. Yes.

Donald E. McCullough vividly remembered the night of January 3. He had been on the main floor of Carl Hoelscher's haberdashery in Pasadena when two men had entered the store. When he had asked them whether he could help them, one had pulled a .45 automatic out of his belt and ordered him to "open up the cash register."

Q. Do you see the man that had the gun in his belt, in the courtroom?

A. Yes. Mr. Chessman.

After the clerk had opened the register, Chessman had instructed him to take out all the large bills and to put them in the other man's pocket. While McCullough did so, Chessman had reached into the till "and took out what other money that was left." When the register was empty, the witness was ordered to go to the back of the store. When he turned around, both men had disappeared with about eight hundred dollars in cash and checks.

Some two weeks later, he was asked to come to the Hollywood Police Station to identify a suspect. Accompanied by a Pasadena gendarme, he arrived at the Spanish-style building at 1358 North Wilcox, where he was taken upstairs to the Detective Bureau. A few minutes later, Chessman was brought into the room. "After he had gone, they asked me if he was the one and I said yes."

Q. Was there any question in your mind?

A. No.

Q. Is there any question now?

A. No.

"You were the only one I got a good look at," McCullough told Chessman. The other fellow was wearing slacks and a sport coat but he hadn't been able to see him because he kept his face turned away. The taller of the two, who had been dressed in a double-breasted gray suit, was the man

who had pointed a gun at him and who had scooped up the
loose change from the register. He had described this man to
the police as being "about 5-10" and weighing "about 160."
He had "a sallow complexion . . . dark brown, or brown hair
. . . a mustache . . . a medium haircut." Most of all, he remembered the way he talked.

Q. What do you mean? I mean, would you enlarge a
little? The voice, or what the person said?

A. The voice, and also your lips, the way you moved
your lips.

Q. Did you report . . .

A. The large lip.

Q. What?

A. The lower lip being larger.

With Elaine Bushaw, it had been a nose.

Following the afternoon recess, Leavy recalled George
Howell. The witness had previously testified that he had
seen what looked like People's Exhibit 9, the rim nut, on the
spotlight when he had washed his car a few days before it
was stolen. But he had not been sure that it was the same
nut. The best Leavy had been able to get out of him was
that "it looks exactly like it, because it looks like the gray
paint on this Ford." Over his recess coffee, the prosecutor, a
most careful man, decided that the all-important nut deserved better than that.

Mr. Howell, it seems, now remembered that he had taken
a good look at that nut when it was on the spotlight. He
had done this because he had unscrewed the lens rim when
he was trying to remove some rust from the back of the spotlight. It was then that he had taken particular notice of the
nut. Yes, he could now swear that it was the nut in the vial,
Exhibit 9.

Chessman had become increasingly agitated as Howell
testified. He whispered something in Matthews' ear when
Leavy turned the witness over. The public defender then

asked Fricke to permit the defendant to "approach the witness chair" when he cross-examined Howell. Fricke was adamant. There would be no deviation from the ground rules he had established at the beginning of the trial—if Chessman insisted on being his own lawyer, he would have to conduct his interrogations from the counsel table. However, he had no objection if Matthews approached the witness "for the purpose of exhibiting the exhibit to him."

While Matthews was walking toward the clerk's desk to pick up the vial, Chessman fired his first question at Howell. Wasn't it true, he asked, that he had testified before the recess that "you had observed this nut and recognized this nut while polishing your car?" Yes, he might have said that, but "I didn't mean exactly that. I did observe it when I was polishing the car. When I was polishing the car, I tried to get the rust off." This was the first time he had ever removed the lens rim and he thought that it had been four or five days before the car disappeared. He didn't remember what type of rust-remover he had used but it had been only partially successful.

Q. At the time you observed this little nut, was rust around the nut, too, was the nut rusty?

A. I didn't examine it that closely.

Q. You saw it closely enough to be able to identify it, though, didn't you?

A. I said it was a nut similar to the one that is in the bottle.

Howell was excused. A better lawyer might have asked him how he reconciled his post-recess testimony with his earlier statement to Leavy that he had never tinkered with his spotlight, but Chessman let the opportunity slip by. It was never to come again.

When Leavy called out the name of Mrs. Mary Tarro, a heavy-set, middle-aged matron plodded down the aisle. Her house at 3306 Garden Avenue had been broken into some time in January but, for the life of her, she couldn't remember the date. After Leavy showed her a copy of her testimony at the preliminary hearing in February, she recalled that the incident had occurred on January 17.

That night, she had been riding in a car driven by her husband. When it turned into their driveway, they had seen "someone going in our bedroom window." She had leaped from the automobile and run after the nocturnal intruder who was halfway through the window. Even Fricke had to smile at the thought of Katrinka to the chase. Her short legs, however, were not up to the task and her quarry had easily eluded her and escaped by jumping over the back fence.

Q. Did you get a good look at that man?
A. I sure did.
Q. Is that man in the courtroom?
A. He is.
Q. Who is he?
A. Chessman.

Mrs. Tarro had known the Chessman family since the war. As an air raid warden, she had taken a lively interest in everyone in the neighborhood. But she had never met the defendant before. She had gotten a good look at him when she chased him through the backyard. "It was very light for eight o'clock at night . . . it was moonlight, very light." Besides, the houses on both sides of her own were "lit up; lights all over." No, siree, she had never given anyone in the Chessman family permission to climb in through a window.

While Mrs. Tarro was testifying, the defendant was reading through the transcript of her previous statements in Municipal Court. When Leavy said, "You may inquire," he leaped to his feet with the blue-covered transcript in his left hand. Didn't the witness remember that she had told Judge Guerin that she wasn't sure whether the person she saw "was going into the house or coming out of the house." Mrs. Tarro was nobody's patsy. "What would you do," she asked Chessman, "if you saw a man halfway in at night? Wouldn't you run after him? I don't think this person would back out—I don't think he would go in."

She had gotten a good look at him when she chased him toward the backyard. As she had told the police, "He had blue trousers on, gray sports coat, light wavy hair, that he was well groomed, and he could run like a rabbit."

Q. How tall did you say he was?

A. I said 6 foot.

Q. How much did you say this person weighed?

A. I said about 180.

Then, why had she testified at the preliminary hearing that "the first thing that caught my attention was how well dressed the person was, and he was fair complexioned and had, I would say, he was about 160 pounds."

Leavy was out of his chair like a flash. Wait a minute, he shouted, if you're going to read prior testimony, then finish the witness's answer. Chessman supplied the missing phrase: ". . . and he ran like a deer." Leavy asked him to read the next question and answer, but Fricke had had enough. "Wait a minute," he roared, "we have a compound question. Objections sustained. We have two questions without stopping for an answer to the first, without completing the first." Mrs. Tarro, who had been chewing her gum vigorously as the big guns thundered over her head, looked less than happy until Leavy told her, "You may step down."

Colin C. Forbes, a police officer attached to the Hollywood Detective Bureau, was a dapper man who sported a trim mustache. In January, he had been devoting his attention to reports he had been receiving about certain robberies committed by "some person pretending to be a police officer and using a red spotlight on a car." Most of the information that had come his way had originated with the Pasadena police who were being plagued with attacks taking place in isolated areas of their sector. On Friday, January 23, he had finished bulletinizing this information and "about 6:00 P.M. it was put out over the air, and at 7:37 P.M. on the twenty-third it came out over the teletype machines." The broadcast, which had emanated from the Central Broadcast Bureau at City Hall, had been beamed to all cruising police cars.

One of the cars which had received Forbes' APB was 16-T which, with Officers Robert J. May and John D. Reardon, was patrolling the Hollywood area. May recalled that "the description of the car was a 1946 Ford club coupé, beige in color, and they further stated that it might or might not have a red spotlight, but it definitely would have a spotlight mounted on the left front—the left portion of the driver's compartment, and that the car would probably contain a penlike type of flashlight. There was also a description of one suspect that would probably be in this car."

May had seen a gray Ford coupé that answered the APB description traveling north on Vermont shortly before eight that night. Reardon, who was driving south, made a U-turn and brought his car directly in back of the coupé. He followed it through a Richfield service station on the corner of Hollywood and Vermont and back again onto the latter avenue where both vehicles were now southbound. When Reardon turned on his red light and blew his siren, the Ford "took off at a high rate of speed, south on Vermont, in the same direction it was traveling."

When the two cars crossed Sunset, they were racing at more than seventy miles an hour. Before the Ford turned left into Sixth Street, May had fired eight shots, six from his own revolver and two from Reardon's. When Reardon spun around the corner of Vermont and Sixth, he saw the coupé one block east on Shatto Place trying to make a U-turn. As May remembered it, "Officer Reardon ran the police car into the left side of the car the defendant was driving."

Q. Could you see who was in the car as you rammed it?

A. The defendant was upon the driver's side.

Q. This defendant, Chessman, right here?

A. Yes.

Q. Did you see enough with the light from your car, as he was sitting there, to identify him?

A. I did.

Q. Is there any question he is the man?

A. No.

As Chessman jumped out of the rammed car, May had heard "a metallic sound" as if something had dropped on the pavement. After the defendant had been captured at the end of a Shatto Place driveway, Reardon found a .45 automatic lying in the street near the Ford. Knowles, Chessman's passenger, had made no attempt to escape and stood quietly on the west side of Shatto Place until he was apprehended by two other officers.

Some thirty minutes after their capture, May had delivered Chessman and Knowles to the Hollywood Police Station. It was there that he had searched the defendant and found "a nut [which] I removed . . . from the right front trouser pocket." When Leavy showed him People's Exhibit 9, he said that it was the nut he had "personally" taken from Chessman. He had also found $150 and some loose change. With a sublime disregard for the rules prohibiting leading questions, Leavy asked him whether "there was some change in some sort of a paper wrapping." Yes, sir, there was but his partner Reardon had taken care of that. But had he seen this change? Yes, he had.

Q. Were they the wrappings that they usually put change in—the type of wrappings that business firms or banks use to wrap large quantities of change?

A. Yes, sir.

Leavy went after the young patrolman like a hungry ferret.

Q. Did you find any pen and pencil set on the defendant, Chessman, after you caught him?

A. Yes, sir.

Q. Where was it on him?

A. His right hand coat pocket, as I recall.

He and Reardon had found the .45 automatic "lying on the pavement, right where I heard the sound, and I later saw it in the Hollywood station when he brought it in." At that time, his partner had removed the clip which contained seven shells. May had marked each cartridge with his initials, "R.M.," before turning them over to the police property clerk.

Chessman's voice was quiet when he questioned May. Had the witness searched the automobile or examined the spotlight? No, he had not. He and Reardon had heard the APB broadcast "at approximately 6:15 P.M." They had checked out two Fords before seeing his car on Vermont; only one of them had sported a spotlight.

With almost a hint of pride, Chessman asked May whether he thought "I ran rapidly." You were a fast runner, the policeman told him. So fast, that he and Reardon would never have caught him if he hadn't tripped. "After I fired . . . two shots at you, you left this driveway and went under the branch of a tree; right under that branch of the tree there was a little ditch and you had tripped there, and I had slowed down my pace, because I thought I got you. It was Officer Reardon who finally caught you in the backyard . . ."

May had fallen down himself during the chase. When he got up, he saw Reardon struggling with the defendant. He didn't remember if he had struck Chessman or not but, if he had, it might have been with the gun which he still had in his hand.

Q. Was it possible that you struck me more than once with the gun?

A. It is possible.

The nut had been found in "your right front trouser pocket." There was also the "pen and pencil set, $150 in cash and coins, and a wrist watch." In Chessman's right inside coat pocket, he had discovered a wallet. If there was anything else, he couldn't recall, but he had written everything down in a note book. Fricke told him that he was at liberty to look at his notes "to refresh his memory." After a long glance at a dog-eared memorandum, May added "a lot of miscellaneous papers in the right inside pocket" to his list. But there had been no wrist watch. "I took a watch off Knowles. I apparently didn't take no watch off of you."

Just as Chessman expressed some curiosity as to the names of any other officers who might have witnessed this search, Fricke called a halt. "Just a moment, Mr. Chessman," he barked, "We have run past our normal adjourning time." Tomorow would be a short day, he announced, until noon only, because he had a meeting to attend. Before leaving the bench, he warned the jury "not to talk about the case, or form or express any opinions." As Harte and his colleagues filed out, the defendant sat staring at the vacant witness chair. The long day was over.

7

THE TRIAL—OF NUTS AND BOLTS

(MAY 5, 1948)

On Wednesday morning, while Los Angeles was reading about Senator Robert A. Taft's resounding defeat of Harold E. Stassen in Ohio's Presidential primary, Officer May resumed the stand. A good night's sleep had apparently done wonders for Chessman, who seemed to have regained the buoyancy that had deserted him during the last two hours of the previous afternoon. The "good morning" with which he greeted Fricke, who arrived some fifteen minutes late, was as warm as one could expect from a man on trial for his life.

Today, he was vitally interested in the search that had taken place on the second floor of the Hollywood Police Station shortly before 9:00 P.M. on January 23. First, there was the little matter of the two wallets. May had found one in Chessman's coat pocket but there was another that Reardon had brought in. The arrest report that May had prepared indicated that both wallets belonged to the defendant. But the policeman couldn't recall whether there had been anything about the second billfold to indicate its ownership.

Then Chessman got down to cases. He wanted to know whether the nut which May claimed to have found in his right front pocket was fastened to the paper clip "that it does now have." No, it was not—"it was all by itself." He hadn't seen any other officer "attach that clip to the little nut." What about a handkerchief? Had May found one on his person?

A. I don't recall that, because that would have been turned back to you.

Q. I didn't understand.

A. I say I don't recall that, because that property would have been returned to you.

Q. Well, was it returned? You do not recall because it probably would have been returned to me, but do you remember taking it out?

A. No.

When Fricke ordered him to get on to something else, Chessman came back to the crucial nut. With the arrest report in his hand, he asked May whether he had personally prepared it. The policeman replied, "No, I prepared that report in conjunction with my partner, Officer Reardon." Then, if there was no paper clip attached to the nut, as he had previously testified, why did he state "in this report that found in the right front trouser pocket was one twisted wire and nut?"

A. I mentioned it in the report that way, because the wire was put around it so as to keep it intact, the nut itself was so small.

Q. Isn't it true that you just testified that you did not remember of ever seeing a clip or wire being put around this nut?

A. I saw the clip around it when I booked it, but I didn't see it put around there, no.

Q. But when you found the nut it did have a wire on it; is that right?

A. Yes, sir.

Fricke looked up at that one and, despite the clear contradiction in May's testimony, told the defendant that he was repeating himself. "Mr. Chessman, he just answered that three questions back," he informed him. But Chessman was not to be deterred. "Did this report include," he asked May, " 'Following described property found on person of suspect No. 1, Caryl Chessman. One of the items found in right front trouser pocket was one twisted wire and nut' "? That's correct. Leavy jumped up and wanted to know what May meant by his answer, "that it was found there, or that is what the report says?" Fricke put a sudden end to the fracas. "It has already been asked and answered," he intoned, "this is the second time it was asked. It appears in there that is not the situation in which it was found. If the wire was attached some time after, in the manner it is, the witness does not know. It is already covered by the testimony." The defendant started to say something, thought better of it, and sat down.

May was followed by Melvin Waisler, an excitable little man in his early fifties, who owned Town Clothiers at 106 South Pacific Avenue in Redondo Beach. He had good reason to remember the night of January 23. Just before seven o'clock, two men had entered his store, and Joe Lescher, his salesman, had waited on them. A few minutes later, the men had pulled out guns and announced in unoriginal but hardly ambiguous language that "This is a stick-up." One of the robbers had been David Knowles.

Q. Is the other man—not Knowles—the other man who robbed you, is he in the courtroom now?
A. He is.
Q. Where is he?
A. There he is.
Q. This is the man, Chessman here, seated here where you are pointing?
A. That is right.

Chessman had ordered him and Joe to get into the back room and stand against the wall with their hands in the air. Shortly afterwards, Lescher was told to come out and "open up the register." Then Knowles had brought him back to the rear room where he took his place next to his employer.

Q. What next occurred? Was there any talk about throwing out of wallets or articles out of your wallets?

A. Yes. "Throw out your wallets."

Since Waisler was not in the habit of carrying a wallet, he had thrown out "a bundle of cards with a rubber band around them." Lescher, however, had reached into his rear pocket and tossed out a black billfold.

Knowles, who was standing near the entrance of the back room, had warned his captives not to turn their heads. When Waisler tried to sneak a look into the store, the bandit had brought the butt of his gun down on the haberdasher's balding head. For a moment, the latter had slumped against the wall and then managed to pull himself erect, blood streaming down his face. "Don't turn your head again or I'll let you have it," Knowles had snarled.

Several minutes later, Waisler had heard one of the men say, "Don't forget the 38-size suede coat." Then it was quiet. Out of the corner of his eye, the witness had watched the two men walking toward the front of the store. When they reached the door, he had bolted after them. They had climbed into "a Ford or Mercury coupé" which was parked at the curb and started down Pacific Avenue before the bleeding store owner staggered out onto the sidewalk. He had shouted at Lescher to call the police while he hailed a cab and chased the two thieves "as far as 101 Road and Pacific." But by the time the taxi had reached the highway, their car was out of sight. Waisler had ordered Lescher to close up, and continued on home where his doctor put six stitches in his lacerated head.

When Leavy showed him a photograph of the Ford coupé in which Chessman and Knowles had been captured, he shouted, "That is the car here; this is the car!" As for People's Exhibit 19, a toy gun with white buttplates, he was "sure," with a little prodding by the district attorney, that one of the men had been carrying it, although he first admitted that "all we saw was the stick-up gun." On Sunday, January 25, when he was taken to the Hollywood Police Station, he had quickly identified Chessman as one of the men who had held him up. He had also seen some three-hundred-dollars worth of clothing which had been taken from his store.

After establishing that it had been Knowles alone who had struck the haberdasher, Chessman had no further use for Waisler and the witness was excused. His place in the witness chair was taken by his portly salesman, Joe Lescher, who had little to add to his employer's story. The .45 automatic and the toy gun which Leavy showed him certainly looked like the weapons he had gaped at that night. When Leavy handed him a wallet and asked him if it belonged to him, he thought that "the outside of it looks like it." Somewhat impatiently, the prosecutor urged him to "open it up." When Lescher did so, he found that it contained his son's picture, his Social Security card and his General Petroleum credit card. Now he was certain that it was his wallet. Leavy threw him a warm smile.

As Waisler had rushed toward the front of the store, Lescher "ran after him, very cautiously." He, too, had noticed "a Mercury or Ford just pulling out." When his employer had ordered him to telephone the police, he had gone back to the office and placed the call. After checking the register, he had discovered that more than two hundred dollars had been taken.

Q. At the time you opened it for Chessman, was there greenbacks, currency, in there?

A. Yes, there were checks, money and all that.

Q. Was there a good many coins wrapped up in—

A. Yes. We always have a reserve of change from the bank, with bank covers.

Apparently it was the answers and not the questions on which the little salesman was concentrating. A flicker of annoyance marred Leavy's normally impassive countenance.

There was no doubt in Lescher's mind that the defendant had been one of the men who had come into the store that Friday night. After all, he had been the one who had waited on them and he had spoken to both of them.

Q. Did you get a good look at their faces?

A. I did.

Q. Is Chessman one of them?

A. Chessman was sitting down and I waited on the other fellow.

He had heard them say, "This is a stick-up" when Mr. Waisler had come out of his office onto the selling floor. When Leavy asked him, "Which one of them said that, Knowles or Chessman?", the witness replied, "I think so, yes." For some reason, the ambiguity of this answer escaped the district attorney who, with a benign "Very well," turned to something else.

After the midmorning recess, Leavy read into the record the testimony of Floyd C. Ballew which had been taken at the preliminary hearing before Judge Guerin in February. On Tuesday, Elaine Bushaw had informed Fricke that Ballew had returned to Custer City, Oklahoma, and would not be available to testify. Under the circumstances, would the defendant consent to having Mr. Ballew's previous testimony read aloud by Leavy? Chessman had no objection and the prosecutor began reading in a sonorous monotone from the earlier transcript.

Like Miss Bushaw, the car salesman had identified Chessman as the man with "a sort of protruding underjaw" who had robbed the couple. "I could see your face very good," he had assured the defendant, "because the street light was reflecting in it. I would identify your appearance anywhere." As for the car, he was certain that it had been "a two-door or a four-door sedan."

Q. You are positive of that?

A. Yes.

The gun and the pencil flashlight which Rose had shown him were "similar in appearance" to the ones he had seen in the bandit's right and left hands respectively that night.

With Ballew out of the way, Leavy called John D. Reardon. It had been Reardon, May's partner, who had caught Chessman near some garages on the east side of Shatto Place. He had grabbed him from behind and, with May's help, pushed him up against a small fence. The defendant had struggled frantically to get loose and Reardon had shouted to May, "Grab him!" "We placed Chessman in a position over the fence," he told Leavy, "to get him off balance, while we put the handcuffs on him." Then the two officers had dragged him back to the gray coupé where they found Knowles in the custody of Officers Cremins and Childs.

Reardon had noticed that a California license plate—8Y1280—was dangling from the Ford's rear plate bracket. It had been attached "with approximately two or three twists on this speed nut; loosely attached."

Q. So it could be easily removed with that speed nut?

A. It took about two or three turns on each nut to remove the plate.

Under the back seat, he had found another set of plates—7P5618. Those jurors who had followed Fricke's recommendation to take notes thumbed through their papers to see whether this was the Howell registration number. It was.

Reardon had thoroughly searched the coupé before turning it over to Unit 14-T. Outside of "numerous articles of clothing," he had also discovered Joe Lescher's wallet on the front seat, a half-cocked .45 caliber automatic lying on the pavement near the right running board, and a toy pistol and a pencil flashlight in the glove compartment. Under the front seat, there was "a small red ribbon . . . a hair rat . . . and a pair of gloves." The clothing had consisted of three hats as well as several suits and some slacks on hangers. When Leavy held up three hats, Reardon agreed that "they could be the hats, yes." There had been a coat "lying on top of the other articles of clothing." All of the clothing had borne price tags.

Leavy walked back to the counsel table and picked up the spotlight. Had Reardon noticed how the metal rim had been fastened around the lens? He most certainly had. "It was attached in the same manner in which it is now, without a bolt locking the bottom of the rim." While Reardon was answering his last question, Leavy slipped the glass out of the spotlight by spreading the rim which encircled it.

Q. Did you remove it easily as I am now doing?
A. Yes.
Q. Removed the glass front or lens, as I am now doing?
A. That is correct.

But he had not unscrewed the spotlight from its mounting. No, he didn't know who had done that.

It was almost noon when the district attorney relinquished the witness. In view of Fricke's obvious eagerness to call it a day, Chessman snapped out his questions so rapidly that reporter Perry had difficulty in following him. Had Reardon seen either fugitive drop anything when they left the Ford? No, he had not. Did he think that the defendant had been hit by one of the two shots May had fired during the chase on Shatto Place? That had been his impression, yes. Had he noticed "a fresh, superficial wound over my right eyebrow or right forehead?" No, sir, he had not. No, there had been no red lens in the car; "the only red article I found was a red ribbon."

The courtroom clock read 12:29. Fricke waved Chessman to his seat and adjourned for the day.

8

THE TRIAL—MARY ALICE MEZA

(THURSDAY, MAY 6, 1948)

It wasn't until 10:15 the next morning that the People of the State of California versus Caryl Chessman got underway again. Although the defendant had indicated on Wednesday that he was finished with Reardon, he told Leavy that he had a few more questions for the police officer. As a starter, he wanted to know just what a hair rat was. Reardon's description left a great deal to be desired. He depicted it as "a little appliance women use to put in their hair." When he fumbled for more expressive language, Fricke came to his rescue. With a broad smile, he said he thought that "the ladies on the jury probably will know what it is." Several of Foreman Harte's charges nodded knowingly. As a matter of fact, the judge continued, "It is almost a matter of common knowledge. It originated back in the Gay Nineties." And, as far as he was concerned, that was that.

Chessman was primarily interested in the wallet that Reardon had found in his pocket at the Hollywood police station. It had been a large wallet, the witness recalled, and he had pulled it "partially" out of his interrogator's pocket. He couldn't recall whether it was hand-tooled or not; it was what he would call "a book-type wallet." He had made no record of the dimensions but "it was a large type of wallet."

78

However, he hadn't looked at it very closely because he hadn't actually removed it from Chessman's pocket.

Leavy had been doing a little bit of meditating himself, overnight. On redirect, he wanted to know if, when the witness first saw the spotlight, the rim which held the lens could be removed "without relieving the tension on it." He looked somewhat surprised when Reardon replied that it could not. "It is completely secure," he assured the prosecutor.

Q. Was it then?

A. Yes.

Ten seconds later Leavy, whose tenacity was unparalleled in Civic Centre circles, repeated the question. Reardon's "It was secure" couldn't have been more emphatic.

The district attorney promptly shifted to another subject. He showed Reardon a photograph of the dashboard of a car. The witness thought that it looked like that of the Howell's coupé. The numerals on both the speedometer and the clock had been painted red.

Q. It causes a red reflection, does it?

A. It does.

Q. As you look at it?

A. It does.

Chessman only wanted to know if all 1946 Fords were equipped with red numerals. "From my observation," Reardon answered, "I would say in the minority."

The next witness, Dr. Kearney Sauer, had been practicing medicine for twenty-two years. For eighteen of those years, he had been a police surgeon for the City of Los Angeles. In the course of his duties, he had seen scores of women who had been sexually assaulted. At 7:17 A.M. on January 22, he had examined one Mary Alice Meza at the Hollywood Receiving Station, which was located in the same building as the police station. When Leavy asked him if he saw Miss Meza in the courtroom, the physician pointed to a slight brunette in a blue sweater sitting outside the rail.

Mary Alice had been accompanied by her mother and two detectives when he first saw her.

Q. State what kind of examination you made of Mary Alice Meza.

A. An examination was made of the vulva and the entrance to the vagina for damage, in that she stated that she had been attacked.

Al Matthews came to sudden life. "I object to that as hearsay," he informed Fricke. Objection sustained. The judge ordered everything the doctor had said after "in that" stricken from the record.

Mary Alice had been given a thirty-minute examination, the results of which had been entered on a record card which Sauer consulted as he testified. The first thing he had noticed was an abrasion of the perineum. Leavy looked appropriately confused.

Q. What is the perineum?

A. The perineum is that area of the individual between the anus and, in this case being a woman, the vagina.

There had also been a "swelling and discoloration of the hymen." The hymen "did not admit the small finger, my fifth right finger, and no attempt was made to force it because the hymen was intact." In other words, the girl was a virgin.

Sauer thought that the hymen could have been bruised by "the pressure or force of a male penis or private part against the hymen." Leavy was now ready for the hypothetical question that would pit feminine hygiene against a negative sperm count. "Assuming, Doctor," he asked, "that some sexual attack on this young lady that you examined here, but after the sexual attack and the emission of semen, male discharge, in the region of her private parts—assuming that the young lady after the attack and the emission of semen in the region of her private parts had gone home and wiped her private parts, in your opinion, could it be unlikely you would find any semen or spermatazoa at the time of your examination?"

It would be quite improbable. Fricke interrupted to ask if any smears had been made. Yes, they had and the slides sent to the Pinkerton Laboratory, but the physician did not know the results.

When Chessman took over, he asked Sauer whether he had looked for any evidence of semen on Mary Alice's clothing.

A. No, I did not.

Q. Did anyone in your presence?

A. Not that I know of.

Had the doctor found "any conclusive evidence of penetration?" Leavy objected to the question as calling for a legal conclusion but Fricke, although he termed the query "inartificial," ordered Sauer to answer it.

A. There was apparently a penetration of some firm
   object past the labia majora and minora, yes.

Could it have been a finger, Chessman wanted to know. Sauer didn't know. "My opinion in this case was there was a firm object pressed against this hymen," he said. "Whether that happened to be a firm penis or whether it was a finger, I am in no position to state." If it had been a finger that had caused the girl's bruises, he hastened to add, it had not been his. "They were there previous to the examination."

Had the doctor been able to determine how long Miss Meza's condition had existed? He thought that it had occurred "within a few hours." The answer did not satisfy Chessman. "What is the longest period of time," he wanted to know, "that it could possibly have been—that condition could have existed?" Sauer protested that he was being forced into a speculative answer. Fricke helped him out. "We are asking you to determine, Doctor, from the black and blue marks, how long they had been there."

A. It varies directly with the individual.

THE COURT: In other words, there are so many factors involved that you could give only the vaguest kind of an answer?

A. That is right, Your Honor.

The most he could say was that the bruises had occurred within "three or four hours, possibly."

The doctor was excused. Although Fricke indicated that it was about time to take the usual morning recess, Leavy insisted on calling his next witness, Officer John J. Cremins of the Accident Investigation Division. Emphasizing his point by tapping the palm of his left hand with his right index finger, a gesture that had characterized his courtroom demeanor, he reminded the judge that "We started late." By the time Fricke had stopped spluttering, Cremins was ensconced in the witness chair.

On the night of January 23, Cremins and his partner, Officer Childers, had been driving southbound on Hillhurst when they picked up the APB from Central Mike. They crossed Sunset and proceeded down Virgil, running parallel with Reardon and May, in car 16-T, who were pursuing a suspect down neighboring Vermont. When they reached Sixth Street, they turned right and found that 16-T had collided with "a light-colored Ford club coupé" on Shatto Place. After Reardon had removed some things from the coupé, Cremins had sent it to the police garage at 237 South Figueroa Street.

Chessman got more out of Cremins than Leavy had bargained for. The witness had examined the spotlight on the Ford. He believed that the lens rim had been fastened with a nut and bolt at the time he had looked at it. "There was a nut and bolt in there," he told the defendant, "but I don't think it was screwed or tightened as tight as it could be." All that Leavy could do with this was to point out that, since it was their case, Reardon and May, and not Cremins, were responsible for "the securing and retention of any evidence."

After the belated morning recess, Leavy called Frank Hurlbut. The soft-spoken Loyola student had taken Mary Alice Meza to a church dance on January 21. Shortly after midnight, the couple had been parked on Mulholland Drive overlooking San Fernando Valley. At 1:00 A.M., another automobile with a red spotlight had driven up Mulholland and parked directly in front of Hurlbut's Plymouth, "bumper to bumper."

A man, who Hurlbut thought was a policeman, had gotten out of the car and walked over to "Mary's side, the passenger's side of the car." The stranger had pointed a gun at the couple and informed them that "This is a stick-up." Hurlbut had noticed that the man "had a hat on, pulled down over his face." In addition, he had been wearing a dark-colored handkerchief over the lower portion of his face, "about halfway up on the bridge." When the student told him that he didn't have any money, the bandit had ordered "Mary to get out of the car and get in his car." Hurlbut was then directed to drive his vehicle a few feet away and park.

He thought that the man's car had been "a dark car, or some gray or green." When Leavy repeated the question, he described it as "some kind of gray car." Hurlbut had started his automobile and, instead of stopping as he had been ordered, pressed his accelerator to the floor and begun to speed down Mulholland Drive. In his rear view mirror, he saw that the other vehicle was following him. For several minutes, the two cars had raced along the winding road at fifty miles an hour until Hurlbut noticed that his pursuer had given up the chase. He had stopped at a nearby house and telephoned the Hollywood Police Station to report the incident. When a patrol car arrived, he told the officers that the man who had abducted Mary Alice was "5 foot 9 to 5-11 or 5-12, that is all."

Leavy moved in for the kill. Had the witness gotten a good enough look at the man to be able to identify him. No, he had not. The district attorney reframed his question.

Q. I show you the defendant, Chessman, down at the end of this table here. Does he look like the man?

A. He could be the man; he looks like him.

Q. Does he resemble the man?

A. He resembles the man.

Q. Which came up to your car, with a handkerchief over his face and stated, "This is a stick-up?"

A. He resembles him.

He didn't recall whether or not he had seen a flashlight in the man's hand.

Hurlbut admitted, on cross-examination, that he had no idea about the man's weight and height. Outside of the brown felt hat, the only other article of clothing he had observed was a knee-length salt-and-pepper overcoat with "some sort of design." But he was certain that the kidnapper's car had been "a dark gray," and that the spotlight had been mounted "on the right hand side."

After Hurlbut had told the bandit that he had no money, the latter had made no attempt to search him or look into his companion's purse. No, he hadn't seen him search Mary Alice either.

Q. After you had advised him that you had no money . . . did he indicate that he was taking Miss Meza forcibly for the purpose of robbery?

A. He didn't indicate anything. He just said to get into his car.

Q. He didn't tell her to take her purse with her?

A. No.

Q. He did not tell her to take her purse?

A. No.

The witness had been unable to give the police a better identification of the man who had attempted to rob him because "it was too dark." Chessman appeared puzzled.

Q. What is there, then, about me that resembles this bandit that you saw?

A. Just of average height and average weight. That is as far as I can go.

When the defendant sat down, he looked happier than he had been at any time during the trial.

When Leavy called out the name of Mary Alice Meza, there was an excited murmur in the courtroom which the judge promptly gaveled into silence. After the slight brunette had dutifully promised to "tell the truth, the whole truth and nothing but the truth," the prosecutor explained to Fricke that her name had been mispelled as Miza in counts X, XI, and XII of the information. Would the judge please amend the papers to indicate the correct spelling of her name? Fricke cheerfully did so.

Mary Alice, who pointed out that her name was pronounced "Meeza," said that she was a student at Los Angeles City College and that she had just turned eighteen on April 3. A painfully thin girl whose soft brown hair was cut rather short, she spoke in a quiet, almost detached, voice that was barely audible beyond the rail. According to Al Matthews, it wasn't difficult to foresee that, within a little less than two years, she would be committed to Camarillo State Hospital as hopelessly schizophrenic.

Leavy was very much the Dutch uncle as he gently steered her through her story. On January 21 she had gone to a dance with Frank Hurlbut. "It wasn't exactly a date," she insisted, "We went to more or less of a dance, and I knew him, and he was going to take me home." After the dance, Frank had suggested that they park for a while on Mulholland Drive and she had agreed. When Leavy asked her whether the road on which the couple had stopped overlooked San Fernando Valley, she replied, "It was overlooking somewhere; I wasn't sure; I suppose it was."

Some twenty minutes after they had arrived, another automobile had pulled up in front of them. She thought that it was a police car because she had noticed "on the righthand side, facing us, there was a light shining." No, she didn't recall what color it had been—"I know it was some kind of spotlight, but I don't know what color."

Q. Did someone get out of that car that came up in front of you?

A. Yes, a man got out of the car and came to my side of the car. I rolled down the window, and when I did he had a gun and said, "This is a stick-up." That is the time I said I didn't have any money. So he took me over to his side of the car.

Q. What did this man say, if anything?

A. He just said, "Get over there."

Q. Did he motion with the gun?

A. That is right.

Q. Toward this car with the spotlight on it?

A. Yes.

While she stood petrified at the side of the bandit's car, she had watched him talking to Hurlbut. She had heard him tell the boy to drive down to the first bend in the road and park. Then he had returned to his car, forced her into the front seat, and started the motor. She had seen the tail-light of Hurlbut's car as it moved slowly along Mulholland Drive. When, instead of stopping at the first curve, the Plymouth had begun to pick up speed, her captor had angrily pressed the gas pedal to the floor and chased Hurlbut down the perilous winding roadway. As both cars raced toward the valley, the man beside her had said, "Do you want—shall I kill him, or do you want me to take you?" When the terrified girl answered, "Well, take me," he had turned around and sped off in the opposite direction.

As they drove along, she had noticed that two instruments on the dashboard gave off "a red light illumination." In their glow, she saw that the driver had "a white handkerchief over his nose, about in the middle of his nose."

Q. When you got into the car did this man still have a handkerchief over his face, and did he have a hat on
at that time, when you were first with him?

A. Yes, he had a handkerchief on the whole period of time.

When he had asked for her name and address she was so frightened that she readily gave them to him. She thought that she had also given him her telephone number. She had a suspicion that something terrible was about to happen to her but "I didn't know exactly. I wasn't thinking particularly well." "You weren't thinking what?" Leavy asked her. "Well," she told him. "I mean, I was kind of dazed, I suppose." The prosecutor looked appropriately sympathetic.

Mary Alice had sat huddled in the front seat of the car as the man drove rapidly through the night. She recalled that, after some twenty minutes, he had turned left onto a dirt road and backed into "a sort of ravine . . . a kind of crevice in the mountain." When the car had stopped, she looked around but could see no houses or lights in the area.

Between racking sobs, the girl had asked him what he planned to do with her. When he replied, "You know," she pleaded with him to leave her alone. "I never did anything to you," she cried, "Why do you do this to me?" As soon as she told him that she was menstruating, he said, "Show me," and she lifted up her skirt and showed him that she was wearing a sanitary belt, but "that didn't make any difference then." For more than ten minutes, she begged him to take her home but "he just sat there and waited until I was finished."

Q. Had you been making any effort up to that time to note his appearance?

A. Oh, yes.

Q. His facial appearance, in spite of any mask or handkerchief over his face?

A. I tried to notice what he looked like.

Q. Were you making an effort to remember him?

A. I was noticing what he looked like, out of curiosity, in case I might have to tell anything about it afterwards.

Even though he told her not to look at him, she had managed to steal several glances at his face. In particular, she had observed that he had "a hooked nose." "I remember that," she told Leavy, "a curved nose. I saw it profile. It was a large nose, a long nose."

Q. Did you have an opportunity to study the shape of his nose and the shape of his face, in spite of the mask or handkerchief over the nose?

A. Yes, sir.

When her tears had subsided, the man had opened his pants and exposed his penis. "He . . . made me put my mouth down on it. He told me he would kill me, strangle me, if I didn't, so I did." Leavy, who evidently felt that the facts of life came late in Southern California, asked her whether she had studied physiology in school. Yes, she had learned all about the male and female anatomy "as well as the names used with respect to . . . the private parts."

Q. When you referred to "penis," you were referring to the male organ or private part?

A. Yes, I was.

Then, her captor had ordered her to take off her clothes and get into the back of the car. When she had done so, he had undressed himself and joined her on the vehicle's rear seat. He told her to lie on her stomach with her legs spread apart and then "he got in back of me."

Q. In back of you; you mean what?

A. On top of me, in back of me.

She had felt his body moving back and forth and "then there was an emission . . . through my legs, between my legs."

A few minutes later, he told her to go behind the car and get dressed. "He threw my clothes at me, and I got dressed. Then he got dressed and he drove out of the mountains there, and he drove devious ways around. Finally, he took me within a block of my home." Was the man who had done these things to her in the courtroom? Yes, he was.

Q. Who is it?
A. That man over there in the blue pin-stripe suit.
Q. This man right here, that I am pointing to?
A. Yes.
Q. The defendant, Chessman?
A. Yes.
Q. Is there any question in your mind?
A. No, there is no question. It is definitely him. I know
   what he looks like.

While she was putting on her clothes, she had gotten a
good look at the car. It was a "gray-beige" Ford club coupé.
She remembered that it had a split front seat and red numerals on the dashboard. As far as the spotlight was concerned, "It was on the driver's side, definitely." She was
certain that the car she had seen in the police garage on
January 30 was "the same car."

When she had finished dressing behind the car, she
noticed that the defendant was shining his flashlight in the
vicinity of the spotlight. Leavy, who had long since given up
any pretense of avoiding leading questions, asked her
whether "after you heard or could tell in some way that the
defendant was putting a light on the spotlight, could you
hear the rustling or the sound of anything in the defendant's
hand being placed into some compartment of the car?" Why,
yes, she had heard "the sound of tools around—it was like he
had some kind of metal he was jangling together. It was at
the back seat of the car; he removed the seat and put something in there. I couldn't see what he was doing, but I remember the sound of tools."

The diminutive prosecutor looked unfulfilled. Hadn't she
also noticed him doing something in the glove compartment?
She smiled sheepishly. Oh, yes, just before he had fooled
around with the spotlight, he had taken something out of
the glove compartment. "It was—sounded like tools being
bumped against each other." Leavy's sigh of relief was profound.

Q. Did the defendant return to the glove compartment after flashing the flashlight on the spotlight?

A. Yes, he did.

Q. Was it after you saw or heard the defendant do something with the glove compartment that he went to the rear of the car?

A. Yes, he did. That was after the incident occurred; I mean, just before we went home.

She hadn't been able to see what he was doing because he had ordered her to turn the other way. "But I kind of turned around," she said, "and saw him, more or less."

Shortly before 4:00 A.M. Chessman had dropped her off a block away from her home on Sierra Bonita Avenue. During the drive home, the defendant had avoided a passing police car on Wilshire Boulevard by turning into a side street. She didn't remember whether it was at that time that he had removed his hat, but she was certain that he had done so at some time during the ride from the ravine. "He removed it while we were going home," she told Leavy, "I saw his hair and his forehead."

As she stepped out of the car, Chessman had told her "not to look back." The moment she heard his car drive off, she had run to her house. As soon as she arrived home, she had gone into the bathroom and removed her clothes.

Q. Did you . . . make an effort to clean yourself up with reference to your private parts?

A. Yes.

Q. Did you clean your private parts in some way?

A. Yes. Not very well, I don't think. I mean, I was just kind of dazed. I just went to bed, that is all.

When she awoke the next morning, she noticed that she had a rash on her chin which gradually spread over all her face. By noon, her mouth was so swollen that she had difficulty in swallowing. Leavy clucked sympathetically.

Q. Were you mentally and physically upset as a result of your experience?

A. Yes, I was.

Q. Did you suffer a personal outrage to your feelings as a result of your experience?

A. Yes, I did.

In fact, she had been so upset that she had not been able to leave the house until January 30, when she had been taken to the police garage to look at a car.

Had she worn a hat that night? No, she had not. Her hair had been longer at the time and she had been wearing it loose, "about the way it is now."

Q. Was your hair loose and of the same description when you were forced to get into this back seat and lie on your face?

A. Yes.

Q. Was your hair, your head or your hair, in contact with the upholstery or cushion when you were in the back seat?

A. Yes, I believe it was.

Two police officers had come to her house the next day and, with her mother hovering nearby, had removed some hair from her head. She was sure that this had taken place "that same day it happened to me." When Leavy pointed out that it might have occurred on January 29, she said, "I don't recall."

Miss Meza looked frightened as Chessman stood up to question her. But he was, if anything, even more solicitous than Leavy had been. How did she know what time the bandit's car had pulled up in front of Hurlbut's if she wasn't wearing a watch? She had "a vague notion of the time." Had she been wearing lipstick? She thought that she had "had some left on." No, she couldn't remember when she had last applied any but she was sure that it had been before she stepped into the Plymouth at midnight. By the way, she added, somewhat irrelevantly, that was only the second time she had ever been in Hurlbut's car.

She remembered testifying about the case in Judge Guerin's court in early February. When she had been asked then what description she had given to the police on January 22, she had replied: "I told them your coloring, sort of brown hair and light brown skin, sort of, and brown eyes; shorter than the usual man." She had gone on to add that the defendant had been "just a little bit" taller than her own "5 foot 4 or 5." Under no circumstances could he have possibly been six feet tall. Standing as erectly as he could, six-footer Chessman looked up from the transcript from which he had been reading.

Q. As far as your memory serves you, directing your attention back to this January 22 date, in the morning, is that still the correct impression you have?

A. Yes, that is the impression.

Hadn't she also told the police that "this bandit had a scar over his right eyebrow?" Yes, she had noticed "a fine, a very short, fine line" on his forehead. It had extended "maybe a quarter of an inch from the right eyebrow" in the direction of his ear. It had seemed to be slightly more ruddy than the rest of his complexion. She had only observed it for a moment. "We were in the car and I remember I saw a glimpse of that—I saw something that resembled a scar. It was dark." Juror Vamos noted that there was no scar over Chessman's right eye.

Mary Alice couldn't recall whether her assailant had had any hair on his chest. No, she had not seen a tattoo on his right forearm. In fact, she just remembered his face. "I don't know anything about the rest of his body."

Q. Were this person's pectoral or chest muscles flat, or were they highly developed?

A. I don't remember.

As a student of physiology, had she noticed "if his latissimus dorsal muscles were highly developed"? Fricke broke in and, with the observation that "there is no muscle by that name," told Mary Alice that she didn't have to answer that question.

Chessman decided not to argue the point but, according to *Blakiston's New Gould Medical Dictionary*, the latissimus dorsi muscle is "used to pull the body up in climbing." The Folsom push-up champion should have stood his ground.

She had been able to see the "hairline on his forehead, his profile and his hair," because he had turned on the dome light when they were parked in the ravine. He had switched on the light just before she had started to undress. She thought that he had turned it on "while he was fooling with the spotlight."

Q. Did he fool with the spotlight before you were disrobed or after?

A. Before.

She had been sitting in the car when she had seen him do something with the spotlight. Out of the corner of her eye, she had watched him standing by the left hand door of the car with a flashlight in his hand. Then he had reached in through the window and opened the glove compartment which was directly in front of where she was sitting.

Q. Then, he, standing outside of the car, reached across you and into the glove compartment, is that correct?

A. Yes, he—yes.

If the defendant remembered that Miss Meza had told Leavy that she had been "standing in back of the car" when this incident occurred, he gave no sign.

While she was dressing behind the car, she had not been able to get a good look at the car. She couldn't remember what type of tires or bumpers it had or whether there had been "any identifying trade names" on its rear. No, she hadn't seen any license plate. On second thought, "there might have been a license. I just didn't observe it, if there was."

Q. Do you remember of ever telling the police or testifying that you did see a license plate on the car, but you did not have an opportunity to observe the number?

A. Yes. Yes, there was a license. I remember of seeing it after he let me off by my home. I was going to try to look at it, but he told me to turn the other way.

Her face had begun to itch early on the morning of January 22. Within a few hours, it was "considerably swollen." So bad, in fact, that she could "hardly see out of my eyes." But she was still able to identify people "if they were standing in front of me."

Q. Could you tell at a distance of 50 feet?

A. Oh, yes, I could. I wasn't blind. My eyes were just swollen; they weren't completely shut.

On Saturday, the twenty-fourth, a policeman—she thought it had been Officer Forbes—had come to her house and asked her to identify a suspect who was standing on the sidewalk. "I was in this—in the second story, and I was looking down —I was looking out of the window on the first floor, at the man," she told Chessman. She thought she had been as far from him as she was from the courtroom rail. Fricke, who knew his preserve, murmured that "that is exactly 22 feet."

Q. You were in the second floor of this house?

A. Yes, I was, and I looked out through both windows, the first floor and the second floor window.

When Chessman said, "No further questions," Leavy was on his feet again. Had Miss Meza identified the man whom Officer Forbes had brought to her house? She certainly had —"I identified him right there, Chessman."

Q. That is the man you were talking about, is that right?

A. That is right.

Q. When he has been using this term "that man that they brought there that day," you were referring to Chessman, in your answers?

A. Yes, I was.

There had been some other men whom the police had brought over to her house but "they weren't the men—it wasn't the man." Chessman was "definitely" the one she had identified. There was no doubt in her mind that he was the man.

On the ride home, she had had a conversation with the defendant. She had asked him whether he was Italian and he had said that he was. She was certain that Chessman's voice "sounds exactly the same" as the one she had heard in the car, "just a monotone all the time."

Q. Is that one of the means by which you identify him, in addition to his facial appearance?

A. That is right.

Chessman had a few more questions. Wasn't it true that "during the conversation with this bandit that he asked you directions how to get home, and that he said he was not familiar with Los Angeles?" Yes, it was. He had said he was from New York. She had told the police all about that. When she had asked him, "Why did you do these things?" he blamed his actions on an unfaithful wife. "He said something about his wife deserting him while he was in the Navy or something," she testified.

Q. Did you ask this person if he was an Italian?

A. Yes.

Q. Previous to the time of asking this question, did you have the impression he was Italian?

A. Yes.

When Fricke told Mary Alice that she was excused, the girl made no move to leave the witness chair. Finally, he leaned over and, in a sharp voice, said, "Miss Meza, you can go home now." She stared at him for a moment, arose and, without looking to either side, walked quickly through the rail gate and out the back door of the courtroom. For a moment, it was difficult to believe that she was gone.

A. W. Hubka, a career police officer attached to the Hollywood Detective Bureau, was a tall man with sharp features who bore a striking resemblance to Jack Webb. He had arrived at the Hollywood Division shortly after Chessman and

Knowles had been brought in by May. Since he and his partner, Sergeant Colin C. Forbes, were in charge of the "red light bandit" investigation, he had been informed by headquarters that a likely suspect had been captured by Reardon and May after a wild chase through Hollywood.

Yes, he had been present while Chessman was searched. He had seen May remove "a small nut, elongated" from the defendant's pocket. It was his impression that it had been "longer than the standard nut and beveled on one end, and covered with a grayish-appearing paint or plating."

Q. Did you see May actually take that from Chessman?

A. I did.

He had watched the officer put his hand in Chessman's right front pants pocket and pull out the nut together with some loose change.

When he saw the nut, Hubka had told May, "Here is something that is significant in this case, inasmuch as it appears to be a nut off a bolt that holds a clamp on a spotlight." In order to safeguard it, the witness had "picked up a paper clip on the desk there and put it through the nut to facilitate its handling." When Leavy showed him People's Exhibit 9, he stated that it looked like "the nut which May took from Chessman."

He had first seen Exhibit 10, an automobile spotlight, on a 1946 Ford coupé in the police impound garage on South Figueroa on the morning of January 24.

Q. Did you ever see the rim and the glass?

A. I . . . observed the rim and the glass about nine o'clock on the evening of Friday, the twenty-third of January, this year, in a room—adjoining the room occupied by Chessman and Officer May. The rim and lens were lying on top of the overcoat that is one of the exhibits in this case.

He had found a screwdriver and a pair of pliers in the coupé's glove compartment, which, together with the spotlight and the nut, had been turned over to Lieutenant Lee

Los Angeles Times Photo

Caryl Chessman (right) and David Knowles in the Hollywood Police Station following their arrest after a mile long police chase through Hollywood.

The police identification photograph of Caryl Chessman taken shortly after his arrest.

Brad Williams

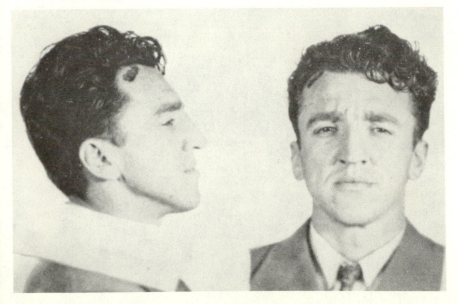

Sergeant E. M. Goosen displaying the money found in Chessman's possession after his capture.

Mary Alice Meza.

Superior Court Judge Charles W. Fricke.

Deputy Public Defender Al Matthews and Caryl Chessman.

Jones of the Scientific Investigation Division on January 29.

He and Forbes had also discovered "six or eight" strands of hair in the car's back seat. After turning them over to Lieutenant Jones, he had driven out to the Meza home in West Hollywood and taken Mary Alice and her mother to the police garage. When the girl had identified the Ford coupé, he had accompanied her to the Scientific Investigation Bureau at 324 West First Street where, with Mrs. Meza's help, "I removed some hair from Mary Meza's head." He had immediately taken the strands to the Crime Laboratory.

Chessman was intensely interested in the hairs Hubka had found. What color had they been? They were various shades of brown. Who had been with him when they were found? Sergeant Forbes and a garage attendant. Where had the hairs been placed? In a white envelope which Forbes had obtained from the attendant. Where had the hairs been found? The first ones had been located on the right and left sides of the rear seat. No, he couldn't say where each individual hair had been found—"I do know that Sergeant Forbes would say, 'Now here is one right here,' and then he would pull it loose from the tufting or upholstery, and he would say, 'Here is one that appears to be a lady's hair; it is long.' "

Forbes confirmed his partner's story. Because it had been so dark in the police garage, he had borrowed a flashlight, and he and Hubka had carefully inspected the car's rear seat. He thought that they had found "around ten or twelve hairs" instead of the "six or eight" Hubka had mentioned. It had been Forbes who had taken Chessman to Mary Alice's house at 11:00 A.M. on Saturday, January 24. The day before, he had shown her another suspect but she had said "that he wasn't the man," although his car "looked similar."

When the defendant took over, his face was impassive. Ignoring the little smile of recognition which Forbes threw his way, he wanted the police officer to tell him all about the visit to Mary Alice's home on Saturday morning, January 24.

Forbes was happy to oblige. He had gone to Sierra Bonita Avenue at eleven o'clock or so and told the girl that "I had a suspect I wanted her to look at. I had to wait about four minutes for her to come downstairs. When she came down I told her I had a suspect for her to look at. She said, 'Where is he?' I said, 'Look through the window.' You were standing with Sergeant Goosen, who she didn't know was a police officer."

There had been a uniformed policeman present but he had been standing some "30 or 40 feet" away across the street.

Q. How close to me was Sergeant Goosen standing at the time this identification was made?

A. Side by side.

The moment Mary Alice had looked out the window, she had identified Chessman. With a little cry, she had turned to Forbes and said, "That's him." When the detective asked her, "Which one?", she had replied, "The man with the crooked nose."

Q. What was the distance between this window you were looking out of to the place where Officer Goosen and myself were standing?

A. I would say 30 feet.

Q. How long had Miss Meza looked out the window when she did identify me as the suspect?

A. Not over three seconds.

The clock read 4:05 when Leavy called Leland V. Jones, a forensic chemist in charge of the Scientific Investigation Division of the Los Angeles Police Department. A chemistry major, he had attended Utah State University, UCLA and USC and was presently teaching Scientific Criminological Investigation at the latter school. For almost thirteen years, he had been almost exclusively engaged in comparing footprints, hair, and other physical evidence for use in criminal and civil trials. As he started to describe the microscopic equipment in his laboratory, Fricke broke in and asked him how much space his division occupied. Jones had no idea, but he did know that he had "close to $75,000 worth of equipment." The judge, who was used to pennypinching legislatures, sounded incredulous when he asked, "You get almost everything you want?" When Jones reassured him that he had to fight for his appropriation each year just like anyone else, His Honor nodded knowingly and waved Leavy on.

But the district attorney, with one eye on the clock, had only a question or two more. He just wanted to know whether Jones had ever testified in court before "concerning your comparison and studies." Yes, sir, he certainly had. More than fifteen hundred times in many of the counties of California as well as in general courts-martial. Fricke interrupted to state that he believed that Leavy had qualified the witness as a scientific expert and that this was as good a place to stop as any. Nobody disagreed with him.

9

THE TRIAL—THE PEOPLE REST

(FRIDAY, MAY 7, 1948)

On Friday morning, for the first time since the trial began, it started on time. At exactly 9:30, Lieutenant Jones, whom Al Matthews described as an "old-school type of police chemist," settled himself in the witness chair. When Leavy showed him Exhibits 9 and 28, the nut and a pair of pliers, he recalled that Forbes and Hubka had brought them to his laboratory on January 29. He had studied both exhibits under a low power microscope, and it was his opinion that some flakes of silver and bronze metal that he had found on the gripping jaw of the pliers were "similar to the material on the nut."

The two detectives had also brought Jones an envelope containing some hair, on the twenty-ninth. The next day, he had received some loose hair from Hubka which he had placed in a glass tube. He had made a slide of two strands from each sample and compared them under a wide field binocularscope. "I found that the hair was similar in appearance in that the granular appearance was the same, that the pigmentary granules had the same appearance. The medulla was both present and missing in certain portions of it, but that the medullary appearance was again the same color, was

100

the same. From that I arrived at the conclusion that they could have come from the same head."

Fricke suggested that some time might be saved if Jones would tell the jury "something about the characteristics of hair, the differences that you found, and the significance of the similarities that you observed." The witness explained that hair was composed of a center known as the medulla, a cortex which was the space between the medulla and the cuticle, the "outside portion of the hair." The pigmentary granules, which gave it its color, were found in both the medulla and the cortex. By a study of these and other general characteristics, it was possible to "point out points of similarity." But, it was impossible to "definitely state that a hair came from any one individual."

At the conclusion of Jones' dissertation, Juror Graves stood up and asked Fricke whether she was entitled to question the burly chemist. The judge was quite expansive—not only could she ask her question but she could do so sitting down. "You don't have to be that formal," he assured her. She wanted to know whether hair that had never been bleached "can be of . . . different variations of the same color." Yes, it could. "Sun can bleach hair out. Hair can be of various colors, a slight difference in color in the individual's head."

Mrs. Graves, who sported a lovely head of hair, told Jones that she had noticed that hair which had never been dyed, like her own, "will have different colors—that is what makes it beautiful—which is the condition of my hair." Fricke, ever the gentleman, gallantly observed that "Nature has been kind to you." The motel operator was only too happy to agree with him.

Chessman directed his attention to Jones' microscopic examination of the hair which Hubka and Forbes had brought to the laboratory. Had he been able to ascertain from what portion of the body the samples had come? From their length, he thought that they had been head hairs. "They are long enough" he explained, "that I do not think they could possibly have come from any other part of the body." It had been "rather fine hair" which he would classify "as a brown." He thought that he had seen roots on some of the hairs but it was impossible to tell how recently they had been pulled from their owner's head.

During his examination, had he found anything which might indicate that any of these hairs "had been in contact with a fabric of an automobile?" Jones, with a quick glance in Leavy's direction, opined that "if there had been fiber adhering to it, that fiber could have come from an automobile, or it could have come from clothes or from any place." But he hadn't noticed any fibers on the samples. If there had been any, he would have had "to compare those fibers with other sources."

Q. Were you looking for this foreign debris? Did you make tests for it, actually?

A. No, I looked for any type of adhering debris. I always look over the material, that is, to see if there happens to be something on there that has a different appearance. If so, then I try to run it down to see what is the origin of it. I saw nothing adhering to the hair that had the appearance of a foreign substance that I could run down or identify.

Now, as to the Exhibits 9 and 28, was it his testimony "that these pliers have been in contact with this nut?" Not at all. "I said that there was some marks on the nut that indicated an instrument similar to those pliers had been on it. In other words, a series of scratch marks on the surface, and I stated that I found certain materials on the jaws of the pliers that had a similar appearance to the outside coating of the nut and the inside, possibly, of the nut." He couldn't say whether he had found any paint on the pliers —merely some "light substance" that had a "metallic appearance."

Q. Do you think, then, that the substance that is on the

pliers and the substance found on the outside of this little nut are the same?

A. No, I couldn't make any such statement. I simply stated before that I found materials of the same appearance.

Leavy, with Fricke's permission, made Jones retrace some of his steps. It was true, wasn't it, that the two hair samples he had examined could have come from the same head? Yes, it was. The prosecutor couldn't resist asking one more question. "In all cases," he asked, "you are able to say when it does not come from the same head, is that correct?" "You cannot always say that it does not come from the same head," replied the chemist. Leavy looked stunned. "Do you in this case say that it does not come from the same head?" he stammered. Jones retreated into a double negative. "No, I don't say it does not come from the same head." He was promptly excused.

Sydney Jones, who described himself as "a truck driver," worked at the police impound garage on South Figueroa. He remembered that Forbes and Hubka had visited the garage in January and inspected a Ford coupé. In fact, they had borrowed a flashlight and a small envelope from him. He had watched the two officers pick up hairs from the vehicle's rear seat with a pair of tweezers. Because he was "in and out of the garage," he had only seen them find two hairs.

Jones told Chessman that he hadn't watched Hubka and Forbes too closely because, as the only attendant in the garage, he was "supposed to watch what goes on in the building." During the search, he had been standing "about a foot from the car." Was he sure that they were placing hairs in the envelope? "Well, I wouldn't say what it was exactly," he said. "It was fine. My eyes ain't the best in the world, so I wouldn't say it was just a hair, but it was something in there; it was fine. I seen that much." He recalled that some other people had searched the car on another occasion, but he "didn't pay any particular attention at that time."

Jones was followed on the stand by Nicholas Raya, the owner of a Hollywood cocktail bar. Speaking with a strong Italian accent, he said that Forbes and Hubka had approached him in late January when he was parking his 1947 Ford on Highland Boulevard. After a stop at a police station, the two detectives had taken him "past La Brea about five or six blocks."

Q. Did Officers Forbes and Hubka tell you they were taking you some place to see if you could be identified?

A. Yes.

Q. Have some girl look at you?

A. Yes.

After they had made him "stand on a street somewhere," he was released.

Chessman merely wanted to know what conversation had taken place between the policemen and the witness. Raya became quite voluble. "When I got down from the car, the two deputies here asked me about the car, whose car it was, and I said it was mine. So I show him the slip, the pink slip and everything. They looked all over the car, the pink slip and everything else, and then they took me to the police station. We stayed there about half an hour, I think. Then they called up the Automobile Club, or where I got the car —I don't know what they do—so Mr. Forbes asked me, 'We want to take you some place, to some girl,' but I don't know anything about it, you see. I said, 'I will go with you.' So they took me some place, five or six blocks past La Brea, and he gets me down out of the car, and I stand up on the sidewalk and some girl look from a window—she look at me. I think he tell me to turn around, and I turned around. After five minutes, he released me and said, 'Go ahead.' That is all I know."

After Ernest A. Wolker, who operated a gas station on East

Seventh Street, testified that the front license plate of his 1937 Chevy—California 8Y1280—had been stolen around Christmas time, Leavy called Robert Rittenhouse, a Los Angeles police photographer. Mr. Rittenhouse had taken most of the pictures of the Ford coupé which the prosecution had introduced into evidence. With the exception of a shot of the car's dashboard, all of his photographs had been taken during daylight hours in the police impound garage. As for the dashboard, "I took this picture about 8:30 or 9:00 o'clock in the evening."

Following a short recess, Leavy read into the record the preliminary hearing testimony of Gerald Stone, the truck salesman who had squired Esther Panasuk to Mulholland Drive on January 20. Mr. Stone, it seemed, was presently plying his wares in Manila, and the defendant had no objection to the district attorney's recitation. As Leavy droned on, only the jury was listening to him. Fricke took advantage of the lull to sign some orders in another case, while Chessman and Matthews conversed in low whispers at the counsel table.

Shortly after midnight on the twentieth, Stone and Miss Panasuk had been parked on the drive above Laurel Canyon. A few minutes later, "a car . . . pulled up in front of me with a red light, parked bumper to bumper, and a man walked over and said he wanted to see my identification." Stone had gotten out of his car and opened his wallet when the man said, "This is a stick-up."

Q. Did he have anything in his hands at that time?

A. A .45.

The bandit had seized the salesman's wallet, removed the money in it, and then taken the girl's purse. "He stuck his finger in her purse and pulled some money out of her purse and asked me if I would stay there for an hour and would she take the keys with her. I said I would stay around for an hour. He told me not to follow him. He got in the car and

turned around and went back down the canyon." The pickings had been pretty poor— "He took a dollar from me and
. . . a dollar and some change from my girl."

He thought that the man's car had "appeared to be a light
color," but he had not gotten a good look at it because the
spotlight was shining in his eyes. As for the gun which the
prosecutor had shown him, it looked "exactly like" the one
the thief had been carrying.

Q. I will ask you to take a look at this counsel table and
see if you can recognize anyone as being the person
who pointed that gun at you.

Stone had pointed his finger at Chessman. "I would suspect
it was him," he had said. But he couldn't be certain because
the man who robbed him had been wearing a hat and "a
handkerchief over his face." Rose had tried another tack.

Q. I will ask you to take a look at this defendant and
state whether or not the portion of the face which
you could see on this person resembles any portion
of the face of this defendant.

A. It does, yes.

Q. What is it about him which resembles the defendant.

A. His hair, his eyes, and particularly his nose.

On cross-examination, Stone had sworn that the car he
had seen "wasn't a club coupé."

Q. You are certain of that?

A. I am positive.

But hadn't he identified Rittenhouse's photograph of a
club coupé as the car he had seen that night? Yes, he had
but he had been influenced by the angle from which the
picture had been taken.

Q. In other words, then, you are not certain what type
of car it was?

A. It was a '47 Ford coupé.

As far as Stone had remembered, the bandit had been
dressed in army suntans, a snug-fitting windbreaker and a

hat. He had worn a handkerchief over his face "just to the bottom of his nose." He had testified that the man had been "six feet tall" and weighed "between 170 and 180 pounds." His most outstanding physical characteristic had been "a sharp nose."

Q. And you say that you are reasonably sure it is me but you are not able to positively identify me, is that correct?

A. That is correct.

Q. In other words, under oath, you couldn't say for certain it was me that accosted you.

THE COURT: He has testified to that and he is under oath now and the record will speak for itself.

Q. Then you can't positively identify me?

THE COURT: Don't ask repetitious questions. You have elected to represent yourself and you will be limited to the strict rules of evidence and you can't ask the same things over and over again.

What was there about the Colt .45 automatic he had been shown by the district attorney that made him so sure it was "similar" to the one the bandit had brandished? Nothing that he could recall. He had been certain that the flashlight he had seen in court was the "exact type" the thief had used, but it "could have been . . . another light similar to it in type."

Rose, who had been obviously nettled by Stone's insistence that the bandit's car had been a 1947 Ford, had asked him whether he knew "the difference in the appearance of a 1946 and 1947 Ford." The witness had been certain that he did. When the district attorney had tried to pin him down as to the difference, Judge Guerin had broken in. "Are you cross-examining your own witness now?" he had wanted to know. Rose had apparently decided that discretion was the better part of valor and, with a resigned shrug of his shoulders, had announced, "Well, that is all."

But Guerin's curiosity had been aroused and he had asked

Stone whether he was "quite certain you could not be mistaken about the year or model of the car?" The truck salesman had beaten a strategic retreat. The spotlight had been shining in his eyes, he had explained, and he couldn't be sure about the car's vintage.

THE COURT: You are not sure then whether it was a '46 or a '47 Ford?

THE WITNESS: No, sir. I was under the impression— it was only an impression though—that it was a '46, but I couldn't say for sure.

THE COURT: Is the same true with respect to your testimony that it was a coupé and not a club coupé?

THE WITNESS: The same is true, sir.

Rose, with a grateful smile in the direction of the bench, had excused the witness. Stone who, fifteen minutes earlier, had been "positive" that the car had been a 1947 model and not a "club coupé," had looked slightly bewildered as he left the stand.

Leavy had one more transcript to read into the record. Dr. Thomas B. Bartle, a dentist who maintained an office in the Hollingsworth Building, had sailed for Hawaii just prior to the trial. At the preliminary hearing, he had testified that, early on January 18, he had been driving with a girl named Ann Plaskowitz on the Pacific Coast Highway toward Malibu Beach, when a car with a red light had forced him over to the side of the road. "I thought it was an officer," he had told Judge Guerin, "and I stopped and this man got out and posed as an officer and wanted my identification." When Bartle, who was wise to the ways of the world, had asked to see his badge, the man "showed me a .45 automatic which scared the daylights out of me, and said, 'Start shelling out,' which I did."

Q. How much money did you give him?

A. I don't know exactly. I thought it was probably in

the neighborhood of $15, but I might have had more; I don't know exactly.

Bartle had thought that the bandit's car had been "a 1947 or thereabouts, a Ford coupé. It was gray in color." He had appraised Rittenhouse's photograph as "a true, correct and fair representation of the automobile." The gun that had "scared the daylights out of me," looked very much like the one Rose had asked him to identify. "I would say it was a gun very similar to that," he had told the district attorney, "if not the same gun."

When he was asked whether he could recognize "anyone seated at this counsel table as being the person who pointed that gun at you," he had looked directly at Chessman and stated, "I do; that man right there." After he had handed over his money, he had been told to "Get going," an instruction he had promptly obeyed. He had turned into Malibu Road and called the police from the first service station he saw.

Chessman had confined himself to Bartle's identification of the person who had robbed him. How tall had he been? About five foot ten. And how much had he weighed? Between 160 and 165 pounds. Two weeks earlier, in a police report, the witness had described his assailant as "Age 30, Height 5 foot 6, Weight 150, Build stocky, Complexion tan, crooked teeth in front." As for his clothes, he had been dressed in "a gray hat with a black band, and, as far as I could tell, khaki-colored clothing." He had also been wearing "a short jacket but not a coat."

Was there any doubt in the dentist's mind that the defendant was the man who had accosted him? None whatsoever.

Q. Do you recognize my voice? Does that seem to be a significant factor in the identification?

A. I recognize you in whole, in all parts.

Q. Well, that is general. That doesn't answer the specific question. Do you recognize any particular features of mine when you made your report to the officers?

A. I told the officers you had a protruding lower lip and I think you will find it in the report.

Q. And anything else. Did you mention the fact that my nose had been broken or anything like that?

A. No, I wouldn't know about those details. All I know is that you are the man. All human beings have minds, and you can't go into great detail as to why I know it, but I just know it, that is all.

Chessman had looked incredulous. "You just know it?" he had roared at the witness. Bartle had stood his ground. "Definitely, you are the person," he had told him, "I recognized you immediately when I went to the police station the other night." This had been quite enough for the defendant who, with a barely audible "That is all," had sunk back into his seat at the counsel table.

Leavy's voice was hoarse after reading Stone's and Bartle's testimony aloud for more than an hour. He decided to give it a rest and asked Fricke to help him in making sure that all of his thirty-three exhibits had been marked in evidence. With the exception of a letter from Floyd Ballew to Elaine Bushaw explaining that he could not leave Custer City, Oklahoma, for the trial, a photograph of some money taken at the Hollywood police station, and a pen and pencil set, the judge admitted all the rest.

The state's last scheduled witness was Ruth Meza, Mary Alice's mother. Mrs. Meza, an older edition of her daughter, was employed by the County of Los Angeles as a clerk in the Probate Court. To Al Matthews, she was "a professional Hollywood mother type"; Leavy saw her as "a plain, nice-looking little woman." Several years after the trial, she was to divorce her husband and marry a building superintendent named Charles Shaw.

The morning of January 22 was still very fresh in her

mind. She had received a telephone call from the police just before 4:00 A.M., telling her that her daughter had been kidnapped on Mulholland Drive. Five minutes later, Mary Alice had walked into the house in a state of near hysteria. She had helped the girl undress and get into bed. The next day, Mary was so ill that Mrs. Meza had called the Probate Court and asked for a week's leave of absence.

Because her daughter could not bear to be left alone, the witness had had to remain in her room while she was awake.

Q. What was her condition, without giving us any conversation with her?

A. She had a swelling, which started in a day or two—the same day, and continued to get worse for several days. I was very frightened.

By the next morning, her daughter had developed such a tremor that Mrs. Meza had to feed her by hand.

On January 24, Sergeant Forbes had come to the house and asked whether Mary Alice could come downstairs and identify a suspect. Because the girl was in no condition to leave the house, Forbes had suggested that she go to her bedroom window and look at a man standing on the sidewalk.

Q. Did she, in your presence, identify Chessman as the man who had assaulted her?

A. Yes, she said, "That is the man."

Chessman had been standing next to another man in civilian clothes and she had had no idea which one had assaulted her daughter until the latter had pointed him out.

A week later, Sergeant Hubka had accompanied Mary Alice and herself to the police garage on Figueroa Street. After the girl had identified "the car driven by the defendant," Hubka had taken them to the police laboratory on First Street. While they sat in the car, Mrs. Meza, at the detective's request, had pulled out several hairs from her daughter's head and given them to him.

Q. Did he leave you with those hairs between his fingers, walk away and go into that building?

A. That is right.

Chessman had no questions for Mrs. Meza and she was excused. Leavy informed Fricke that he had no further witnesses to offer and that, with His Honor's permission, he would rest the People's case if he was allowed to bring Reardon or May back to identify Exhibit 16, the photograph of the money which the judge had earlier excluded for lack of connection. "I will allow you to reopen so far as that is concerned if the occasion arises," Fricke told him. He glanced up at the clock. "I think we will take our recess at this time, and give the defendant a chance to prepare his opening."

After lunch, before Al Matthews could call his first witness, Leavy interrupted and informed Fricke that he wanted to recall Sergeant Forbes to identify Exhibit 16. The detective had seen Rittenhouse take the picture of the money in the Hollywood Police Station some time on the afternoon of January 29. The money, along with the clothes that had been found in the Ford coupé after Chessman's capture, had then been returned to Melvin Waisler, the owner of Town Clothiers. When Forbes stepped down, Fricke, with the observation that "I think that connects it sufficiently," admitted Exhibit 16. One of Leavy's loose threads had been tied.

Reverend J. Roy Harris, a part-time clergyman who worked for the Department of Employment, was the first witness for the defense. After being sworn, he remained standing during Chessman's first few questions. When Fricke noticed this, he asked the minister whether he was from Canada. "Originally," Harris replied. The judge reminded him that local custom permitted witnesses to testify from a sedentary position and, with a grateful smile, Harris sat down, crossed his long legs, and looked quizzically at the defendant.

Carl Hoelscher's Pasadena clothing store had been held up at 7:00 P.M. on January third. That was the day, Harris recalled, when he had conducted burial services for Lillian Cottle, Chessman's grandmother, at Forest Lawn Cemetery. The funeral had begun at 10:30 that morning and ended at noon. He had then visited the Chessmans at their home at 3280 Larga Avenue, just a few blocks away from the cemetery, where he had seen the defendant and his parents.

Q. How long did you remain there?

A. Approximately 30 minutes.

He thought that he had left Larga Avenue at 12:30. No, he told Leavy, he had no idea where Chessman had been "before or after that."

Mrs. Gerda Adair, a secretary at the Ambassador Hotel, who was one of Mrs. Chessman's friends, had not been able to get away from work to attend Mrs. Cottle's funeral. As soon as she had returned home that evening, she had called the Chessman home and spoken to the defendant. "It was after I came home from work," she explained. "It was somewhere between seven, I believe—six-thirty and seven-thirty; somewhere in through there." She remembered that Chessman had answered the telephone.

Q. You say I answered this call, is that correct?

A. You did. I talked with you a few minutes and then I asked to talk to your mother. I talked with her quite a while. I was anxious to know how she felt, because I knew she was terribly upset through her mother's death. She wasn't able to attend the funeral.

Was there any doubt in her mind that she had spoken to the defendant? None at all. "I talked with you and then I talked with your mother afterwards."

Leavy wondered how Mrs. Adair was able to remember "the exact date you called that telephone number." "I know I called," the witness insisted, "because I was anxious to know how she [Mrs. Chessman] felt." But hadn't her memory been refreshed recently by somebody who "spoke to you [to] . . . ask you if you remembered making that call?" Oh, yes, she had been reminded of it "a couple of weeks ago."

Q. That was really the first time you were called upon
to throw your memory back to when you made the
call, isn't that right?

A. That is right.

Q. You had no note or memorandum of the exact hour,
did you?

A. No, I have no way of telling the exact hour.

With a look of profound disbelief on his face, Leavy excused
the witness.

The district attorney took advantage of Matthews' request
for a fifteen-minute recess to recall Officer May. What had
happened to the money he had taken from Chessman's
pocket at the Hollywood Police Station? He had booked it as
evidence. Did Rittenhouse's photograph, which had already
been admitted by Fricke as Exhibit 16, "look like the appearance of the money, that is, as to quantity and the nature
of the currency, that you booked?" It most certainly did.
However, he told the defendant that he could not swear
that the money in the photograph was "the money . . . removed from [his] pocket."

Mrs. Winona Phillips announced, with some degree of
pride, that she was "writing a novel." She had known the
defendant since he was two years old. On Tuesday, January
13, the day that Mrs. Howell's car had been stolen in Pasadena, she had seen Chessman at her house at 3527 Greensward Road. "It must have been about two o'clock or
thereabouts," she recalled, "between two o'clock and three
o'clock." She remembered the time because she had already
finished her lunch and was back at her desk. The defendant
had told her that he had just visited the parole board. "I
was surprised," she confessed, "because I didn't realize that
you had to go to that place, and I remember of making the
remark that, 'Well, that is an unlucky day; it is the thirteenth!'"

Caryl, she said, had only stayed an hour. She had next

seen him on the nineteenth, "just as dark time came in— early." He had come to help her edit her novel, a chore he had been performing for her for several months. He had not left that evening until "around ten o'clock; maybe eleven o'clock; shortly afterward; something like that."

Q. You are certain that I was there at the times you have testified to and on these days; there is no doubt in your mind?

A. No, there is no doubt in my mind.

Q. You are certain you could not be mistaken?

A. I am certain I could not be mistaken.

A very definite lady, indeed.

Leavy was visibly nervous as Mrs. Phillips testified. If Chessman had been at her house at the times she had indicated, he could hardly have heisted the Howell's Ford on the thirteenth and attacked Mrs. Johnson on its front seat six days later. When the prosecutor rose and walked over to the witness chair, his expression was grave. Just when was it, he demanded, that Mrs. Phillips had first recalled that Chessman had visited her on the thirteenth? Why, Mr. Chessman had reminded her of it only yesterday when she had visited him in the county jail. But she would have remembered it without any help from him. If a thing had happened, how could a person forget it? The expression on Leavy's face betrayed a certain lack of faith in her mnemonic powers.

Wasn't it true that she hadn't thought about the defendant's visit to her on the thirteenth until she had talked to him yesterday? No, sir, it was not. She had read of his arrest in the papers and she had remembered then that she had said something about the thirteenth being "an unlucky day."

Q. There wasn't anything in the paper that called to your attention that he had been accused of committing a crime on January 13, was there?

A. No, not that I can recall.

At this point, Juror King wanted to know whether "the witness knows what time it gets dark on that particular day."

Leavy, who obviously did not relish the interruption, asked her to be patient and he would get to that point before he was through with Mrs. Phillips. "We will let Mr. Leavy do all the work," Fricke admonished the inquisitive Mrs. King.

Mrs. Phillips was adamant. No, Caryl hadn't asked her yesterday "to remember what happened on January 13." He had merely requested whether she could recall "any of the times when he was at my house."

Q. And you immediately recalled January 13?

A. I said I didn't think I could remember but about two days that he was there, the day or evening he was there—some days and some evenings.

He had begun coming to her home shortly after he had been released from prison—"come down from the North," as she delicately put it. She was positive that he had arrived after two o'clock on the thirteenth and that he had stayed with her an hour or so.

Leavy, ever mindful that Mrs. Howell's car had been stolen in neighboring Pasadena at 3:55 on January 13, suggested to Mrs. Phillips that perhaps her visitor had been gone well before three o'clock. If he had come to her house, say, at 1:45, he could have left by 2:45. No, she was "pretty sure" that he had not arrived before two o'clock.

Q. Well, would you say he could have been gone within 45 minutes?

A. I would say an hour.

Q. It could have been under, couldn't it?

A. It might have been over.

Q. It could have been well under, couldn't it?

A. It wasn't well under. I should say it was over an hour or maybe a little more.

The prosecutor shifted his attack. If Mrs. Phillips was so certain of her times, she must have made "a particular mental note." "My mind works, a lot of times, in funny ways," she informed him. In what ways, he wanted to know. She smiled ingenuously. Oh, funny ways, baffling ways.

Q. Conveniently, sometimes?

A. Well, about as well as yours would work, I guess.

If he was implying that she would lie to help a friend, she wanted it clearly understood that "I am under oath here and I am telling the truth. I never do anything against the law, and lying in court is against the law."

Leavy looked weary. He turned to January 19. Had the witness made any mental or other memorandum of that day? No, sir, she had not. She only knew that it had been a Monday. When had she first called upon her memory "to recall what happened on the nineteenth of January?" Well, she had started thinking about it when she heard that Caryl had been arrested. She thought that he had been picked up on the twenty-ninth but she hadn't known of it until a week later.

Was it her best recollection that she had last seen Chessman a week before the twenty-ninth? Fricke broke in to ask whether Leavy didn't mean ten days before. "The nineteenth would be ten days," he reminded him. The district attorney struggled to keep his voice calm. "I am questioning her, Your Honor. Your memory is good; hers isn't." The judge, with an apologetic little smile, busied himself with some papers on the bench.

It had been Mrs. Phillips' mother who had told her that Caryl had been arrested. "She . . . asked me if I had read about it, and I said no. She had brought a clipping and showed it to me."

Q. Well, do you remember what date it said in that paper?

A. No.

Then how in the world was it possible for her to tell when she had last seen the defendant if she couldn't even fix the date of the newspaper clipping? "I will tell you why," she snapped. "When I heard about it, naturally I was shocked and I felt sorry, and I thought I would see his mother. So I called her immediately." That was how she remembered the date.

Q. Well, do you remember the date?

A. I remember the day.

Q. The date or the day?

A. The day, a Monday.

Leavy looked properly stupefied. "Monday comes every seven days, Madam," he reminded her. She had an answer for that one. "It just happens," she told him, "I had a birthday on the twenty-second. That also called it to my mind."

Q. Is that the same day his mother called you and told you he had been arrested that day?

A. No.

The prosecutor shook his head. I don't understand, he told her, why you can't tell me "how you fix what you believe or what you heard to be the date of this defendant's arrest." She could if he would let her explain. "I'm not asking for an explanation," he shouted, "I am asking you to tell me first what day it was someone told you Chessman was arrested." As far she could remember, her mother had said that Caryl had been arrested "yesterday."

Suddenly, Mrs. Phillips' face brightened. She was sure that he had been at her house on Monday, January 19, because she had plotted a new ending for her novel after his visit and she had been eager to have him come over as soon as possible. "I was anxious to talk to him and get his opinion of it," she said. However, she remembered that, when she had seen him Monday, he had asked "if he could come on my birthday." She had told him then that she was going out for the day. "I was wishing," she said, "he would come over after my birthday."

Q. When did he come over?

A. The last time he was over, on Monday before my birthday, on the nineteenth.

If she was so sure that she had entertained Chessman on the nineteenth, what had she done on the twentieth? Leavy looked almost gleeful when she mused that "the twentieth was a Sunday, and I probably had company there—" He broke in to ask whether she wanted the jury to believe that "Monday was January nineteenth and the twentieth was Sunday." No, she had made a mistake; "the twentieth would be a Tuesday." As to exactly when Caryl came to see her that day, she couldn't say but it was "6:00 or 6:30; something like that." A writer, she never paid much attention to time. Leavy let it go at that and Mrs. Phillips tripped lightly out of the courtroom to resume her sadly interrupted writing schedule.

Harold Ostran, Chessman's supervising parole officer, was next. The defendant had indeed reported to him on January 13. Leavy had only a few questions. At what time had this interview taken place? He had seen the parolee at 10:00 A.M. for "about 15 or 20 minutes." Did he know if Chessman was working? He was supposed to be; "he was released to employment at his father's nursery located on Fletcher Drive near Glendale."

Q. Was he privileged to drive a car, a 1946 Ford car, on the night of January 23, either in Redondo Beach or around Vermont Avenue?

A. He had no permission to drive any car.

Q. Did you know he was doing that?

A. No.

Mrs. Cottle's funeral had taken place at the Atwater Park Baptist Church on the corner of Tyburn and Perlita. Mrs. Lillian M. Fleming, her great-niece, had attended the services and then joined the procession to Forest Lawn Memorial Park. After the graveside ceremony, she had gone to the Chessman home where she had remained until 12:30. During her brief visit, she had spoken to Chessman and his mother.

Her sister-in-law, Cora A. Fleming, had attended the funeral with her brother. Toward evening, she had arrived at the Larga Avenue house. "It was daylight," she recalled, "late afternoon, because I went through the neighbor's yard, and when I left it was dark, because I came down the street instead of going through the yard; the street lights were on." Just before she left, she had seen Caryl, with a handful of books, going into his room.

Q. When you left it was dark on that day?

A. It was dark, because I couldn't go through the yard on account of the rose bushes.

Leavy was fully conscious that the robbery at Hoelscher's had taken place at seven that night. His opening gambit was much the same as it had been with Mrs. Phillips. Hadn't Mrs. Fleming discussed her testimony with someone before the trial? Yes, Chessman's father had asked her to try to recall when she had been at the house. "That is the only time I have been approached," she insisted. When had this occurred? "I couldn't tell you," she replied, "I don't remember." Leavy's tone was caustic. "That is about how good your memory is, is that right?" he asked her. Mrs. Fleming was not one to get rattled. "That is right," she told the prosecutor. But she was absolutely certain that the street lights had been turned on when she had left the Chessman house that night. "You can call up and find out," was her parting shot.

At 7:30 P.M. on January 17, a half hour before Mary Tarro said that she had seen Chessman crawling into her bedroom window, Harold Lloyd Doty, an operating engineer's helper, had knocked on the front door of 3280 Larga Avenue. An amateur electrician, he had come to repair the invalided Mrs. Chessman's small table raido. After he had replaced a tube and restrung the dial cable, he remained to listen to *Gangbusters* with the family. He thought that he had been there "roughly, four or four-and-one-half hours."

He, too, had been consulted by Chessman's father after the defendant's arrest. "His father asked me if I would be willing to testify, and I told him I would if it was necessary." Leavy was interested in discovering when Mr. Doty had first remembered his January 17 visit. It had been last week when he was subpoenaed to appear in court. He had fixed the date by looking at a calendar. "It was a day or two following the funeral," he said, "that I went over to repair one of their other radios, and two days later, which would be the ninth, I went again and picked up parts for the radio, at which time I was with Mr. Chessman about two hours in the afternoon. And then it was the following Saturday that I went back to make the final repairs on the little radio."

Q. You mean the nearest Saturday from the ninth?

A. That was the seventeenth, yes.

Leavy scratched his head. Wasn't Mr. Doty aware that January ninth was a Friday and the next day would be the nearest Saturday to it? The witness refused to backtrack. "I know it was a week before I came back," he retorted. The district attorney handed him a calendar and asked him if he wanted to change his testimony that he had repaired Mrs. Chessman's radio "the very next Saturday after the ninth." No, he did not. "I merely misworded it the first time. It was a week later."

Doty had a remarkable memory. By reckoning back to the day of Mrs. Cottle's funeral, he knew that he had picked up one of the Chessman radios on the following Wednesday, January 7. He had not been able to return it for a week because he had been working and couldn't get the necessary parts. He had done some work on the radio that day at the repair shop he maintained in his back yard. On Saturday, the seventeenth, he had returned to Larga Avenue and worked on Mrs. Chessman's small radio. Leavy surrendered the witness.

Chessman stood up again. Did Doty remember what "I showed you in the rooms of the house?" Yes, he did. "You showed me the front room—that would be to the right as you go in—where you had—where you told me you had just finished laying the linoleum." That had happened on the same Saturday on which the witness had come to repair his mother's radio.

Q. Did you see this linoleum?
A. I did.

The room had been "a medium-size bedroom."

It was Leavy's turn again. He wanted to know whether Doty had seen the linoleum laid. "I merely know what he told me, that he had just finished laying the linoleum that day." He didn't know exactly when the linoleum had been laid except the week before "I had seen the room without linoleum." While he was fixing Mrs. Chessman's radio that Saturday, had the defendant been in the room with him all the time? No, part of the time Caryl was out of the room.

Q. As far as you know, he might have left the house?
A. He could have.
Q. You did not keep track of him, to see that he stayed in the house, did you?
A. No, I didn't.

How far was 3280 Larga Avenue from the Tarro home on Garden? Doty estimated that it was "roughly, two blocks."

Leavy returned to the linoleum. He wanted to know the dimensions of the front bedroom. Was it bigger than the jury box? Doty thought that it was "a little bigger than that, I believe." Juror King had a question. Had Doty noticed any peculiar odor before he had left the house that night? The witness knew exactly what Mrs. King was driving at. "Not that of glue, if that is what you are referring to," he answered.

Q. You don't remember any glue odor?
A. No, I don't.

William E. Simpson had been the district attorney of Los Angeles County since December 1, 1946. A florid, heavy-set, gray-haired man who looked like a back-county congressman, he had been subpoenaed by the defense. At the time of the trial, he was running unopposed for reelection. Chessman looked surprised when Simpson claimed that he knew nothing about "the case now being prosecuted in this courtroom." In fact, he had never discussed the matter with anyone. Yes, he had seen some copies of the *Equalizer,* but he knew nothing about the April, 1948 issue.

What about lie-detector tests? Had Mr. Simpson's office ever administered them? The witness started to answer when Fricke, who had been hovering over him like a mother hen, interrupted. "Just a minute, Mr. Simpson," he said, "I sustain an objection to that question as having absolutely nothing to do with this case." Simpson looked amused when the judge apologized for objecting on his behalf. He assured him that "It is all right with me, Your Honor."

Leavy had no questions. "I don't want to have to cross-examine my boss," he explained. When Matthews called out the name of his next witness, one Archie Pauff, the clerk informed Fricke that, because of the late hour, he had excused him until Monday. Matthews had no objections. "I don't think we would have gotten through anyway. I think it is almost the hour when the court calls recess. It is ten minutes to four." Court adjourned until Monday morning.

10

THE TRIAL—ALIBIS GALORE

(MONDAY, MAY 10, 1948)

During the Mother's Day weekend, negotiations in Washington over the impending rail strike had deadlocked. Just before Mrs. Hallie L. Chessman, the defendant's mother, was wheeled into the courtroom in a bed chair, at 9:50 A.M., word came through that President Truman had signed an executive order seizing the nation's railroads. But, in Department 43, the electrifying news from the White House was overshadowed by the spectacle of a wisp of a woman who, with her tired eyes fixed on the ceiling, was doing what she could to save her son's life.

Mrs. Chessman's back had been broken in an automobile accident when Caryl was nine years old. The jurors, who could look into her lined face as she testified in a quiet but strangely fervent voice, saw the unmistakable imprint of almost two decades of physical pain. The cancer, that would end her life a little more than a year after the trial, had already begun to sap what little vitality she had and, by the end of her stint, she seemed on the brink of collapse. "She looked like a very sick Whistler's Mother," was Al Matthews' comment.

Chessman could not bring himself to question his mother, and Matthews informed Fricke that, with His Honor's permission, he would conduct the examination of this witness. Mrs. Chessman had seen her son on January 3, "because that was the day of my mother's funeral." He had been with her all day long. "I remember," she said, "that Mrs. Cora Fleming was over in the evening and that Mrs. Adair called up that evening, and he answered the telephone, and he referred her to me. She wanted to see how I spent the day, and I had requested particularly that he stay with me during the time of the funeral. I had quite a number of others who had dropped out there, but I particularly wanted him to stay with me the day of the funeral."

On the afternoon of the seventeenth, her son "had been laying the Congoleum rug that we had gotten that day—Congoleum or linoleum that we had gotten." She recalled that Harold Doty had dropped in as well as Willman and Lucille Greene who had come for some of her mother's furniture.

Q. Do you remember whether your son was there that evening?

A. Yes, he was there very definitely all day and all evening because I—he did not leave me at all that day.

Mary Alice Meza had been kidnapped early on the morning of January 22. Caryl, Mrs. Chessman said, had been home on the night of the twenty-first. She was sure of that because she had had a severe attack earlier that day. So severe, in fact, that her husband had to call her physician, Dr. J. Mark Lacey. Lacey had given her a sedative and she had slept all that afternoon. Her son had stayed home "because I had been so dreadfully ill that he wanted to be sure —have me to be sure that I was all right after I would have to take a hypodermic. They gave me a hypodermic, so I could sleep all afternoon."

On the night of the twenty-third, she had asked Caryl to "go over to Gerda Adair's . . . to see her for me, and he had gone over there and he had called me up and told me that he had been over and was starting home, and he would be

home within an hour or an hour and a half." She thought
that she had spoken to him "between six and six-thirty." Matthews thanked her and sat down.

Now, Mrs. Chessman, Leavy purred, do you mean to say
that your son was never once out of your sight on January 17?
No, he had gone to the drugstore to get some cotton around
four o'clock and he had returned about an hour later. He
had been home during the rest of the day because he had
been working on the Congoleum rug. On the twenty-third,
she had not seen him after he had telephoned from Gerda
Adair's. But she was positive that he had not driven to Mrs.
Adair's house. "He went up by street car," she insisted. "He
walked up to the boulevard to take the street car."

Leavy was getting nowhere with Mrs. Chessman. How
about the twenty-first, was she sure that her son was in the
house when she "woke up at 6:00 P.M."? She certainly was.
And he had stayed home all that evening? Yes, he had.

Q. That is definitely true, is it?
A. Yes. He was very anxious about my condition. I had
   had a very severe attack that day.

There was no doubt in her mind that Caryl had remained
with her from the time she awakened "through the rest of
the evening of January 21." With that, Leavy called it quits
and the exhausted witness was quickly wheeled out of the
courtroom.

According to Gerald Stone's testimony which Leavy had
read aloud on Friday morning, he and his companion, Esther
Panasuk, had been robbed on Mulholland Drive at 12:10
A.M. on January 20. But Mrs. Helen Denny claimed that
she had seen Chessman at 12:20 that night in Bradley's,
a bar on Hollywood Boulevard. Mrs. Denny, a plain, soft-
spoken young lady who was a typist employed by the Hollywood Rental Service, had gone to Bradley's on the twentieth
with Ollie Treon, a fellow boarder at Joe Keene's rooming
house on Hawthorne Boulevard. There she had met a man

named Kenny Marsh who was sitting at the bar with two other men.

Q. Do you know—identify anyone sitting at this counsel table as one of the two other men?

A. You look like one of them.

She recognized Knowles, who had just been brought into the courtroom by two burly deputies, as the third member of the triumverate.

Mrs. Denny was a very thorough young woman. She kept track of all the money she spent in a stenographer's note-book. On Tuesday, January 20, her records indicated that she had gone to see *Golden Earrings* at the Hollywood Theatre. Later, at Bradley's, she had ordered a "Sloe gin coke, French fries and coffee, candy" and made one telephone call, all of which added up to an expenditure of ninety-one cents.

Q. Is there anything else written on January 20? Have you got a statement down there, "Met Kenny."

A. Yes, I have.

Mrs. Denny told Leavy that she had been working as a waitress in the Pig'n Whistle on January 20. Before she had gone to Bradley's, she had stopped for a cup of coffee "in a little malt shop after the show on Hollywood Boulevard." She couldn't remember where she had been prior to that but she thought that she had gone to church earlier in the evening, "about eight-thirty." On second thought, she was sure of it because she had been wearing a new hat which she had picked up at Reed's the week before.

Q. If you made a novena on January sixteenth, or the fourteenth, or the twenty-third, you would still have worn a hat, would you not?

A. Yes, sir; that is right.

Leavy kept pressing her. Where else had she been that night? She had dropped in at a little book shop "on some side street."

Q. How do you come to remember that now?

A. Do you have to have a reason for remembering things?

Q. Well, I do not know. I leave that up to the jury. How do you?

A. I just happen to remember, because I have never been in that book store there.

There was another place. Just before she had gone to the malt shop, she had drunk a sloe gin coke in the Circle Bar at the corner of McCadden Place and Hollywood Boulevard. In fact, she had been there twice that night.

Q. You made no note or memorandum that it was the night of January 20 that you also went in the Circle Bar, did you?

A. No. I saw my friend, Ollie, in there before I was in the Malt Shop.

She had begun to think about the night of January 20 when she had received a telephone call from a Mr. Pat Dailey over the weekend. He had tried to contact her on Saturday but she had not been home. Ollie Treon had informed her that someone was trying to find out whether she had been in Bradley's on January 20. Yesterday morning, she had spoken to Mr. Dailey and had told him where she had been that night.

Q. So you cannot go past Saturday, just past, to fix any day that anybody asked you to recall to your memory what you did on the night of January the twentieth or the morning of January twenty-first, is that right?

A. Yes, sir.

Leavy thumbed through Mrs. Denny's notebook. "I see," he observed, "that you have a penchant for green ink, is that right?" No, she had once filled her pen from a former roommate's bottle and she had used it "until it ran out."

Q. When did you run out of green ink?

A. About a week after I left there.

Q. Then you changed to some other ink?

A. Blue ink.

The prosecutor looked almost benign when he inquired whether the witness made her entries "on the same night these things occur." No, sometimes she had waited as long as a month before she wrote things down.

Q. Don't you forget, eventually, whether you are going back to write it in your memorandum, put it in there?

A. I do not forget.

Leavy looked incredulous. "What did you do two weeks ago today?" he demanded. The witness had a ready answer. "I went to City Hall," she told him. What about two weeks ago yesterday? She had stayed home all day. And two weeks ago Friday? She had gone to church. The district attorney took one more plunge. "What did you do two weeks ago Wednesday?" he asked. "I was out looking for a job two weeks ago Wednesday."

Then he turned his attention back to her notebook. Her last entry had been made yesterday. Since she entered every important happening, did she make any notation of Dailey's Saturday or Sunday calls? No, she had not. What about her girl friend Ollie's reminder on Saturday about "a message from a man as to refreshing your memory as to what occurred on the night of January twentieth or the morning of the twenty-first"—hadn't she considered that important enough to write down? Mrs. Denny shook her head vigorously. "No, I did not," she replied.

With the exception of the notations "Golden Earrings" and "Met Kenny," all the entries for January 20 were written in green ink. Leavy pounced. Did this mean that Mrs. Denny had gone back "and made those entries in your January 20 memorandum?" Yes, she supposed that it did. But she frequently went back and included things that she wanted "to remember . . . particularly." I see, murmured the prosecutor.

Mrs. Denny apparently led an active nocturnal life. Some man had bought a drink for her at the Circle Bar on the twentieth. Then, Kenny Marsh, who had been sitting at the bar with Chessman and Knowles, had picked her up at Bradley's. In fact, he had taken her home. Leavy had difficulty in keeping a smirk off his face.

Q. You talked to Marsh after he escorted you home, did you not. I mean you became acquainted with Marsh, did you not?

A. What, pray, has that to do with this?

Q. Madam, I am not trying to embarrass you. I have a purpose, and it is not to embarrass you. Did you become acquainted with Mr. Marsh by talking with him, befriending him? Did he befriend you? Whatever it was?

A. No, I did not.

It had been a short-lived friendship. She hadn't seen Marsh again until today, when she noticed him in court.

Leavy had only a few questions more. Was Mrs. Denny prepared to swear that Chessman and Knowles were the men she had seen with Marsh at Bradley's. "They look like them," she replied.

Q. You would not say positively that Knowles and Chessman are the men that were with Mr. Marsh the night you met Marsh, would you? They just look like them, do they not?

A. Of course they look like them.

When the prosecutor pressed the point, Mrs. Denny had her dander up. The man sitting at the counsel table, she retorted, was positively the man she had seen drinking beer with Marsh and Knowles at Bradley's that night.

As Mrs. Denny flounced out of the courtroom, one of the ladies in the jury box whispered something to Leavy. "Your Honor," the latter said, "an alternate juror is inquiring of me. I did not want to answer." Fricke agreed with the prosecutor's discretion. The alternate wanted to know what had happened to Esther Panasuk, the girl who had been sitting in Stone's car when he was robbed. "She is outside the State of California," she was informed. There was also another missing girl, Ann Plaskowitz, who had been mentioned by Dr. Bartle at the preliminary hearing. Before Fricke took the morning recess, he told Leavy that he would permit him to show later that his process server had been unable to locate either woman within the state.

Ollie Treon was a saleslady at the Hollywood Outlet at 6760½ Hollywood Boulevard. On January 20, she had worked until midnight and then met her friend, Helen Denny, in the Circle Bar. After finishing her drink, Mrs. Denny had left the bar first and, several minutes later, Mrs. Treon saw her next door in the Malt Bar. "She waved at me," she told Chessman, "and I went in and I had a cup of coffee with her then."

Q. Did you remain with her from that time until the time you went to Bradley's?
A. Yes, I did.

The two women had entered Bradley's "about 12:20 or 12:30, somewhere around there."

Q. While you were in there in Bradley's, did you see anyone seated at the counsel table here, at this table?
A. Yes, I did.
Q. Who?
A. You.

Chessman had been with "two other fellows." As far as Knowles was concerned, she wasn't sure that he had been there. "I am not sure about him," she testified, "I remember the other two, but one of them was very quiet, and he was the one that was very quiet." When Matthews asked Marsh, who was sitting in the rear of the courtroom, to stand up, Mrs. Treon said, "I definitely recognize him."

After her friend had left with Marsh, Mrs. Treon stayed until the bar closed at 2:00 A.M. She had seen Chessman and the other man with him leave "before two, but not much."

Q. While you were in the bar, do you remember my

kidding you about your resemblance to Beulah Louise Overell?

A. Yes, I do.

Unlike Mrs. Denny, Mrs. Treon did not keep a notebook of her activities. Mr. Dailey had called her over the weekend and asked her to try and remember what she had done on the night of January 20. After she had spoken to him, she had talked it over with Mrs. Denny and she assured Leavy that everything her friend had said in court was true.

Q. This time you saw Chessman and Knowles, whom you saw brought out here, was this the first and only time, is that right?

A. The only time.

When one of the jurors asked Leavy to find out where the Outlet Store, the Circle Bar and Bradley's were located, the district attorney repeated the question to Mrs. Treon. They were all within two blocks of each other. "Does that answer your question?" Leavy asked the juror. No, it did not. Since the witness had quit work at midnight and said that she arrived at Bradley's between 12:20 and 12:30 after stopping at the Circle Bar and the Malt Shop, "it seems to me the time is very short." Leavy, with a sheepish expression on his face, quickly took the hint.

How long had Mrs. Treon spent in the Circle Bar? "I should imagine I was in there about two minutes," she said. No, she hadn't had a drink there; she had only gone in to see one of the bartenders. Helen Denny had been there when she arrived "but she was just getting ready to leave when I went in." After a brief stop at the Malt Bar, where she had met Helen again, both girls had gone to Bradley's where, Ollie figured, she had drunk three John Collins before she left at 2:00 A.M. Mrs. Denny had departed with Kenny Marsh shortly after one o'clock and "she was in bed when I got home."

A JUROR: I would like to ask how she knows her friend was in bed if she was in another room.

THE COURT: Did you see her in bed or did you figure it out?

A. I said I did not know whether she was there or not.

Kenneth Marsh, an embalmer for Pierce Brothers in Van Nuys, had been listening intently while the two women testified. Yes, he had met them both in Bradley's on the night of January 20. When he and Knowles had arrived at the bistro, they had run into Chessman at the front door. The three men had sat at "the end of the bar" where they had a beer. "Then we sat there for some twenty or twenty-five minutes, and I excused myself and left." He thought that he and Mrs. Denny had walked out "around one o'clock sometime."

Leavy asked stenographer Perry to read back Chessman's last question and Marsh's answer. "What happened," he then wanted to know, "about one o'clock of what day?" The witness shook his head. He did not know what day it had been.

Q. You cannot fix it?

A. I do not know dates. That is the first and last time I was ever in Bradley's.

No, he couldn't even say whether it had been January 20 or February 20. He could not remember "that far back."

He had run into Knowles, with whom he had gone to school ten years ago, on Highland Avenue in Hollywood the day before he had gone to Bradley's. The two men had agreed to meet the next day and Knowles had called for him in Van Nuys at three the following afternoon. They had spent the rest of the day together until Marsh had left Bradley's with Mrs. Denny. This was the first time he had seen his former classmate since high school.

Oversights were very much the order of the day. As soon as Marsh had left the stand, Leavy decided to bring Mrs. Denny and Mrs. Treon back for one question. He wanted to know whether they had known Pat Dailey "before last Saturday." Neither woman had. Then, the defense recalled Harold Doty. Matthews showed the amateur electrician an R.C.A.

Electron Tube Reference Book for 1947. Yes, this was his book; he had given it to Mr. Matthews last Thursday.

Q. Did you have occasion to keep various records of yours in there?

A. I keep a record of addresses and calls that I make in connection with a hobby, more or less, of radio.

Now, there was an entry for January 17 which read "Chess radio finished one twelve, SK7 delivery 3.20, 1.00, 4.20, 1-17-48." Was that in his handwriting? Yes, sir, it was—he had written it when he had delivered Mrs. Chessman's Stewart-Warner table radio.

Leavy strolled over to the witness chair. Was this the only record book Mr. Doty maintained? No, it was not. When he had been repairing radios on a regular basis, he had used a receipt system. He had sold all of his equipment a year ago when he had gone to work for an engineer, and he now used only the book that he had given to Mr. Matthews. It was just a hobby with him now.

Q. What is this hobby you had? Just an isolated occasion when you repaired a friend's radio?

A. I stopped this work entirely except for Chess where his mother is bedfast; she needs her radio repaired when it goes on the bum, regardless of the time of day or night when it wears out.

Wasn't it a fact that the only entries in the R.C.A. book concerned the Chessman radio? "That is not correct," Doty replied, "You will find entries in there for another radio." Leavy wanted to be shown. The witness thumbed through the book and pointed out a notation for November 24, 1947. This was for Mr. Tunkie's radio which he had repaired that day. If Mr. Leavy cared to look further, he would find other entries concerning the replacement of some weak tubes in the large Chessman radio. In fact, he had repaired the family's radio "roughly six or eight times."

Leavy's tone became quite cordial. You treated the Chessmans pretty nicely, didn't you? He certainly did. "In fact, you were very kind to Mrs. Chessman and you kept their radio in repair, is that right?" Doty smiled broadly. "That is correct."

Q. You are a friend of the family, are you not?

A. I believe that is correct.

"Including this defendant, isn't that right?" Leavy demanded, his voice suddenly heavy with insinuation. Doty's grin vanished abruptly. Yes, sir, he was.

The district attorney suddenly noticed that the R.C.A. book "starts by the printed form in January, 1947." Doty nodded. So the notation for Friday, January 17, was for the preceding year "so far as the printing in this book is concerned." The electrician admitted that that was so.

Q. I do not mean your handwriting; I mean the printing on this refers to when it came out, the reference book that you use as your memorandum?

A. That is correct.

Juror King had a question. She wanted to know if she was correct in remembering that Mr. Doty had testified on Friday that the defendant had been laying linoleum on January 17. "He showed me the linoleum and said he had just laid it," Doty answered. "He did not say that day." Had it been linoleum or Congoleum? The witness didn't know. "I call it one of those names. It is similar to linoleum, but I think it is the same thing." Leavy wanted no more talk about linoleum. "Does that answer your question," he asked impatiently. "If you think that it does not, give me another, lady, and I will ask it." Mrs. King subsided. "At present it does," she replied tartly.

Wilbur M. Callahan and his brother operated a small garage behind a Shell service station on Los Feliz. At 10:00 A.M. on January 21, Chessman had brought in a gray 1947 Ford club coupé. Callahan recalled that the car's right front fender was "marred up" and that its front spring was collapsed.

Q. Did you repair the right front spring?

A. Yes, sir.

Q. Who asked you to make this repair?

A. You did.

It had taken the mechanic several hours to fix the spring. He had also removed the Ford's defective speedometer and sent it to Psenner-Pauff, Inc. in Glendale. It had been returned to him the next day and he had remounted it in the car's dashboard. Mrs. Vamos interrupted to ask him whether he had made a record of the mileage at the time he had removed the speedometer. No, ma'am, he had not. It was customary to do so but "whether you do depends on how busy you are that particular day."

Matthews picked up the People's Exhibits 3, 4 and 5, the photographs of a 1946 Ford taken by Rittenhouse at the police garage. Did Mr. Callahan think that "the automobile shown on these pictures and the interior of that automobile are similar to the automobile that you repaired for Mr. Chessman?" The witness took a long look at the photographs. "I would say," he replied, "it was the same car or a similar make, either one." Chessman broke in. "If you were to see this car again," he asked, "would you have any way of positively identifying it?" He would. Because of the work he had done under the car's body, he could recognize certain marks he had made on the stabilizer.

Mr. Callahan had brought with him copies of his receipts for January 21. He didn't have any invoice for the spring because "we had it stocked." When Fricke asked him where the bill was for the speedometer, the witness admitted that he had forgotten to bring it. "That was the twenty-second we replaced the speedometer," he told the judge, "I forgot to bring that bill. I brought that for the twenty-first."

Q. Have you got it available?

A. It is home.

Q. Will you bring it to court?
A. Yes, sure.

After lunch, Chessman took over from Matthews. Did Mr. Callahan remember the color of the speedometer's numerals? He thought that "they were red." The other dials on the dashboard had been "kind of blue-gray." He was certain that the car did not have a radio because he had asked Chessman "why he did not put a radio in it." In fact, when he saw that the defendant was interested in a radio, he had checked the price of one with a Ford agency. But, his customer "could not see his way, though, when he came for it."

Leavy began slowly. He understood that the brothers Callahan did not keep as detailed records as the big garages. The witness owned that this was so. But he did write up every repair job. "In this particular instance here," he reminisced, "I filled them out for the spring, and he told me at the time that his speedometer was not working, and I removed it when he came in. When he came back I just more or less charged him for what the speedometer cost me. I did not write a bill for it. I figured he was our customer. We do favors for them." Leavy supposed that Chessman had been a regular customer. Callahan's definition was quite flexible. "He is a customer as far as I am concerned," he announced, "when he came in before."

Q. That was the first time that you had seen him, when this occurred?
A. Yes, sir.

He hadn't thought about this job until he had received a telephone call last week from a Mr. Bliss, an investigator employed by the public defender. "He asked me if I had not worked on a 1946 Ford on such and such a day, and I told him I did not remember, and he said, 'Well, now, think hard, because it is really important.' So, I thought around, thought I remembered a 1946 Ford that I had worked on.

And he said, 'Well, it is something about a spring,' and I thought, 'that is the only 1946 Ford we ever put a spring in.' " He had also told Mr. Bliss that "we had worked on the speedometer, too."

Mr. Callahan, Leavy mused, you and your brother have a very busy garage? The witness beamed. Oh, yes, there was more work than they could handle. Then, it would be impossible, wouldn't it, to "carry in your memory from day to day who you put a spring in for?" Callahan looked blank. "I do not get that," he said, "I don't understand it."

Q. I will put it another way. Your principal interest is to get the repair job and get the money for it, is that right?

A. That is right.

But of one thing, he was certain— "That is the only 1946 Ford sedan I ever remember at the garage."

Callahan thought that all of the dashboard dials had been "illuminated with red." But when Leavy prodded him for his "best independent recollection," he hedged. "I cannot recall if it is red," he confessed, "I only had the speedometer out."

Q. You say the speedometer was red. Wouldn't you have the others lighted?

A. I do not think any of them were lighted. If you know whether they were red, perhaps they was red. If it was light it would show it, but I do not know whether that was lighted up in red, blue or green.

Besides, he had worked on the speedometer in daylight only and he had never seen the dashboard illuminated.

When Mr. Bliss had spoken to him about the Ford's owner, he had had no difficulty in recalling "that particular fellow." His hobby was automobile racing and Chessman "seemed to take an interest in my race car." "Do you still have it?" Leavy inquired. When Callahan said that he did, the prosecutor, with a dark look in the direction of the de-

fense table, murmured, "You're lucky." The witness, who
had been bridling under Leavy's persistent questioning, took
the observation as a personal insult. He wanted it clearly
understood that he hadn't come to court to be ridiculed.
The district attorney was all apologies. "Nobody is ridicul-
ing you," he assured the irate Mr. Callahan. When the latter
muttered, "That is all right," the storm was over as suddenly
as it had begun.

The garage had kept no record of either the Ford's license
number or its owner's name. We usually do that, Callahan
stated, and "I catch holy heck from my brother when I
don't." But he was still sure that Chessman was the man
who had brought the car in. No, he had no memorandum
to substantiate when the car had arrived at his shop or when
it had been picked up by the defendant. He just remembered that Chessman had driven in at ten that morning
and returned in the middle of the afternoon.

Although the defendant had told him to fix the speedometer, Callahan had forgotten to do so. When Chessman
returned to the garage that afternoon, he was disappointed
to find that this had not been done. The abashed mechanic
had told him, "I will take it out. It isn't much of a job to
take out." He had then removed the speedometer, and his
brother had taken it over to Psenner-Pauff's which was some
five blocks away. It was brought back the next day and the
witness had installed it in the Ford.

Juror Vamos returned to the wars. She wanted to know
how much the Callahans had charged for replacing the front
spring. $9.00 for parts and $5.50 for labor. Leavy, who had
already released the witness, was spurred to greater efforts
by Mrs. Vamos' curiosity. Springs break from driving too fast
and hitting some obstruction, don't they? Mr. Callahan reminded him that "the spring was not broke; it was sprung."
Well, sprung or broke, wouldn't hitting a curb, for example,
at a high speed, put any spring out of commission. The

garageman looked bored. "Sure," he agreed, "anything could do it."

The ubiquitous Pat Dailey was next. A former O.S.S. man who tipped the scales at two hundred pounds, he was a student at the University of California, majoring in International Relations with Asiatic States. Just before the trial, he had been employed by the defendant's father, at Al Matthews' suggestion, to do a bit of sleuthing for the defense. It was in this connection that he had interviewed Ollie Treon and Helen Denny. Leavy had only a question or two. Had he been informed of certain dates before he went out and talked to witnesses? He had—by Mr. Matthews.

Q. You did the best you could, with what facts Mr. Matthews gave you with respect to those dates and with respect to this, did you talk to those witnesses? Is that right?

A. Yes, sir.

Lucille Ruth Greene had been left three chairs in Mrs. Cottle's will. On Saturday, January 17, she and her husband had driven over to the Chessman's to pick them up. The couple had arrived at the Larga Avenue house "in the early afternoon" and had stayed for "about half an hour or forty-five minutes." The witness had a vivid memory. "When we arrived, Mr. Chessman and his father were working in the front bedroom preparing it for his mother who, as you know, is ill. They were laying, placing linoleum; they had been cleaning the room; the windows had been washed, and I believe there was new wallpaper had been put on. The woodwork had been cleaned. The room was being thoroughly done over for her occupation."

Mrs. Greene was only "vaguely" related to the defendant, she told Leavy. Mrs. Cottle had been her great-aunt and she had seen her at Larga Avenue more than fifteen times. The only visits that she could remember clearly were the three she had made after Mrs. Cottle's death to pick up the

chairs, a stove and some other articles that had been bequeathed to her. No, she had made no note or memorandum
of her visits but she could easily figure it out by reckoning
from the reading of Mrs. Cottle's will which had taken place
on Wednesday, January 7.

Q. When, with respect to the seventh, would you say
you went back to make the next visit, to pick things
up?

A. It was the week following; not on the Saturday following, but the week following that.

Leavy had a stubborn witness on his hands. Mrs. Greene
was "positive" that she had picked up the chairs on the seventeenth. No, she did not know that the defendant had been
charged with a crime that had occurred on that day. "I do
not know now," she insisted, "just what the charges are
against him." She only knew that she had visited Larga
Avenue on the seventeenth and nobody was going to change
her mind about that. "I know it was on Saturday," she explained, "because my husband works during the week. It
would have been the morning after his next day off. It was
not Sunday because our Sundays are full. It would have been
morning, to have gone down and picked up the chairs. It was
not the following Saturday after the first week we went
down being on the seventh. It was just as I say the next Saturday after that, about a week and a half, because it was on
a Wednesday we went there before. That is how I am sure
it was on the seventeenth." If the district attorney didn't
understand that, she didn't know how she could put it any
plainer.

Her husband, a stoop-shouldered machine operator, confirmed her story. He, too, had been in the front bedroom
of the Chessman home on January 17, where he had watched
the defendant laying some linoleum. No, he didn't know the
difference between linoleum and Congoleum.

Q. Well, I mean, in other words, say it is linoleum or

Congoleum, being tacked down or was it being glued down? Do you remember that?

A. It was being fitted to the room at the time.

It was during this visit, he said, that he had met Mrs. Chessman for the first time.

It had been his wife who told him that Chessman had been arrested. He remembered that she had tried to figure out just when it was that they had last seen him. "There were two Saturdays," he told Leavy. "It was the second Saturday after the first time we were there. It was the seventeenth."

Q. Well, if you met them on the tenth or the third of January, it would have been no more important than any other date, would it?

A. No more important to me, no.

Q. Or of any importance?

A. No, sir.

How long before his wife had told him of Chessman's arrest had he picked up the three chairs? He thought it had been "several weeks. I could not tell you exactly."

Dave Knowles had already been convicted of the Redondo Beach robbery and sentenced by Judge Harold B. Landreth to life imprisonment without the possibility of parole. A handsome, affable man in his early twenties, he was destined to serve the next eleven years in Folsom. He was finally admitted to parole in 1959, after the California legislature had amended Section 209 of the Penal Code to eliminate "standstill" robberies from the purview of the kidnapping statute. When he took the stand, he was still dressed in the same clothes he had been wearing on the night of his arrest.

Matthews picked up the People's Exhibit 21, an overcoat that had previously been identified by Melvin Waisler as one that Knowles, with the words, "Don't forget that 38-size suede coat," had taken from the racks when he and Chessman had run out of his store. "Will you try it on?"

the public defender asked the witness. Under the watchful eyes of two deputies, Knowles donned the garment and then walked in front of the jury box. Leavy looked surprised when Matthews said, "That is all." "Is that all the questions you have?" he asked the lawyer. That was all.

When Leavy started to take Knowles through the chase on Vermont Avenue, Fricke intervened. "You know the direct examination was strictly over clothes!" he barked at the prosecutor. "I think it is objectionable and that you ought to know that much!" Leavy's face reddened. "I understand," he told the angry judge, "and I understand that he was codefendant and these were the clothes he was wearing. And he had on this coat. Is that your opinion, Your Honor?" It seemed that it was.

The district attorney turned back to the amused witness. Was it his contention that the coat he had tried on did not fit him? "I don't know whether it fit me or not, Mr. Leavy," was Knowles' answer.

Q. What size do you wear?

A. I think I wear a 36. If I am not mistaken, the last time I had a coat made, I think that is what it measured.

Q. You do not think this fits you?

A. No sir, it does not.

"Put it on again," the prosecutor ordered.

As the convict slipped on the coat once more, Leavy watched him closely. "Just drop your shoulder," he ordered Knowles. "Relax a little bit. That is not a bad fit, is it?" The witness didn't think so. "It is a good fit, maybe, in your judgment?" he shot back.

Q. You cannot ask me questions. I asked you if it is a good fit.

A. I do not think it fits me at all, what I can see of it.

Leavy's voice was heavy with sarcasm. Perhaps the coat "has been altered to fit your hips now." "If it was a coat taken

in the robbery," Knowles retorted, "I do not think I would
have time to get it altered."

When the prosecutor announced that he was through with
the witness, Fricke looked astonished. He hoped that Leavy
was not being inhibited by his outburst at the beginning
of Knowles' cross-examination. "I did not mean I was pre-
venting you if you intend to ask an impeaching question, if
you have that in mind," he told him. As an old hand, His
Honor well knew that the credibility of a witness was always
open to attack, no matter how irrelevant the inquiry appeared on the surface. Thus reassured, Leavy returned to
the witness. When had he met Chessman? In the penitentiary. Hadn't he been convicted of burglary in 1944, and of
receiving stolen property in 1945? Yes, sir, he had. What
about the Redondo Beach robbery? Knowles lost his temper.
"That's a bum beef," he shouted, "that is one that I am innocent of!"

After Knowles stated that there had been a third man in
the Ford coupé during the chase down Vermont, a man who
was introduced to him only as Joe, Chessman recalled Colin
Forbes. He was interested in the bulletins that the detective
had prepared on January 22 and 23. In particular, he wanted
copies of the interviews with victims which Forbes had later
bulletinized and sent to Central Broadcast Bureau. Leavy
jumped to his feet. "Those are confidential papers," he protested, "That is part of the robbery evidence here. I do not
propose to disclose it to this defendant. When I get my robbery evidence in, I might permit it, but up to this point
they are confidential." With the exception of the broadcasts
themselves, Fricke sustained the objection.

Chessman read the APB of January 23 to the jury. As he
came to the suspect's description, he raised his voice and
carefully enunciated every word. "Male, Caucasian, possibly
Italian, swarthy complexion, 25 to 35 years, 5 foot 6 inches
to 5 foot 10 inches, 150 to 170 pounds, thin to medium
build; dark brown wavy hair—close cut; dark brown eyes;

crooked teeth; narrow nose with slight bump on bridge of nose; sharp chin; possible scar over right eyebrow."

It was 3:40 when he finished. When Matthews advised Fricke that he had one more witness who would not be available until the morning, the judge offered the remaining time to Leavy. It was refused. "I would rather not start my rebuttal," the prosecutor explained, "until I have heard all the defense." There was only one thing to do and Fricke did it. "Court adjourned until 9:30 tomorrow morning," he intoned.

11

THE TRIAL—THE DEFENDANT'S STORY

(TUESDAY, MAY 11, 1948)

Promptly at 9:30 the next morning, Arthur Pauff, who had played on the Manual Arts High School's 110-pound basketball team with Leavy, sat himself down in the witness chair. He was one of the owners of Psenner-Pauff, Inc., an automobile repair shop at 620 South Brand in Glendale. On January 21, Callahan Brothers had sent over a defective speedometer which needed a new cable. He had brought with him the "original job card" which Matthews offered in evidence as Defendant's Exhibit "G."

If Leavy recognized his former teammate, he gave no sign of it. No, Mr. Pauff had not handled this transaction himself; the job card had been filled out by Al Algots, one of his eighty-six employees. But he was sure that it was correct because it was "our normal routine and practice." When this job came in, he explained to Leavy, the pencil clerk jotted down the pertinent information "for the purpose of checking with the Auto Parts Delivery Company to verify it for delivering this particular speedometer."

The speedometer had been repaired by Algots and the two men who worked under him. Pauff was sure of this because the "53" which appeared on the job card was Algots' number. "They are asked to put their number on the job card," he explained, "because we keep a record from this of the amount of labor they turn in."

Q. Do you have any system when speedometers come in to be repaired of dating it somewhere in the speedometer?

A. Yes, sir.

Q. And the speedometer might be dated, is that right, if it was repaired at your place?

A. In the normal course of business the speedometer should be dated by our man who repaired it.

That was the only way his company had of protecting itself "against kick backs."

Eber (Al) Algots, a thin, middle-aged man, acknowledged that he had prepared Exhibit "G." But he couldn't remember the particular job. "We put through so many in a day's time," he said, "and it is away back in January." The best he could say was that his department had repaired the speedometer mentioned on the job card of January 21, 1948. Leavy extracted nothing further from Mr. Algots except that a job of this type took "forty-five minutes average."

Charles H. Morrison, a truck driver for Auto Parts Delivery, followed Algots. He had delivered a speedometer to Callahan Brothers on January 22. He had brought his delivery record with him, a document that promptly became Defendant's Exhibit "H." It indicated that Mr. Callahan had receipted for the speedometer on "1-22-48" and had acknowledged that it was "received in good order." Leavy could do little with the witness but suggest that everybody makes a mistake once in a while. Mr. Morrison looked annoyed. "It could happen," he admitted grudgingly.

After Matthews had introduced a letter from Charles H. Cleminshaw of the Griffith Observatory and Planetarium as to the condition of the moon on January 17 and 19, Chessman read into the record Broadcast 9 which had been aired by Central Mike at 5:24 A.M. on January 22.

BROADCAST 9 1-22-48   5:24 AM   DM
KIDNAPPING   (HOLLYWOOD)
VICTIM MARY ALICE MIZA   1568 S SIERRA BONITA
OCCURRED 2:05 AM DATE MULHOLLAND DRIVE
VICTIM WAS SITTING IN CAR WITH MALE FRIEND
WHEN SUSPECT DROVE UP WITH RED LIGHT ON THE
RIGHT SIDE OF HIS CAR BURNING, STOPPED HIS CAR,
CAME OVER TO VICTIM'S CAR PULLING RIGHT DOOR
OPEN AND PUSHING .45 AUTOMATIC INSIDE STATING
"THIS IS STICKUP" VICTIM'S ESCORT (FRANK J. HURL-
BUT) SAID HE HAD NO MONEY SO SUSPECT ORDERED
VICTIM TO GET OUT OF THE CAR AND GET IN SUS-
PECT'S CAR. THEN ORDERED ESCORT TO DRIVE
STRAIGHT AHEAD AND AROUND THE NEXT CORNER
AND STOP. WHEN ESCORT STOPPED AROUND CORNER
SUSPECT HAD DRIVEN ON DOWN MULHOLLAND. CAR
USED BY SUSPECT 1946 FORD SEDAN DARK COLOR WITH
RED SPOT LIGHT ON RIGHT SIDE OF VEHICLE SUSPECT
MALE CAUC 35 YEARS 5-10 175 LBS MEDIUM BUILD
SWARTHY COMPLEX CLEAN SHAVEN VERY SLIGHT AC-
CENT WORE GRAY HAT GRAY CHECKERED OVERCOAT
(OR COULD BE SALT OR PEPPER DESIGN) VICTIM WAS
DRIVEN AROUND FOR 2 HRS THEN DROPPED OFF AT
UNKNOWN LOCATION AT APPROXIMATELY 4:05 AM
WALKED HOME ARRIVING THERE AT 5 AM
DR 426   758
FINIS

The discrepancies between the January 22 bulletin and the testimony of both Frank Hurlbut and Mary Meza visibly worried Leavy. He decided to recall Sergeant Forbes. Who had given the detective the information from which he had compiled the bulletin? It had all come from Frank Hurlbut.

Q. According to the record, not from Mary Meza?

A. That is right.

Forbes hadn't spoken to the girl until he saw her in the Hollywood station that morning "about quarter to eight." The prosecutor looked somewhat relieved.

It was a little after eleven o'clock when the defendant stood up and walked briskly to the witness stand. When the clerk asked him, "What is your name, please?" he answered "Caryl W. Chessman" in the slightly slurred metallic voice that had become so familiar to the courtroom regulars. Al Matthews, with a stubby pencil in one hand and a pad in the other, stationed himself in front of the jury box. He started to ask a question but stopped in the middle when he was disconcerted by the sound of Leavy's chair being moved nearer the front of the room. When the prosecutor had settled himself, Matthews began again.

"Caryl," he asked, "you are the defendant before this court at this time?" That was correct. "How old are you?" He was twenty-six. "When were you born?" On May 27, 1921. "How tall are you?" Six feet. "How much did you weigh at the time of your arrest?" 190 pounds. "Are you married?" No, he was not, he was divorced. "Where were you married and to whom?" Leavy uncurled. "I object to that," he barked at Fricke, "It is immaterial." The judge thought so, too, and ordered Matthews to get on to something more relevant.

On January third, Chessman had stayed home with his mother. That was the day of Mrs. Cottle's burial services which had been held in the morning, and "there had been several people there that afternoon, and talked to my mother and telling how beautiful this funeral had been for my grandmother." About 5:30, Mrs. Cora Fleming had come over and remained for an hour or "perhaps a little longer." At seven, Gerda Adair had telephoned and he had spoken to her "about four or five minutes." Then, Mrs. Adair had talked to Mrs. Chessman on the bedroom extension.

Q. Did you on the third day of January, 1948, rob one Donald McCullough?

A. No sir, I did not.

Q. Or on any day in your life did you rob Donald E. McCullough?

A. No, I did not. I heard the witnesses testify. I had never seen the gentleman before in my life.

What about the thirteenth, did he remember what he had done that day? Yes, he did. Mr. Ostran, his parole officer, had instructed him to report to the Bureau of Parole on the third floor of the Homer Laughlin Building at 315 South Broadway. He had taken a street car into town that morning and talked to Mr. Ostran "at approximately ten o'clock." After the interview, he had met a policeman downstairs who had asked, "Well, how long have you been back in town, Chessman?"

Q. Did he threaten you in any manner?

MR. LEAVY: I object to that as immaterial.

THE COURT: Objection sustained.

MR. LEAVY: Even if it was true.

Later that morning, he had gone to the Hall of Records and the Hall of Justice to check some real estate that had been owned jointly by his mother and Mrs. Cottle. In order to have the property transferred from his grandmother's executor to Mrs. Chessman, "it involved getting some tax receipts and going to the Guaranty Title and Trust Company . . ." The County Tax Collector had given him two forms, "one of which showed that the tax was due and the other was a receipt for the taxes that had been paid." When Matthews showed him a small piece of paper, he identified it as the tax bill he had received at the Collector's office.

After lunch, he had taken the street car back home. "I stopped on my way home," he remembered, "just a couple of blocks from where I lived and saw Miss Winona Phillips." He thought that he had stayed at her house "roughly an hour." Matthews looked up from his notes. Had he on that day stolen Rose Howell's car in Pasadena? Chessman shook his head emphatically. "No, sir," he replied, "I was not in Pasadena on that day."

On the sixteenth, he had had his breakfast at nine-thirty and, with his father, had gone to Glendale to pay a parking ticket and do some shopping. After paying the ticket, the two men had gone to Sears Roebuck, where they purchased some curtains and a Congoleum rug. Matthews showed him Defendant's Exhibit L. Yes, this was the receipt they had received when they bought the rug. And the piece of Armstrong's Congoleum Rug that the lawyer asked him to look at was the type they had selected. "That is the pattern, yes, because I had occasion to examine it very closely prior to the purchase. It is, of course. I laid it."

He had done that on the seventeenth. "I know when I made the purchase, and I know it was the next day that we laid it, because we found that the room that Friday, the sixteenth, was not square. We had assumed it was so when we took the measurements of the room so we—yes, by that time we took the measurements and everything and tried to fit the rug that afternoon. We found it would not work. So the next day then, subsequently, why, we did lay the rug." They had not used any glue. "We used tacks . . . that was purchased for my grandmother's room."

They were still working when the Greenes had arrived to pick up the chair "that my grandmother had included in her will." The Chessmans had offered them two other chairs. "We were planning to refurnish the house, so we decided if they could use those chairs we would give them to them." Before they left, Mr. and Mrs. Greene had watched the two men working on their hands and knees in the front bedroom.

At five-thirty, he had gone to a drug store in Glendale to pick up some cotton rolls for his mother. On the way home, he had run into Harold Doty who was on his way to Larga Avenue to repair Mrs. Chessman's radio. Doty had stayed "until about ten o'clock because he wanted to wait and see. He was not sure that he did a good job, or he wanted to wait and see if it would stick." He had not left the house while Doty was there.

Q. Did you in particular on the seventeenth of January,

1948, on or about 8:00 or thereafter burglarize a building occupied by Mary Tarro located in Los Angeles?

A. No, I did not.

The next day, he had gotten up late and, after giving his mother her breakfast, cleaned the house. "I always used to do that on Sundays" he confided to Matthews, "and lots of times during the week, too, that my father was not able to come in time." He had left the house "about five-thirty or six o'clock" and gone to 10960½ Broadway to see Philip Daniels, an old friend of his. Daniels was not in and he had decided to take in a movie in Hollywood. He had changed his mind and, after having his supper at a place on Sunset Boulevard, had gone home. He remembered that two police officers had entered the restaurant while he was eating, and sat at the bar. No, he had not robbed Thomas B. Bartle or anybody else that night. Matthews winced at the negative pregnant.

Q. You have robbed people in the past, have you not?

A. That is correct.

Q. You have been a thief most of your life, have you not?

A. I have been a thief most of my life.

He had spent the evening of January 19 at Winona Phillips' house. "I was helping her to write a book," he acknowledged, "I was working on it with her." Had anything unusual happened to him that night? Well, he recalled that, just as he had knocked on Mrs. Phillips' door, "a police car went by and threw the spotlight on me and left it there for perhaps five seconds." The same thing had happened to him when he arrived home at midnight. Did he rob Jarnigan Lea, Regina Johnson, or Gerald Stone that night? Of course not. How could he? He had been with Mrs. Phillips all evening.

He had spent most of the twentieth working in the backyard. His father had sold his florist shop on New Year's Day and most of its equipment had been stored behind the house. "We were trying to get it straightened out or sorted," he testified. "He was going to sell this equipment because he was no longer in the retail flower business, but he was contemplating going into the wholesale florist business." He even had a prospective customer, the floral group that had purchased his store.

After working all day, he had gone to Hollywood where he had seen *The Swordsman* at a "large" theater on Hollywood Boulevard. Yes, it might have been the Pantages. He left the theater shortly before midnight and was on his way to Bradley's when he had heard someone shout, "Hey, Caryl. Hey, Caryl." "I looked around and I did not see anybody I remembered, but the fellow came running over with his hand out and shook hands with me and he said, 'Don't you remember me,' and I told him, 'Frankly, no,' I said, and he introduced himself as David Knowles and he discussed when he met me, and I did have a vague recollection of him; and he was in the company of a man I had never seen before. He introduced him as Kenny Marsh, a friend of his. They invited me into the bar at that time. We went into the bar."

This was the start of a big evening. Before it was over, the three men had been joined by Helen Denny and Ollie Treon. The latter had reminded him of a girl he had once known by the name of Beulah Louise Overell * and he remembered kidding her about it. At 1:00 A.M., Kenny Marsh had departed with Mrs. Denny, and he had gone home an hour later. He thought that it had been "approximately closing time," when he left Bradley's because "the bartender had just started to take his apron off." There had been no Mary Meza, no Frank Hurlbut, no robbery and no rape that night.

On Wednesday, the twenty-first, Mrs. Chessman had had one of her bad days. Suffering from cancer of the spine and

---

* Beulah Overell and a man named George (Bud) Gollum had, some nine months earlier, been acquitted of the murder of her parents who were killed when their yacht mysteriously blew up at Newport Beach, California.

the intestines, she had awakened in agony. "She was suffering very acutely on this day from this condition, and the doctor had to call in the afternoon and give her a shot. While she was asleep I did go out for a little while. My Dad said he would be there, and I had previously made arrangements to see a friend of mine, and I got back about five-thirty or six o'clock, I would say."

He had stayed with his mother all that night and it was not until three the next morning that she began to feel better. "Because we were very concerned that she might die that night," he said, "we had a doctor ready, you know. We were prepared to call him if she did look any worse." On the twenty-second, he had visited Phil Daniels at his Broadway apartment and he had remained there until "very close to midnight." He was sure of the time because he remembered kidding Daniels about the fact that he had to get up early to go to Glendale the next morning.

Yes, he had been arrested the following evening. He had been driving a car when he was picked up by Officers Reardon and May. When Matthews showed him Rittenhouse's photographs of an automobile, he was sure that they were "representations" of the Ford he had been driving that night.

Q. On that automobile, did you have a spotlight?
A. There was a spotlight.
Q. On what side, do you remember?
A. On the left side, the driver's side.

Matthews walked over to Leavy's table and picked up the .45 automatic. Had he ever seen People's Exhibit 1 before? He had. "I saw this gun or a similar gun the early part of January, but I cannot say it is the same gun. The first time I definitely remember seeing this particular gun was in the Hollywood police station subsequent to my arrest." What about Exhibit 2, a pencil flashlight? He also had seen that for the first time at the station house. Leavy, who was having difficulty hearing Chessman, asked him to repeat his last answer. Matthews read it back from his notes.

On the day that Mary Alice had identified him, he had been standing in front of her house next to a plain-clothes man. He had been handcuffed but the officer had not. Matthews showed him a gabardine topcoat. Had he ever seen it before? Yes, it was his coat. "I bought it in Harris and Frank's, Hollywood. I mean they handle that particular type of top coat. It is size 46. I remember it at the time I purchased it." He had been wearing it when he was captured on Shatto Place.

Now, Caryl, did you make any telephone calls on the evening of January 23? Yes, he had called his mother from Hollywood. He thought that he had made the call "about six, between six and six-thirty." He had been expecting his parole officer to visit the house and he wanted to know whether "he came or anyone came." He had actually spoken to his mother, who had informed him that Mr. Ostran had not shown up.

Matthews asked Leavy for People's Exhibit 9, the little nut attached to a paper clip. "To the best of your recollection," he asked, "did you have in the pockets of your pants a little nut?" Chessman was "positive" that he did not. What about a paper clip? Yes, he had carried a paper clip in his wallet. "I have one ear that runs," he explained, "and I used it to clean out my ear." Had he ever seen Exhibit 9 before? He had seen it "Saturday morning, January the twenty-fourth, in the Hollywood police station lying on a desk along with some things that were taken from my property." One of the police officers had "picked this little clip up and put it around it at that time."

Q. Do you know where . . . the little nut came from?

A. No, I have no idea where it came from.

Matthews was almost through. Had he ever used a red spotlight on any car under his control? Chessman looked over at the jury box. "No, sir," he said solemnly, "to the best of my knowledge there was never a red spotlight on the automobile."

Q. Did you ever use any red cellophane?

A. I did not, sir.

The lawyer walked over to the witness chair. He looked directly into Chessman's eyes. "Caryl," he asked softly, "are you the red spotlight bandit?" The defendant wasted no time in answering. "No. If it involved using a red spotlight or robbing those people that I am alleged to have robbed, I am not, no." Matthews turned to Leavy. "You may cross-examine," he said, and sat down.

The sudden end of the direct examination caught the prosecutor unawares. He started to ask one question and then withdrew it. After a hurried glance at his notes, he began again. Where did Chessman get the $150 the police had found in his pockets when he was searched in the Hollywood Police Station? Part of it had come from cashing a bond for his father on January 23 and the rest "from working." Where had he cashed this bond? "At the bank in the corner of San Fernando Road and Grand Boulevard." Because the bond had not been in his name, the clerk had referred him to the branch manager who had taken care of it for him. He had received twenty dollars for the bond.

He had accumulated the rest of the money by "working for my father steadily since I have been out. I sold some parts that I had in back, floral parts; and I had also sold some bonds and automobile parts and something else." The sale of some fender skirts and floral equipment had netted him $75. The rest of the money had been saved from the thirty dollars a week his father had paid him for trucking. There was also some four or five hundred dollars which the latter was holding for him at home.

$150 was quite a bit of money to be carrying around, wasn't it? Chessman didn't know. A man feels a little more secure, more confident with a roll in his pocket. "Well, did

you feel that evening you were going out and engage in some
revelry, a night club, or something, when you went out on
the night of the twentieth?" Leavy wanted to know. No, he
had had nothing like that in mind. Well, just what did he
have in mind? Nothing at all. He had been carrying large
sums of money ever since he had been released from Folsom.

Q. For what purpose?

A. Just to be a big shot or something, be somebody. I
   just wanted to have character.

Q. It inflated your ego, did it?

A. Perhaps.

But there had been another source of the money. Leavy's
ears perked up. "What source is that?" he asked. Chessman
smiled. It had come from a bookie "out in the Firestone
area." No, he hadn't been betting. "I just told him that he
lost, he lost his bet." The prosecutor looked genuinely in-
trigued. Just how had he obtained this money? Chessman
wasn't very enlightening. "We had occasion to walk into
his establishment," he replied, "and I told him that he had
lost on a particular horse." The gentlemen in question had
responded by handing over $2,300.

Leavy was completely confused. If Chessman hadn't been
betting, just why would the bookie give him $2,300? Well,
it seemed that there were "some other factors involved."
When the district attorney egged him to "tell me more,"
Matthews jumped to his feet. "I object to any further questions along this line," he argued, "on the ground possibly
the defendant may incriminate himself." Fricke didn't quite
see it that way. After all, the defendant had "opened the
door." He has also testified part of this $150 came from a
bookie. Objection overruled.

Leavy turned back to Chessman. "Tell us," he urged
gently, "about these other factors where you got the $2,300
from some bookmaker because he lost." That was easy. "He
lost because maybe I had a pistol in my hand. So maybe did
a couple of friends of mine."

Q. So, you stuck him up?

A. Yes, sir.

Leavy looked up at the clock. It was almost twelve-thirty. Since the defendant had given the jurors a choice conversation piece, he wasn't going to delay their enjoyment of it. "May we take the recess, Your Honor?" he asked. Fricke agreed and, with a warning to the members of the panel not to do any private investigating of their own, excused them until 1:45.

After lunch, Leavy returned to the attack. So the gun was one of the factors involved? The repetitious questions seemed to nettle Chessman. "I said there was a gun involved," he barked. "That is correct." The holdup had taken place "in the afternoon" on January 9 or 10. His share of the loot had been $800. At the time of his arrest on the twenty-third, he still had $600 left.

Q. Where was it?

A. That is what I have been trying to find out.

The prosecutor looked surprised. "You had more than $150 on your person the night of your arrest?" he asked him. That was right; he had had "about $600" on his person when Reardon and May had picked him up. "Part of it was in my pocket, my front pocket," he asserted, "part of it was in my wallet." The innuendo in his voice was hardly subtle.

Leavy took an earlier tack. Why had Chessman been carrying such a large sum of money that night? He was "just carrying it." Why? The reason that any other person would carry money. Why? There was no specific reason. He had it and he was going to "put it to work."

Q. Can't you give me more particularly why you were carrying $600 on the night of January 23?

A. No, sir.

The prosecutor's face was expressionless. Now, you didn't commit any crime on the night of January 23, did you? The defendant's "I did not" could hardly be heard. "Speak up please," Leavy urged, "these folks want to hear you." Chessman repeated his denial. The only crime he had been guilty of that night was a violation of a traffic regulation against speeding.

Q. Forget about those things—I am not inquiring about this chase. Had you committed any crime on the night of January 23, the night of your arrest?

A. I did not, no.

Then why, when he was asked, during Knowles' trial for the Redondo robbery, what he had been doing on the night of January 23, had he refused to testify on the ground that "it might tend to incriminate me?" The defendant looked over at Matthews for a moment. "I mean it was really immaterial because of my plea that was pending, and that is why I positively refused to discuss it at that time at that hearing."

Now, he was prepared to be more loquacious. He had called his mother at six that night from a pay station on the corner of Sunset and Highland. He had been waiting there to meet a man named Joe Terranova who finally drove up at 6:45. He had met Terranova through a fellow convict at Folsom whom he remembered only as the "General." Up to January 23, he had seen Joe some five or six times since he had first met him in early December. Suddenly, Mrs. Vamos, who sat in the next to the last seat in the jury box, leaned over and whispered something to Leavy. The district attorney nodded. "This juror, Mrs. Vamos, says she would like to have you speak up." Chessman nodded in her direction. He would try to talk a little louder.

Just what did Joe Terranova look like? Well, he was "5 foot 10 or 5 foot 9 maybe." He weighed between 150 and 160 pounds and he had "dark brown or black wavy hair." No, he was not particularly good looking. How old was he? Around thirty.

Q. Not over, is that right?

A. That is my opinion.

What did Joe do for a living? Well, he drove a 1946 Cadillac, but he didn't know anything about his business.

Q. Didn't you ask him?

A. Well no. I don't have a habit of asking people what they do for business.

He had met Joe at Bradley's at 6:00 P.M. on January 20. Terranova had asked him whether he knew any mechanic who could fix a Ford that was "all tipped over." "He wanted to know if I could get it fixed, if I knew any mechanic who could fix cars like he wanted to get it fixed." When Chessman told him that Callahan Brothers could do the job, the two men had arranged to meet in Hollywood the next morning. At the appointed time, Joe drove up in his Cadillac, while a friend of his, a stocky gentleman known only as Tubby, was at the wheel of the Ford.

The witness had brought the car into the Los Feliz garage "about ten o'clock that morning" and picked it up some five hours later. He had been driving it near Bradley's when he happened to see Terranova standing in front of the bar.

Q. In other words he was standing in front of Bradley's and you drove along there with this Ford that he had turned over to you?

A. No. I had parked it on a side street.

Q. Coming on afoot?

A. That is right.

When he had turned the car over to Terranova, he had explained to him that "the speedometer had been taken out of it, it would be picked up the next day, so he said he would be around the next morning . . ."

Didn't he realize that driving a car violated the conditions of his parole. Well, he had asked Mr. Ostran whether he could drive in connection with his work but he guessed that "this probably was not in connection with any of my work." Leavy was exasperated. "You knew, didn't you, that as a parolee you should not be driving that car?" he demanded. "Oh, sure, yes," Chessman whispered.

On the twenty-second, he had met Joe and Tubby again at the same place on Hollywood Boulevard. Tubby, he thought, had been between 5 foot 8 and 9, and weighed "about 190 pounds."

Q. Does he look anything like you?

A. No, I would not say that.

But Terranova did look "vaguely" like him; he had "the same kind of nose, anyway."

Q. He has a nose, in other words?

A. Yes, he has a nose.

Did he talk like you? No, he didn't think so. What about his lower lip—"does it move up and down when he talks like yours does?" Chessman shrugged his shoulders. How could he tell? He had never looked in the mirror when he was talking. Leavy grimaced. "You do not know," he asked, "that your lower lip moves around like this when you talk, do you?" No, sir, he most certainly did not.

He had driven the Ford over to Callahans' garage while Joe and Tubby waited in the Cadillac on Glendale Boulevard. It had only taken ten minutes for the speedometer to be installed, and he had driven back to where the two men were parked and turned the car over to them. No, he hadn't been paid by Terranova for his services. "I was asked to do it," he stated. "He told me why he wanted me to do it and so I did it. He said he did not want to acquaint his face in that particular area."

Q. What is that?

A. He said he did not want to acquaint his face in that area. Just that he did not want to make himself known around there.

Terranova had told him that the car belonged to a friend of his and that "he had wrecked it, and he wanted to get it fixed before he had to return it." But he hadn't really believed that. He had thought that it was a hot car, but he hadn't been sure.

Q. Well, you had a suspicion when Joe showed up and

asked you if you would handle this car, that it was hot, did you not? Is that it?

A. That is right, originally, yes.

Q. Hot means that maybe the police are looking for it?

A. That is right.

Mrs. King raised her hand. She just wondered why the defendant had not taken the car to Psenner-Pauff himself instead of making Mr. Callahan go to the trouble of removing the speedometer. Well, he hadn't known it was going to be such a big job. "I didn't know the cable was broken until they took the cable out of it, and Jim Callahan got a model 1939 cable in it—in the car." Leavy picked up where the juror had left off.

Q. You know that there were other places where they repaired speedometers, such as Psenner-Pauff's, did you not?

A. Oh, yes.

Q. But you preferred to take it to this little fellow, whatever his name is, Callahan, is that right?

A. Yes, that is right.

With Mrs. King satisfied, Leavy turned to January 23. At the time that Chessman had delivered the Ford to Terranova, the latter had told him to "see me the next morning." On the twenty-third, Joe had come to his house before lunch and arranged to meet him that evening at a drive-in on the northwest corner of La Brea and Hollywood. The reason for the rendezvous was to settle accounts once and for all with reference to the robbery of the Firestone bookie. It seems that there was another five hundred dollars owed to Chessman which had been paid by "some people in this county that were not interested in seeing him stay open." Leavy raised his eyebrows. "You were closing the bookmaking place for law enforcement agencies?" he inquired. No, siree, he and Terranova had been employed by another bookie who wanted to eliminate competition.

Q. Did you get $500 on the twenty-third?

A. No, sir.

Q. You did not get it?

A. No, I got arrested.

It must have been almost seven o'clock when Terranova and Tubby had pulled into the drive-in in the gray Ford "because I had already phoned my mother." Joe had asked him to take the wheel and drop Tubby off near the CBS. Studios on Sunset. "He had said he was going to see a girl friend and we were joking about it and laughing." After Tubby's exit, he and Joe had driven down Sunset to Vermont.

Mrs. Vamos looked worried. She asked Leavy to find out if the defendant knew whether the Ford was registered in Terranova's name. Yes, he knew that it was not Joe's car. He had seen the registration slip on the vehicle's steering wheel when he first drove it on January 21. It was registered in the name of a Rose K. Howell and the number on the license plates—7P5618—agreed with the pink slip. But he hadn't needed these to know that something was amiss. When he had gotten into the car at the drive-in, Tubby and Joe had told him that "they had had a little trouble." He had also seen what "looked like new clothes" on the automobile's rear seat.

Q. It looked a little suspicious, like somebody had stuck up a clothing store, did it not?

A. Well, that would be a conclusion. I mean, they could have gotten in a burglary or receiving stolen property, or the other ways and sources from which it could have come.

He was supposed to pick up Dave Knowles near Sunset and Vermont. On Tuesday night, at Bradley's, Knowles had told him that he was broke and needed $150 to pay back his employer for a loan he had received "when he first got out on parole." He told the frantic ex-con that he would try to help him and they had made an appointment to meet two nights later. When he saw his friend standing near a stop sign on the corner of Sunset and Vermont, he had pulled up for him. Knowles had sat on the front seat between Chessman and Terranova because "he did not know this other fellow, so the other fellow got out to let him in." The three men had then proceeded down Hollywood Boulevard, intending to stop at a gasoline station on the southeast corner of Hollywood and Vermont so that they could use its men's room. When they entered the service station, Terranova got out of the car and started walking toward the lavatory. Chessman had just reached down to turn off the ignition when he "looked into the rear vision mirror and the police car turned around and came in view."

Q. What did you do?

A. I drove away.

Even though he hadn't committed any crime that night, he had pulled Joe's door shut and started off down Vermont. "I did not stop to think, when I saw the police car," he claimed. "I was just intending to vacate that particular area, that is all." Yes, he was sorry that he had to leave Joe behind but he had been thinking only of himself.

He didn't know the extent of the policemen's interest until a "couple of bullets" whizzed by his head. "By that time I was going at a rapid rate," he told Leavy. "I was trying to hold Mr. Knowles in the seat. He had become terrified and was trying to climb all over my lap. I was trying to drive at the same time."

Q. He lost his guts first, is that right?

A. Well, I never thought of losing mine.

He had not seen the police car's red light or heard its siren "until they started to shoot." He had been far more interested in trying to prevent Knowles from jumping out of the Ford.

Leavy smiled benignly. "That was quite a chase, was it not?" he asked. The defendant suddenly became wary. "What do you mean, quite a chase?" Well, this was the first time the police had ever caught him, wasn't it? Chessman couldn't quite keep a touch of pride out of his voice.

Yes, sir, it was. But hadn't he told Forbes that "that was the first time the police ever caught you in a chase, because the car you were driving, this Howell car, was a lemon?" He had not. "I was beat insensible in that station before I had a chance to talk to Mr. Forbes."

At the word "beat," Leavy's ears perked up. Had Messrs. Forbes and Hubka raised a hand to him? No, sir, they had not. "They treated you like a gentleman, did they not?" Yes, sir, they did. "At all times?" Yes, sir.

Q. You were not afraid of them at any time, were you?

A. Well, now, that is a little different question there entirely. I mean they were not mean at any time.

Leavy exploded. Did he mean to say that he was afraid that members of the Los Angeles Police Department would stoop to physical force? Well, he had known several officers "who were capable of doing it!" In fact, by the time he had been taken to the Hollywood substation that night, he "had been kicked a few times in the groin and beat on the head with pistols and everything and . . . was not too interested in what was going on." But he was willing to admit that neither Hubka nor Forbes had touched him.

During the chase down Vermont, he had kept the accelerator pressed to the floorboards. At Sixth Street, he had turned sharply to the left and reached Shatto Place when his car was rammed by that of Reardon and May. Knowles had scrambled out first with the witness at his heels. "What became of the gun?" Leavy murmured. Chessman refused to bite. "What gun?" he asked blandly.

Q. You do not know anything about a gun?

A. No, I do not.

No, he hadn't told Mr. Forbes that he "had a gun cocked and . . . could have picked the officers off like clay pigeons."

After he had run between some houses on Shatto Place, May had caught up with him. The policeman was "rather anxious that I didn't get into the car again, so I got hit in the head. He hit me and pulled a gun." He had stumbled on the curb when he had tried to run behind the houses, which "knocked the wind out of me." When the officers jumped on him, he had struggled to get up but "it was not much of a struggle." They didn't even give him a chance to put his hands up.

The district attorney had had enough of the twenty-third. Let's see what happened on the seventeenth, he mused. That was the day Chessman and his father had laid the Congoleum rug in the front bedroom. The witness had only left the house twice that day—once in the morning to buy some groceries and at 5:30 P.M. to pick up some medical supplies at a Glendale drugstore.

Q. You were home all that day, January the seventeenth, except for getting your mother medical supplies and running to the grocery store? That is your testimony, is it?

A. That is my testimony.

Mr. Leavy pirouetted sharply toward the rear of the courtroom. "Alfred Davis, stand up please," he ordered. A short, middle-aged man, who had been sitting in the fifth row, rose to his feet. Leavy turned back to the witness. "Mr. Chessman, didn't you see this man on the 17th?" Not to his knowledge. He did not remember "ever seeing him." The unrecognized Mr. Davis sank back into his seat.

The prosecutor picked up a package from his table. It turned out to be a pawnbroker's "Buy Book," and he flipped its pages to Item 179, a bill of sale dated January 17, 1948. "Now, Chessman," he said, "you examine very carefully that bill of sale . . . and see whether that recalls anything to you as to what you did on January 17th of this year?" The defendant scrutinized it closely. Yes, the writing on the bill was his signature but he hadn't pawned any jewelry with Mr. Davis on the seventeenth. If Mr. Leavy would look at the document again, he would see that "the date has been obviously altered. There are two dates on top there."

But he had once pawned a little gold chain, a pen knife

and seven stick-pins that had been bequeathed to him by his Uncle Hervey. But this had been done before the seventeenth—he wasn't quite sure of the date—and, as for Mr. Davis, he couldn't remember him at all. "You had forgotten all about it, had you?" queried Leavy. Why, yes, he had. This was the first time "I ever had occasion to think about it."

The Hollywood Police Station was next on the agenda. When he talked to Forbes and Hubka after his capture, had he told them that he had committed any of the crimes of which he was accused? Of course not. They had pumped him for three days solid. "They told me at that time they were only going to file three robberies. They wanted to clear those records. I said, as far as I am concerned you can put down whatever you like as far as your records go, but I am still going into court and plead not guilty, because I am not guilty."

Q. Well, you did know from Mr. Forbes and Mr. Hubka that you were being accused of having committed these hold ups and robberies and some sex crimes in connection with them, with reference to a red spotlight bandit, did you not?

A. I certainly did.

Q. Of course you knew nothing about it because you were not the red spotlight bandit, you didn't know exactly how he had committed the crimes, naturally, isn't that right?

A. That is right.

The trap was set. Leavy picked up his copy of the transcript taken at the preliminary hearing. "Do you have your copy, Mr. Chessman?" he inquired solicitously. Matthews handed it to the witness. The prosecutor smiled politely and asked Chessman whether he would mind turning to page 9. Now, Dr. Bartle had testified that there had been a red spotlight on the car of the man who had robbed him.

But the only one at the preliminary hearing to raise the possibility that there might have been a piece of red cellophane over the lens had been the defendant. Fricke recognized a body blow when he heard one. "I do not think the witness gets the idea," he interrupted, "will you read it back to the defendant." Chessman looked stricken. "I see what you mean in the first place," he told Fricke. "Do you catch on now?" asked Leavy. "Yes, yes," was the answer.

There was more to come. The prosecutor asked Chessman to read from page 61 of Regina Johnson's testimony before Judge Guerin. He did so in a subdued voice. "I got out of the car," Mrs. Johnson had testified on direct, "closed the door, and he drove on, and in the meantime I told him, I grabbed the gun because I thought it was not real, and he told me that was a good way to get killed and if I tried it again he would kill me." That was the only reference she had made to verifying whether the gun was a real one, was it not? Yes, sir, that was all she had said about it.

Leavy struggled to control his eagerness. Turn to page 62, he ordered the witness, to line 13 where he had asked Mrs. Johnson about the gun. "Now listen to this one," he said. "Question: Did this person who committed this crime, did he do anything with the gun to indicate that it was real? I mean by taking out a clip or showing you any shells? Answer: I told him that I did not think it was real and he told me that it was, and he flipped something and I saw the shells." Hadn't he asked Mrs. Johnson that question and didn't she answer as he had read? Yes, to both the question and the answer.

The district attorney had made his point. Now, back to January 19. After Chessman had left Mrs. Phillips' house that night, had he been with anyone "who could establish an alibi as to what happened after you left her until you got up the next morning?" He had been seen by someone as he was closing her front door behind him. A squad car had driven by and flashed a spotlight on him.

Q. They just turned the flashlight on you and you went on your way, did you not?

A. That is all, yes. I did not meddle.

No, the officers hadn't stopped him or taken his name or address. When he got home, everyone at Larga Avenue was asleep and no one had seen him enter the house. So, naturally, he had no alibi for the rest of the night.

While we're on the subject of alibis, Leavy said, why had he prepared one for midnight on January 20, the time of the Stone robbery, when there was no indication during the preliminary hearing of the exact time it had occurred? "Well, I do know where I was at that time. So I think if that was the time he was robbed that he knew where he was, and I knew I was not present and robbed him." Leavy brushed aside the doubletalk. "You were under the impression at least," he asked, "that Mr. Stone was robbed at about midnight of January 20 or the morning of January 21 . . . ?" No, he was not. "I realized before that he may have been robbed on any of two nights. I do not know when the man actually was robbed, so I properly tried to establish where I was on both times."

Is that why he had brought Helen Denny to court, "to establish an alibi for when Mr. Stone was robbed?" The witness shrugged. Of course, that was the reason. But if it had been so important to him to ascertain the time that Mr. Stone had been robbed, why hadn't he asked him at the preliminary hearing? Because "I was not interested in when he was robbed."

Q. You questioned some of the other witnesses about the hour and day when they were robbed at the preliminary hearing, didn't you?

A. I do not know. I may have.

He didn't remember whether he had ever seen the official reports of the Stone robbery. On second thought, he did "have a recollection." He thought that Stone had said "it was on the night of January the nineteenth."

Fricke agreed with Leavy that this was "a convenient place to stop." As the jurors filed out, Chessman was busy thumbing through the blue-jacketed transcripts of the preliminary hearing.

12

THE TRIAL—THE VOIR DIRE

(WEDNESDAY, MAY 12, 1948)

Wednesday was a bright sunny day. The weather, which had been on the cool side during the first two weeks of the trial, gave every indication of an early return to form. By 9:25, the jurors were in their seats, dividing their morning comments between the rising temperature and the news that doughty Queen Wilhelmina had decided to abdicate in favor of her daughter Juliana. Five minutes later, Judge Fricke mounted the bench and motioned the defendant to resume his place in the witness chair.

Leavy lost no time in springing back into action. When Knowles had been picked up by Chessman on January 23, had the former been carrying anything? Yes, he had been carrying a bundle which "was about 12 or 14 inches long, 6 or 8 inches high and 6 or 8 inches wide." He had thrown it in the back seat when he entered the car. The prosecutor showed him a "box with shoes." Did it look like the package he had seen in Knowles' possession that night? "Just about."

Q. The same one, is that right?

A. Yes, that is right.

Had he seen Knowles "at any time on the night of the twenty-first or the morning of the twenty-second?" No, sir, he had not. But hadn't he testified in Knowles' trial before

Judge Landreth two weeks ago that he had seen his friend on the night of the twenty-first and the morning of the twenty-second? Yes, he had said that, but it wasn't true. Then, could he explain why, when Mr. Erwin, Knowles' attorney, had asked him whether he had seen his client on the twenty-third, he had replied, "I had seen him two days prior to that in the evening, the time extended over into the next morning, it was around midnight when I saw him"? There was no explanation. Leavy came perilously close to chuckling.

Did Mr. Chessman remember that, after he had told Forbes and Hubka that he had had nothing to do with the crimes "where the kidnappings occurred or where the woman was assaulted," the officers had asked him who he thought had committed them? Matthews was on his feet with an objection. He didn't think that any statements made by the defendant when he wasn't warned of his constitutional right to stand mute should be paraded before the jury. Fricke overruled him. "There is nothing in the law," he insisted, "that requires those statements to be made to a prisoner." Matthews scowled. He was sure that His Honor was aware of the case of People v. Simmons. His Honor was "quite familiar with it." While Matthews searched through his papers for more effective legal ammunition, Chessman took advantage of the momentary lull to remind Fricke that nobody indeed had informed him of his constitutional rights.

After the judge had delivered himself of the opinion that the Simmons case had been superseded by People v. Peterson, Leavy repeated the question. Yes, he remembered that Hubka and Forbes had asked him who had committed the crimes.

Q. Did you not tell them it was a man by the name of Terranova?

A. No, I did not say that.

Leavy's jaw dropped. Come now, he said, you gave them the

name of a man, didn't you? Yes, he had. He had given them
Terranova's name. When they asked him if he meant a man
by the name of Tuzzolino, he had replied, "It could be."

Q. Then they showed you a picture cf a man, didn't
they?

A. Yes, sir.

Q. Did you not say, "Yes, that could be him. It looks
like him. He hangs around Bradley's in Hollywood."

A. I said it could be.

Q. Did you say what I suggested?

A. Not especially, no.

Leavy changed course abruptly. Let's go back, he said, to
the robbery of Dr. Bartle near Malibu Beach on January 18.
Of course, the witness had had nothing to do with that
crime. No, he "did not commit that robbery." That was the
night he had driven his father's panel truck into Hollywood
after stopping at Phil Daniels' apartment on South Broadway. He hadn't met anyone he knew that evening, but he
did remember that he had eaten his supper at a drive-in
where they were breaking in a new waitress. "She did not
know what to do," he said. "She could not even write the
order on this paper that they had." The episode had been
"amusing."

He had been thinking of "going to a show" and had
parked the truck on a side street near Hollywood Boulevard.
He hadn't found a movie he liked so he had done a little
"window shopping" and then dropped in at Bradley's for a
drink. He had left the bar at eight-thirty and "just went
along the boulevard" until ten o'clock.

Q. You were alone all that night, were you not?

A. Yes, unfortunately.

Q. Very unfortunately, is that right?

A. That is right.

After stopping for a hamburger, he had gone home, arriving
there "before midnight." His father had been sleeping on
the couch in the front room and he thought that the old man

had gotten up when he entered the house but he couldn't swear to it.

The prosecutor picked up a single sheet of paper from his table. Holding it carefully in his hand, he showed one side of it to the defendant. Did he recognize it? Yes, it was a piece of Folsom stationery. It had been in his wallet at the time of his arrest. On its reverse side was a diagram of a house on Old Malibu Road, which had been made for him by Robert Salembier, a fellow prisoner at Folsom. Was this the place he had told Forbes he was headed for on January 18 when he had robbed Dr. Bartle? Not at all. That was sheer persiflage.

Leavy picked up People's Exhibit 1, the .45 automatic. Is this the gun, he asked, that you saw in January? "Wait a minute," the witness protested, "I didn't say it was the gun." Matthews leaped to his feet. "I object to the question as being irrelevant," he told Fricke, "unless it is that gun. If it is not that gun, it has nothing to do with this case." The judge started thumbing through his notes. "I think there was some reference to it in\ the direct examination," he interjected. The district attorney was positive that it had been mentioned. "I have it in my notes," he explained. He read from his pad: "Gun. He might have seen it earlier in January." With the observation that that was his recollection, too, Fricke overruled the objection.

The witness looked at the gun. In early January, he had seen "several .45's" in a gun shop. "Were you shopping for guns?" Leavy asked. Emphatically, no. As a former prisoner, it wasn't legal for him to purchase a weapon. Leavy understood completely. "You have to get them through someone else, is that right?" Chessman thought for a moment before he answered. "Well," he replied, "I am not in a position to answer that question. I don't know. I know you can buy them at gun shops."

Now, in January when you saw a gun "similar to Exhibit 1," just where was it? He had seen it in Terranova's car when it had been parked in front of his house "right after New Year's sometime." Was it the same gun he had seen when the bookie in Firestone had been robbed? It could have been.

Q. You were there when the bookie was stuck up, weren't you?

A. I didn't say the bookie was stuck up. That is a conclusion on your part.

Leavy looked annoyed. He asked Fricke's permission to have the reporter read back "the last answer given by this witness just before the noon recess yesterday." Mr. Perry leafed back through his notebook. "I've got it," he said. "Question: So you stuck him up? Answer: Yes, sir."

After a ten-minute recess, Leavy returned to the piece of Folsom stationery. Who lived in the house that was shown on the diagram Salembier had drawn for him? Walter Wanger. "I was trying to get to know him because I had a book I was writing, and I was trying to get him interested." If he wanted to sell a novel to Walter Wanger, why was it necessary to list every room in the house? Well, he had thought that the fellow who had drawn the diagram for him "might be telling me some hooey about it."

Suddenly, Leavy spun around and barked, "Will you stand up, Mrs. Johnson, please?" Regina Johnson, who had been attending almost every session of the trial, stood up. "Mr. Chessman, didn't you tell that woman that you were from New York?" The witness's tone was defiant. "No, I didn't tell that woman anything." He had never seen her before in his life until the Pasadena police had brought her into the Hollywood substation to identify him. That was the first time he had ever spoken to her. Mrs. Johnson sat down.

Now, after his arrest he had been questioned by a number of police officers? He certainly had. Messrs. Forbes, Goosen and Hubka had been at him constantly. Hadn't he admitted to them that "You got me, yes, that stuff came from the Redondo job?" Before the witness could answer, Matthews jumped up. He objected to any questions relating to what the defendant had told the police "until it is shown it was answered freely and voluntarily." Fricke agreed with him. "The answer to the proposition," he pontificated, "is that the witness is asked whether he committed a particular crime and his answer 'Yes' would be tantamount to a confession and would not be admissible if there is no foundation laid. I think we should lay a foundation before we proceed." He brushed aside Leavy's plea to be allowed to complete his cross examination of the defendant and ordered him to call any witnesses he had as to Chessman's treatment by the Hollywood police. The judge's ruling ushered in the voir dire, the trial within a trial to determine the admissibility of any incriminating statements made by the accused.

Colin Forbes was back for his sixth stint on the stand. After the defendant's arrest, he had talked to him "on the morning of January 24, 1948, at the Hollywood Detective Bureau . . . and on the day of January 25, 1948, at the Hollywood Detective Bureau, and I believe on the evening of the twenty-fifth or twenty-sixth of January, 1948." Officers Hubka, Goosen, or Weaver had been present at every such conversation. Chessman's statements had been "free and voluntary" and nobody had threatened or beaten him.

Chessman told quite another story. On the night of January 23, he and Knowles had been taken up to the second floor of the Hollywood Detective Bureau. There Officer Don W. Grant, who called him "a rapist son of a bitch," had beaten him for "about 20 or 30 minutes and pounded on me until he was physically exhausted. I was up against some lockers, and he pounded on me with his fists and I was kicked in the shins and kicked in the groin, and I felt like retching, and I retched several times, just a dry retch." Grant then went into another room where "he kicked

Knowles around." An Officer Begay * had been present during both beatings, Chessman added.

On Monday, the twenty-sixth, his father had visited him
in jail. "I told him that I was in pretty bad shape. There
was blood in my water. So I was a little worried about it. I
didn't know whether my kidney was ruptured or not. So I
was pretty sick." When Mr. Chessman noticed a scar on his
forehead, he had told him that it had been caused by one of
May's bullets on Shatto Place. There had been an officer
present while his father was in the cell. The policeman had
not been overly sympathetic. "He just laughed at me, some
conversation about 'That's normal.' "

But his father wasn't the only one who had seen him.
Everyone in the county tank knew that he had been worked
over. There was Manuel Fox and Howard Gibson "and another one that came in about three days later after I was,
named Johnny Dillinger." As far as his mental condition
was concerned, he was completely confused after the beating. "I did not know where I was at. I was punch goofy after
that. I figured the best thing to do if they wanted to ask any
questions was to tell them anything they wanted to hear, so
as to get out of there."

Leavy had been making copious notes while Matthews
questioned the defendant. Was Detective Grant the only one
who had touched him? That was correct. Had he been
beaten at any other time than the night of January 23? No,
he had not. Neither Forbes nor Hubka had made any promises to him in order to get him to confess, had they? "Well,
they had made a lot of promises and a lot of statements."
What statements? They had told him that they wanted to
"clear their records." If he would cooperate with them, "they
were only going to file two robberies on me." He had told
them that he refused to go into court and plead guilty to

* The records of the Los Angeles Police Department contain no reference
to any officer by that name.

crimes he had not committed. As far as he was concerned, there were only two kinds of police officers. "The kind that catch you and the kind that don't catch you?" interjected Leavy. "The kind that beat you after they catch you and the kind that testify in the courtroom after you have been beaten," was the laconic reply.

Chessman became expansive. When the officers first talked to him, he had insisted that they let their witnesses take a look at him. "I am not right for this," he had told them, "I may be a thief but I am not a goddamned sex fiend." He had told them to look at his record and the F.B.I. files and "see if you ever find where I have been accused of any sex crimes." Forbes and Hubka had told him that they were only going to accuse him of three robberies "so as to get their books in the clear." But he had refused to plead guilty to anything.

Then they had changed their tactics. "They said I was a pretty good boy, and started buying me meals. Then they came at me, talked about it. They said, 'Do you want to tell us anything?' All this time they kept telling me, 'Do you want to tell me anything? You know it's off the record, confidential, don't you. Let's try and get together.' " He had tried to point out to them that a man with a dying mother would hardly go in for kidnapping young women. Then they had taken him to Sierra Bonita Avenue to let Mary Alice Meza have a look at him.

Finally, he had gotten so tired of the persistent questioning that he said, "I don't care. You write down anything you want. You know it's phony." Then Forbes and Hubka had threatened to send him back to prison as a parole violator, "to refix your sentence at the maximum." They had even asked him about some other crimes, such as "a little boy that was supposed to be snatched out near the beach somewhere." "You are not charged with it?" Leavy asked. Chessman laughed loudly. "No, no. That is one of the remarkable things." Fricke was furious. "Just a minute," he roared. "That laughter is just a little bit unnecessary; it sounds a little bit forced. Just remember that a little bit, please." The defendant looked properly chastened.

It was on Saturday, the day after his arrest, that Hubka "came up with this little nut." The policeman had picked up the paper clip that had been found in his wallet and asked him, "What did you use this for?" He had replied, "I used it to clean my ear. I have a running ear." Then Hubka had twisted the clip through a little nut that was lying on the table. "At that time, I saw no significance in it, but he said, 'Where did you get this?' So I said, 'I don't know.' I said, 'I didn't know it was mine.'"

On Monday, January 26, the police had started talking to him about bookies. "They asked me if I had not had anything to do with putting some of those bookies out of business. I told them I didn't know. I said, 'That is up to you to find out.' They said, 'Well, we want to clear the record, and you know, of course they won't make any arrest reports. So they got us over a barrel. You know how we pick them up. They forget it.' I said, 'I don't know anything about bookies. I am not interested in those bookies right now.' I said, 'Do you charge me with that?' 'No, no,' he said, 'We want to know one thing. Will you tell your two partners to lay off?'" He had replied, "If I had two partners I would tell them."

One night, Forbes had told him, "I have got some bad news for you, Chess." It seemed that District Attorney Simpson had insisted that all the other charges be filed against him. "I just shrugged," he said, "so then I told him, 'You ought to tell that Grant he couldn't punch his way out of a paper bag when you see him next.'" Leavy saw an opening. "You mean that he did not hurt you?" he inquired. "No, I don't mean he didn't hurt me. I meant how weak he was."

Q. You used the expression, told Forbes, "He can't punch his way out of a paper bag"? That expression

means someone has not got a punch and can't hurt;
isn't that what that expression means?

A. That is what that expression means.

Chessman pushed on. Forbes and Hubka had talked to
him about the red spotlight. "They asked me what was being
used, a red light or cellophane used to redden the spotlight?"
He had told them that he couldn't answer that question.
They had never let the subject drop. "It was always, 'Where
is it?' 'What did you do with it?' 'If you haven't got it; who
has got it? Who is he? Where is he?' " When they showed
him a picture of Tuzzolino, he had said, "That resembles
him somewhat."

The witness paused for breath. Go on, Leavy urged, tell us
everything you told Messrs. Forbes, Hubka and Goosen. Well,
there had been some discussion "about those shoes. Dave told
me he had bought them that night. Then they asked me
about it, and I told them I didn't know where they had come
from. Then they specifically started telling me about this
robbery in Pasadena, this Donald McCullough. They said,
'Well, we have got the book finished on this one.' 'Well,' I
said, 'that's wonderful. The only difficulty is that it was the
day of my grandmother's funeral.' "

On the night of January 23, he had been visited at the
Hollywood Police Station by Lewis Drucker, a former member of California's Adult Authority, who had approved his
parole in December. He told Chessman. "It looks like we
made a mistake letting you out, doesn't it?" The prisoner
had answered, "That is yet to be determined."

Q. Go ahead. Tell us just what occurred, anything
whether wise or otherwise, between you and Mr.
Drucker?

A. That is all I remember. He came in and looked at
me.

He had known Drucker fairly well because he had occasion-
ally worked for him in the Folsom administration building.
"I used to take his dictation at times."

Goosen had come into the picture after Grant suffered a slight heart attack. When Chessman had refused to tell him anything new, the police officer had threatened to send him to a basement that was maintained "for people that don't like to talk." That hadn't fazed him a bit. "Let's go to the basement," he had told Goosen, "I have received this treatment before. I have had policemen work on me before for several hours here in 1941. They broke a lot of ribs, broke my nose, but still don't know very much. Maybe you can do a little better." He had then been informed that the officer "was just kidding."

The next morning, he had complained bitterly to Goosen that he wasn't feeling very well. He had requested some urotropin because "I had passed some blood." When he was asked whether he wanted a doctor, he had said, "I don't want a doctor. I just want you to get this stuff for me." After he had received a "couple of urotropin," the officers had taken turns in questioning him. During the interrogation, witnesses were constantly being brought into the room. He remembered "a little redheaded gent who . . . rushed into the room and said, 'That's the man! That's the man! I would know him anywhere.' "

After lunch, Leavy, who was determined to play out as much line as the defendant desired, asked him to "finish your narration of what had occurred between you, Mr. Hubka, Mr. Forbes, and Mr. Goosen." Well, on Saturday they had taken him outside to some house. "They were very casual about it; they did not seem to be concerned with my custody." When they had returned to the police station, Forbes had said, "What's the matter? Aren't you interested in leaving. We were waiting for you to leave. We were all ready."

Q. You gathered from that that they wanted you to make a break so they would shoot to kill you? Is that what you mean?

A. Yes, that is definitely what I mean.

On January 25, he had been visited by Dr. Paul J. De River, a police department psychiatrist. He had complained to the physician about the beating he had received at Grant's hands. "Never mind that," he had been told. He was sure that De River had taken notes about his physical condition. But he had not told him how he had received his injuries. "I told him I had sustained these bruises in an automobile accident. I was afraid if I told him the truth it would start all over again." He had shown him the bullet wound on his forehead but he had not asked for any medical treatment. "It was just a superficial wound," he remarked.

When Leavy taunted him with an observation that a big strong man like Chessman would hardly be upset by a bullet crease, he retorted, "Any time you are shot in the head you are apt to be a little nervous." Furthermore, May and Reardon had added to his misery by "beating me on the head with their pistol butts." But that was caused by the struggle, wasn't it? "No," he replied, "there wasn't much of a struggle. It was one-sided. I was not capable of much of a struggle." Just before they had caught him, he had run into a small guard rail at the end of the Shatto Place driveway. It had hit him "right about at the navel."

Q. You ran into that rail hard, didn't you?
A. Yes, sir.
Q. When you ran into this guard rail, you were going at top speed to try to get away, weren't you?
A. Well, reasonably, yes.
Q. It stopped you, didn't it?
A. It did.

But he hadn't noticed any bruises on his body "until after Detective Grant had had occasion to spend 30 minutes with me in this back room."

Finally Hubka & Company had worn him down. "I . . . definitely decided if I didn't start in better with them that I might not make the Los Angeles county jail, so I figured in the interest of my own welfare whatever they said I would say yes to, by that time." So every time the officers asked, "Well, did you do this?", he had replied, "Well, if you say so, yes, yes."

Let's get down to cases, Leavy urged. Instead of "this" and "that," be frank and give us the very words the officers used. "I don't remember the exact words they used. They asked me in connection with these crimes. In the questioning, they asked me about Mary Meza. They said, 'What color of slacks did she have on?' I said, 'I don't remember. Black slacks, I guess.' They said, 'Well, what side did you go up to this car on?' I said, 'I went up on the right side.' . . . They cursed me and said, 'Why don't you get your story straight?' They said, 'You know you went up on the left side. You know the girl was wearing a skirt.' "

Q. What did you tell them?

A. Well, I believe I said, "I guess I was mistaken." I don't know what she wore.

Didn't you realize that when you told Hubka and Forbes about the Meza incident that you were admitting your guilt? Yes, he knew that. Yet you told us this morning that, when the officers were begging you to confess to certain crimes so that they could clear these jobs up, you did not say that you had committed any of these offenses; do you want to change your testimony now? No, he did not. "Up to the point that I was relating this thing," he testified, "I didn't make any admissions at the time."

Q. Now, you say that you told Forbes and Hubka that you walked up to the right side of the Meza car, is that right?

A. Yes, sir.

That was about the whole story. He had shown Dr. De River the bruises on his body and his legs. He had complained to the county warden but he had been afraid to contact the police jailer out in Hollywood. Yes, he had told Hubka and Forbes that a man with a sick mother couldn't commit the crimes they were talking about. What about the bookie holdup, Leavy asked him. "It was not robbery," was the defiant reply. No, he hadn't admitted anything to Detective Grant. "I have no further questions," said Mr. Leavy.

Dave Knowles was back for a reprise. He vividly remembered the second floor of Hollywood substation on the night of January 23. "They brought us up there with the handcuffs behind us, our hands were handcuffed behind us. Grant came in and started to work on us both. He worked on you first, then worked on me." He hadn't seen Chessman being beaten but "I heard it." He would rather not repeat what he had heard because of the ladies in the jury box. "Not the language," the defendant asked, "just what effect. Did you hear Officer Grant talking?" Well, he didn't know that it was Officer Grant but "somebody was asking you if you were going to give out, come clean. I could hear that in between blows. I heard that. I heard you grunt."

Later on, Grant had come into his room and beaten him unconscious. Most of the officer's blows had been "about the body." When he came to, he was sitting in a chair next to Chessman "and the photographers were taking pictures." No, he told Leavy, despite the beating he had received, he hadn't confessed to a single crime. It was true, wasn't it, that the only confession introduced at his trial before Judge Landreth was Chessman's admission to Mr. Forbes that he had pulled the Redondo Beach job? It was.

Although the defendant had refused to examine his mother when she took the stand on Monday, he had no qualms about questioning his father. Whittier "Serl" Chessman, a direct descendant of John Greenleaf Whittier, was a frail, sad-looking man for whom life had never even remotely lived up to its promises. His health had been permanently impaired by his struggle to feed his family during the depression years and he had, on two occasions during the thirties, tried to commit suicide. When he sat down in the witness chair, one sensed that this was the final indignity in a series from which there was no escape.

He had visited his son at the Hollywood police station on Monday, January 26. He had seen marks and bruises on Caryl's chest and legs. Yes, his son had told him how he had received those injuries. "What did I tell you?" Chessman asked. Fricke interrupted. "I am afraid that is hearsay," he said, "and inadmissible." When Leavy stated that he had no objection, the judge changed his ruling and told the witness that he was free to answer. "Everybody seems to anticipate a good answer," he observed. Serl Chessman remembered exactly what the defendant had told him. "You told me," he said, "they were given to you by a policeman there in the jail. You did not mention a name. You told me a policeman gave them to you, beat you up."

Leavy had only a few questions. Where were those bruises on the defendant's chest? "It was up around all the way down as far as I saw." On his abdomen, too? Yes, sir. Had he undressed? "Well, he pulled his shirt down." Did he tell you all about the running gun fight on Vermont? He did. And that he had run into an iron rail and hurt himself? Yes, sir. He also told you, didn't he, that he "got creased on the forehead some place?" That is right.

Doctor Paul J. De River had been waiting impatiently to testify. Finally, he told Leavy that he had an important engagement at three o'clock, and asked the district attorney to call him out of turn. Since Matthews was waiting for a prisoner-witness to be brought down from the County Jail, Fricke decided to grant the physician's request. A short man in his early forties, Dr. De River, who sported one of the droopiest mustaches in Los Angeles County, was the author of *The Sexual Criminal* and other studies of the same nature. Twelve years later, Al Matthews remembered him best as the prototype of "Gaston, of Alphonse and Gaston."

He had examined the defendant on Sunday afternoon, January 25, in the squad room of the Hollywood police station. He thought that Officers Forbes and Hubka had been present. Although his examination had been "primarily psychiatric," he had looked at the suspect's body. He had found "a slight scar on the right side near the hair line" that "appeared to be a recent scar." He had observed "one large scar on the left knee and a scar on the lower gluteal region—" Leavy broke in. "That doesn't mean anything to me," he remarked. "Where is that part?" Fricke had the answer. "It is where you generally sit down," he informed the prosecutor. "In other words, the buttocks?" Leavy asked De River. That was right. The defendant had also had scars on the right little toe and the left leg. No, he had not noticed any other scars or bruises "about his abdomen," and Chessman hadn't asked him for medical treatment.

Howard Gibson was brought into the courtroom by two deputies. A murder suspect, he had been a resident of Cell Block 10A2, the so-called "High Power Tank" in the County Jail, when Chessman had been brought in on January 27. In fact, the defendant had been put in the cell adjacent to his. The next morning he had had a long talk with his new colleague. He certainly had seen bruises and marks on his body. "It would have been impossible not to have noticed it," he asserted. "The first thing that came to my attention naturally was your face. One of your cheekbones which, to the best of my knowledge, was your right, I remember was swollen and discolored. There was a graze or gash at the hair line, I believe on the left hand side. In addition to that you then showed me, which I had not seen, you called my attention, I believe, and mentioned your thumb, one thumb was dislocated or fractured, was bent back over the back of the hand. It was somewhat swollen. Then you showed me both shins were bloody and raw from your knees to your ankles, the entire front part of your shins, is what we called barked or peeled, had scabs on at that time. Your chest was black and blue as far as I could see by your pulling your shirt down, this undershirt, this cotton shirt, your entire chest was discolored." He clucked sympathetically.

Leavy started slowly. Did this gash he had noticed on Chessman's head look as if it had been caused by a crowbar? You've got it all wrong, Mr. Leavy, Gibson explained, Caryl didn't say that the police had caused the crease on his head. "He did not tell me that it was a prior wound or anything of that sort. He did not single it out. It was one of a group of wounds, as far as I was concerned."

Q. You say Chessman, in addition to the wound on his forehead, had a big wound on his cheek bone?

A. No, sir, I didn't say a big wound. I said the cheek bone was discolored, swollen.

As for the wounds on his shins, he hadn't said that they had been caused when he tried to escape from Reardon and May? "No, sir, he did not. He just said the police officers did it."

The prosecutor handed the witness two photographs of the defendant. Gibson gave them a long look. "This one eye here," he observed, "is pretty near closed. The cheek bone is swollen, and the eye is pretty near closed. One eye is swollen in the picture as compared with the defendant at the present time." While the jury was inspecting the photographs, Leavy asked Gibson whether he had spoken to the defendant in the County Jail. "No more than was possible for each prisoner confined therein," he replied. While we're on the subject of jails, the witness was presently a resident of the High Power Tank, was he not? He was.

Q. That is the tank where they keep prisoners who are charged with high pressure crimes, crimes of violence?

A. Not necessarily, no.

When Matthews objected to the question as calling for a

conclusion of the witness, Leavy had had enough. "I have no further questions," he muttered.

Manuel Fox, a slender man with a pencil moustache, was another sojourner in tank 10A2. Like his fellow tenant, Mr. Gibson, he had noticed that newcomer Chessman had some rather interesting injuries. "On your face the most noticeable bruise was on your left cheek. It was puffed and swollen and about—there was a slight discoloration just below the eye and in the vicinity of that swelling. Then I also saw a thumb that was definitely swelling. And then later on in the course of the conversation which ensued I saw you stripped to the waist, and I definitely saw bruises and discolorations in the vicinity of your chest and ribs. Then you proceeded to raise your pants legs, and I saw your legs from the knees down to the ankles definitely scarred, definitely scratched and scabs. They were a mass of blood, sores, the way I can describe it." Chessman smiled his thanks and sat down.

Leavy stood up. Had the defendant told Mr. Fox just how his legs had been injured? He certainly had. "He said that he had been subjected to a beating at the Hollywood Police Station, that in the course of that beating he had received those scars." Ditto for the swollen left cheek. What about the injury to his forehead, had that been the result of the beating, too? No, it had not. "He definitely said that was from the graze of a bullet," Fox said.

Q. Did he tell you that any bruises on his legs or on his chest might have occurred by running into some object while he was trying to run away from the police that were running after him?

A. No. He was definite about how the injuries had been received. In fact he referred to it the day he came in, in the bunk.

So he was trying to impress you with his injuries. Not at all. "He was more incensed at this blow he had received, and consequently was giving vent to his feelings mostly, and I think that is the reason the man referred to that; not to impress me."

Q. Did it impress you?

A. No, it did not.

Leavy pushed out one cheek with his tongue. "Was it out like I am?" he asked. Fox thought that the swelling had been higher, on the cheek bone. The prosecutor handed him one of the pictures he had shown Gibson. "Tell me," he said, "if you can find on this photograph the injury to the cheek that you are talking about, or the front, the eye?" It was "very hard to show from this photograph." He was sure that the picture "absolutely does not look like he did when he came into the tank." But whether the photograph showed it or not, there was no doubt in his mind that "I seen the swelling on the cheek. It was quite obvious."

Chessman had a few more questions for Fox. Had he seen him do anything peculiar after he had been brought into the tank? The witness thought for a moment. "Well," he recalled, "I saw you retch, and [you] stated that the retching was due to nausea, by the aftereffect of having been kicked in the groin." He had also been shown "a knot . . . in the vicinity of the groin, and I myself was incensed at seeing it." Leavy jumped to his feet. Isn't it possible that the defendant was making a scene so that he could use it in court later? No, sir, Chessman had been "quite weak all that first day."

Q. You do not know what was going on in his mind, do you?

A. Well, I don't believe one can retch just thinking of anything of that sort.

Matthews informed Fricke that he had two more witnesses —prisoner Johnny Dillinger and a newspaper photographer— but that they would not be available that afternoon. Although it was only 3:30, the judge decided to call it a day. As the deputies took Fox out of the courtroom, he waved at Chessman, but the latter was too engrossed in conversation with Matthews to notice the gesture.

13

THE TRIAL—THE ADMISSIONS

(THURSDAY, MAY 13, 1948)

Court resumed at 9:50 the next morning. In Moscow, the Kremlin had just announced that Jacob A. Malik would succeed Andrei A. Gromyko as the Soviet Ambassador to the United Nations. But, in Department 43, on what promised to be one of the warmest days of the spring, the newspaper reporters, oblivious to the news from Russia, were giving odds that Fricke would reject Chessman's contention that he had been given the third degree in the Hollywood Detective Bureau, and admit as evidence any damaging statements he may have made to the police.

To everyone's surprise, Matthews announced that he had no further witnesses on this point. Leavy then called the defendant back to the stand. He wanted to know whether Chessman could remember when a photograph which showed Officer Goosen standing between him and Knowles had been taken. He thought that it had been "the same night I was arrested." Was it possible that it had been snapped on the morning of the next day? It was possible. The prosecutor then offered the shot in evidence. When Matthews objected to its introduction on the ground that it had not been properly identified, Fricke thought that "we should have . . . testimony that actually portrays the subject matter in the photograph."

Leavy grumbled but called Officer E. M. Goosen who had been sitting in the courtroom for several days. Goosen, who looked to epigrammatic Matthews like "Dick Tracy gone to flesh," was a husky, quiet-talking policeman attached to the Hollywood Detective Bureau. He identified the photograph as having been taken at the Hollywood booking office on the morning of January 24. He couldn't remember when it had been snapped but he knew that a newspaper photographer had taken it. That was quite enough for Fricke. He ordered it marked as People's Exhibit No. 41, and Leavy, in high spirits, immediately circulated it among the jurors who looked in vain for the "swollen cheek" and "puffed eye."

With Goosen excused, the district attorney resumed his cross-examination of the defendant. He had a few more photographs to introduce and he showed them to the witnesses. In one of them, Chessman and Knowles were standing next to Reardon and May. "Is that a picture of you and Knowles with your heads hung?" Leavy wanted to know. It was.

Q. You were trying to avoid being photographed, weren't you?

A. Yes.

He hadn't wanted to be photographed because the picture might have appeared in the newspapers. Was that because he was afraid that someone might recognize him? No, that wasn't it; the papers had a police mug they could have used. But this shot "would be more recent, wouldn't it?" Not necessarily. "There was a picture taken of me in jail that would be equally recent." When Leavy and Chessman began to split hairs over the respective vintages of the photographs, Fricke intervened and the witness was excused.

William Albert Thornton had served twenty-four years in the United States Navy as a chief pharmacist's mate. When he retired from the Navy in 1947, he had accepted a job with the County of Los Angeles as a night jail nurse. He remembered that Chessman and another man had been brought into the jail hospital on the fourteenth floor of the Hall of Justice by Deputy Beach at 11:10 P.M. on January 26. No, he had not examined the defendant; he had "inspected him." Because Chessman was a high-power prisoner, he had made "a particular inspection" of him. Since both Mr. Matthews and Mr. Leavy had telephoned him last night, he had brought his records into court.

All of the handwriting in red ink on the Chessman record was his own; the notes in blue ink had been entered by Mr. Arenson, the day man. What had he observed when he had "inspected" the defendant? It was right there in the record over his signature: "High-power inspection reveals no marks, scars or bruises, none claimed." Whenever a high-power prisoner was sent to him, he always looked for "fresh scars rather than old ones," and he knew he had done that in this case.

Q. Do you have an independent recollection of this examination now?

A. Now I do, yes, sir.

At Leavy's request he had consulted his records just before coming into court, and he had, as ordered by the chief nurse, "reinspected" the defendant at seven this very morning. The only scar he could find was "one on the right temple above the hair line." When Chessman claimed that he had another on his right thigh near his groin, Thornton had taken a look at it. He had found a "discoloration."

Q. What else this morning that you have noted here? What did you find the defendant claimed?

A. Nothing.

He remembered this defendant in particular because he had stormed around the examination room yelling to Knowles that "he had nothing wrong with him, he was not a sex maniac, and he wanted to get out of it."

Chessman had been following Leavy's questions intently. Mr. Thornton, he asked, you testified that you have "an independent recollection of conducting this examination?" The nurse was positive that he did. What about Knowles? Did he have "an independent recollection" of him, too? Well, he would have to check his chart.

Q. Is that the way you remember what happened here, by checking the chart?

A. Well, that, and other incidents that happened.

Thornton had to admit that he couldn't remember Knowles or that he might have treated him "for an infected toe and heel." But he was "positive" that he had inspected the defendant and that he had found "no marks or scars or bruises" on his face and body.

How many men had he inspected since January 1? Roughly, between fifty and a hundred each night. During that period, however, he had only seen "maybe ten high-power prisoners." All the rest had been "the regular run." Was it common practice for him to reinspect a prisoner say, four months after his first examination, "and put down in the chart what you remember four months previous?" Only when he was ordered to do so. Chessman had no further questions.

Leavy had an afterthought. He wanted to know just what the procedure was as far as the inspection of "the high-powers" was concerned. Mr. Thornton was quite explicit. "We have them strip. They just leave their shoes and socks on. My policy has been to have the man extend his arms, his hands, his wrists, bend them up and down, move his legs, bend away out and walk to see he has nothing wrong with his extremities. Then my policy is to ask him whether he has any illnesses, marks, or scars. If so, I record them. If the man says that he has not, I put down 'none claimed.'"

Q. Did you do that with the defendant in this instance?

A. Yes, sir.

No, he hadn't seen any scab near Chessman's hair line. But it might have come off when he was showered.

When Leavy sat down, Thornton started to leave the stand. Just a minute, Chessman said, did you find any scars when you inspected me this morning? "I found what you called scars," was the reply, but they were "very slight." As he answered the defendant's last question, the nurse gasped and clutched his chest. "Do you have a heart condition?" Leavy asked. Yes, he did. He had to take a nitro-glycerine pill. Fricke was immediately concerned. If you are the least bit apprehensive, he told the witness, we can take a recess. Thornton accepted the glass of water that Leavy offered him, swallowed a pill, and informed the judge that "I am all right now." But Chessman was almost through. He only wanted to know whether the witness always asked prisoners about their complaints and the cause of any injuries he might find. "Absolutely, I do," Thornton replied. Everyone breathed a sigh of relief when he walked out of the courtroom under his own power.

Patrolman E. D. Phillips was next. On the night that Chessman was captured, he had been in one of the prowl cars that had responded to 16-T's calls for reinforcements. He and his partner, Officer Bradley, had joined the pursuit just "north of Beverly on Vermont." When Reardon rammed the gray Ford in which Chessman and Knowles were riding, the witness had parked his car behind the two collided vehicles. He had seen the two suspects get out of the coupé and had followed Reardon and May when they ran after the defendant. When May stumbled, Phillips had helped Reardon subdue the fleeing man. He remembered that he had hit Chessman with his regulation flashlight but he couldn't recall exactly where he had struck him. "I think it was in the head," he volunteered.

Q. Did you hit at his head?

A. No, sir, I did not hit at his head.

Bruce Doebler, a reporter for the *Hollywood Citizen News* had arrived at the Hollywood substation a few minutes after 9:00 P.M. on January 23. He had seen the defendant in the detective bureau on the second floor, surrounded by a crowd of police officers which included Goosen, Hubka, Forbes, May and Reardon. Mr. Doebler had remained at the station until eleven o'clock, during which time he saw Chessman "continuously." At no times had he noticed that any of the doors to the bureau's three small rooms were closed.

Nobody had used "force and violence" on either of the two suspects. No, Chessman had not made any complaints while he was there. He had seen "one small scratch" on Chessman's head "near the hair line on the right side." He had returned to the station the next morning where he saw the defendant again in Forbes' office. Except for the fact that the suspect's face was washed and his hair combed, he had noticed no appreciable difference in his appearance. When Leavy showed him the photograph of Knowles, Goosen and Chessman, he stated that he had been present when it was taken. It was "a true and fair representation of the defendant and Detective Goosen."

Chessman had just started to question Doebler when Fricke noticed that Al Matthews had slipped out of the courtroom. "Do you want to proceed without him?" he asked the defendant. He did. But he had no luck with Doebler. All that he could extract from the reporter was that the latter had seen Detective Grant in the immediate vicinity, and that he had never had a chance to observe the defendant's "body or chest."

Joe Ledlie, who plied his trade for the *Los Angeles Daily News,* had reached the Hollywood station some thirty minutes before Doebler. He had seen the defendant "seated in the squad room, being interrogated by various officers." He had witnessed no third degree methods and he was sure that none of the squad room doors had been closed at any time. He had no recollection of any injury on Chessman's head

196 / BEYOND A REASONABLE DOUBT?

or body but "it is possible there was, though." Like Doebler, he had been present when the picture of Goosen and the two suspects had been taken by a photographer who, he thought, worked for the *Examiner*.

Leavy, who recognized the practical difficulties of getting a newspaperman into court twice, asked Fricke's permission to depart from the voir dire temporarily and question Ledlie about something other than police interrogation methods. Was there anything special about this particular story? Yes, there was. His editor had alerted him to the fact that Chessman might be "the so-called red light bandit." The reporter had been present when the defendant had been ordered to empty his pockets and place their contents on the squad room table. Among the suspect's effects, he had seen "a small nut." He had heard Hubka say something "about the unusualness of such an item being found in a man's pocket; also words to the effect it might involve a spotlight, or might fit a spotlight, automobile spotlight, which they also thought to be involved in the case." He thought that People's Exhibit 9 was "very similar" to the nut he had seen.

Matthews returned to his seat just as the defendant stood up to see what he could do with Ledlie. The reporter had not seen the nut removed from Chessman's pocket. When he had arrived at the station, "the property was on the table and officers were crowded around . . . I don't know who took the property from whose pocket." No, he didn't remember "a little paper clip." He had mentioned the nut in the story he had written about "this red spotlight bandit."

On January 23, the desk sergeant at the Hollywood Police Station had been Billy B. Alley. He remembered that Goosen and Hubka had brought the defendant down to his first floor office at "approximately 10:00 or 10:45 that night." It was his function to check in a prisoner's personal property and to make out a medical slip if there is a "complaint . . . of injuries."

Q. When you booked this defendant did he make any complaint to you of injuries?

A. No, sir.

In Chessman's case, everything, including "a little nut," had been booked—except his pants—and it had taken Alley until the end of his shift at 1:15 A.M. to complete the itemization. No, he didn't remember any wrist watch.

The cells at the Hollywood station were located directly across from the booking desk. The witness told Leavy that he had talked to Chessman at noon the next day. He had seen his new charge picking at his shin and he had asked him how he had injured it. The defendant told him that "he had skinned his shin as he left his automobile and fell over in the hedge with the officers in pursuit."

Q. That is what he told you?

A. Yes, sir.

When Chessman took over, he was particularly interested in the condition of his shin bone. Alley couldn't remember whether it had been the right or left shin, but he thought that the scab had been "faint."

Q. You mean your memory of it is faint or the scab is faint?

A. My memory is faint on that particular incident.

Q. Your memory is good about asking me how that was sustained, is it?

A. Very good. I remember pretty well the conversation that followed that.

Leavy's next witness was Otis E. Phillips, Jr., a photographer for the *Los Angeles Herald & Express*. It had been Phillips who had taken the picture of Knowles, Chessman and Goosen on the morning of January 24. He had photographed the three men with a Speed Graphic equipped with Agfa Super Pan Press film, "the best film that is made right now." Later that day, he had developed and printed the picture.

Q. That film would show, or disclose if you had a scar, and would that disclose any bruises or any swelling

on the cheek bone below your eye, if there were any?
A. I think in this case it would. If there were any such
wounds or bruises that had turned black or blue.
Fricke had a technical question. Was the film the photographer had used "sensitive to red . . . so a red mark would be
revealed on the picture." It certainly would. "Panchromatic
film," Phillips assured the court, "is a type of film that I
would say more closely resembles what is seen by the eye
than any other type of film."

After lunch, the prosecutor began a parade of police officers that was to last for most of the afternoon. His first offer-
ing was Detective Goosen who had arrived at the Hollywood
station at "approximately nine o'clock" on the night of January 23. He had remained until the defendant had been
booked by Sergeant Alley. He had not used any force on
Chessman and he had not seen any other policeman do so.
He had no idea of what had transpired at the station house
before nine o'clock.

Sergeant Hubka had entered the Detective Bureau at
about the same time as Goosen and had not gone home until
about 11:30 or 11:15. In fact, he and Goosen had taken the
defendant downstairs to the booking office. During his so-
journ, he had not participated in or observed "any force or
violence upon this defendant Chessman."

When Leavy turned Hubka over to Chessman, one of the
ladies on the jury wanted to ask the defendant a question.
She was interested in finding out what kind of bath he had
received at the station. Had soap been used? Yes, it had.
Were you provided with "any alcohol of any kind? I mean
like hair tonic, massages, alcohol for a rub down along with
the bath?" No, you would only receive that kind of treatment if you were in the hospital. But he assured her that he
did indeed have soap. She thanked him. "That is all I want
to know," she said.

On cross examination, Hubka had very little to add to his

direct testimony. Like Goosen, he didn't know what had occurred at the station before his arrival. While he was answering Chessman's questions, Forbes had risen from his seat behind the rail and whispered something in Leavy's ear. Before excusing the witness, the prosecutor asked him if, on January 23, he had been "working on the apprehension . . . of this red spotlight bandit?" He had been. Then you were called to the station that night because a likely suspect had been located? No, that wasn't so. "As I recall it, I merely dropped into the station," he stated.

Don W. Grant, a husky six-footer with prematurely gray hair, was the first police officer to interview Chessman and Knowles when May and Reardon brought them in. He had been at the Hollywood substation some thirty minutes before Forbes and Hubka had put in an appearance. He had been present all evening while members of the Detective Bureau interrogated the suspects. He was most emphatic in his statement that he had not beaten either man.

Chessman was tense when Leavy turned the witness over to him. How long had Grant talked to him and Knowles before Hubka and Forbes had shown up? Approximately thirty minutes. And had anyone else been present during that time? Yes, there had been.

Q. Who was that person?

A. I couldn't say.

Q. Well, I am asking you now.

A. I don't know.

But he was sure that the person had been a police officer. "Uniformed officers and detectives were all up in the office," he claimed, "I don't know which ones were in the room."

He had talked to Chessman for "possibly five or ten minutes" before the other officers had arrived. "I asked you your name, your address, your height, your weight, your age, the color of your hair, the color of your eyes. I asked you about the car, the gun you had, and I asked you about the clothes in the car. I said other things I don't recall." When he had noticed a bulge in the defendant's pocket, he had searched him and removed "a roll of money." No, he couldn't remember in which pocket the money had been.

Who had assigned him to the Chessman case? Nobody in particular. It was general policy for officers on duty in the Detective Bureau to interview suspects when they were brought in by patrolmen. "My capacity in the Detective Bureau when a uniformed officer brings a prisoner in is to talk to him to determine under what section of the penal code he shall be booked, or if he shall be booked at all." But he hadn't been familiar with the charges against the suspect at that time. Fricke tried to help him out. "Had you read police reports in regard to the case of the alleged red spot-light bandit?" he asked him. Of course he had.

The look Chessman threw the judge was withering. He turned back to Grant. But, when you first talked to me, you didn't know that I was suspected of being the red light bandit, did you? No, he did not. Didn't Reardon and May tell him why they had picked him up? They had merely stated that "they had chased you down Vermont, shot at you, that you tried to get away from them, that you had a load of clothes in your car." The defendant's voice was heavy with disbelief. "They did not give you any indication then that this case was related to the red spotlight case, is that correct?" No, not at that time. Later in the evening, someone had told him that this might be the bandit headquarters had been looking for.

He had telephoned the Redondo Beach police department when he noticed that some of the clothing that had been found in the coupé had a Town Clothiers label. He had put in the call after he had finished talking to the defendant. But didn't you discuss the Redondo Beach holdup with me? Yes, he did. Chessman shook his head. If he had first learned about the Town Clothiers job when he had spoken to the Redondo Beach police department and this had taken place after their interview, how could he have possibly asked him anything about it? Grant never answered the question.

Chessman tried another tack. When had he first seen the clothing? He had helped carry it out of the car, "sometime between 8:30 and 9 o'clock." Had he talked to someone about the clothing "before you spent this five or ten minutes talk with me?" He didn't believe so.

Q. It was brought after this, is that it?

A. I didn't say that.

Q. Well, I am asking you, what did you say?

A. I don't recall whether the discussion was before I talked to you, or when we talked the first, second or third time. I don't know when it was.

The defendant crossed his hands behind his back. Wasn't I handcuffed like this when you first saw me, he demanded. "When you came in I remember it," the officer answered, "however, later than that I don't." Do you at least remember "placing me against the wall lockers in that room?" He most certainly did not.

Q. Shoving me against them?

A. That, I did not see.

You must remember kicking me in the groin, Mr. Grant. Fricke broke in. You're assuming something not in evidence, Mr. Chessman. "That is like that question: Are you still beating your wife?" The defendant reframed his question. "Did you shove me against those lockers with expletives and strike me in the chest and kick me in the groin and accuse me of certain specific crimes, and ask me was I prepared to cop out and start telling you everything?" That was a damned lie. He had not done any of those things.

Mr. Grant, when you had this interview with me, did you write down my answers to your questions? He did. Did you write them down in a note book? No, he had not. Just what was it that you put into writing? In addition to your name, "your age, your height, your weight, color of your eyes, color of your hair, your build."

Q. What did you write down for my height?
A. I don't recall.
Q. What did you write down for my weight?
A. I don't recall.

Chessman frowned. "What did you write down for my name?" he asked. Your name. "What is my name?" With infinite relish, the detective spelled it slowly for him.

Now, Knowles had been put into another room, had he not? He had. Who had been responsible for separating the two suspects. He didn't recall but "it could have been" his decision.

Q. You do not recall . . . knocking Mr. Knowles unconscious?
A. I did not do anything like that.
Q. Do you remember bringing me in and showing me Knowles on the floor and in a very vulgar manner asking me if I wanted to get like Mr. Knowles?
A. Nothing like that ever happened.

The defendant looked incredulous. Do you mean to say, he thundered, that you didn't "take me back into the other room and place me again against the back of the lockers?" Grant smiled tolerantly. "Nothing like that ever happened, of course," he repeated quietly.

On January 26, 1948, Howard C. Gibbs, a police photographer, had been assigned to the "mug room" in the basement of the Central Police Station. On the evening of that day, he had taken two pictures of the defendant, both with panchromatic film. One shot had been a full-length photograph while the other had been "what we call a police mug" in which just the head and shoulders were shown.

Q. If there were any defects or bruises, such as bruise discolorations with his eyes, would it show on that photograph?
A. Definitely, yes.

In fact, the two prints clearly showed "a little abrasion on the forehead on the right side near the hair line." He was positive that any noticeable swelling "would show up . . . in the picture."

While Gibbs was on the stand, Grant had been busy drawing a diagram of the second floor of the Hollywood sub-station. Leavy recalled him for a moment but, after the detective indicated the location of the room in which he had questioned the defendant, he was promptly excused and his place taken by Officer May. The patrolman remembered that Grant had ordered him to put Chessman in one room and Knowles in another. He had left the defendant there for "fifteen or twenty minutes" while he had checked in at the front desk. No, he had not seen Grant or any other detective "use any force or violence" on either suspect.

May was followed by Lawson E. Snyder, a traffic officer who had arrived at Shatto Place several minutes after Chessman's capture. He and his partner had accompanied May and his two prisoners to the Hollywood Police Station. When they arrived there, they had gone to the second floor where "Chessman was placed in the southernmost room on the west side of the building, and Knowles . . . in the room next to him." He had remained with the defendant "until the car which investigated the accident that was involved started to make their report."

Q. What time would you say that was, in hours?

A. It would be an hour in the station. About an hour and fifteen minutes.

While he was there, nobody had laid a finger on Chessman. He had listened to Grant's questions but, for the life of him, he couldn't recall any of them.

Sergeant Forbes returned to the stand. He told Leavy that "around 6:30, 6:45, or 7:00 P.M." he and Hubka had escorted Chessman and Knowles to the basement of the county jail where Gibbs had taken their pictures. Then they had taken the two prisoners to the line-up on the ninth floor. "The show-up," he recalled, "lasted about an hour and a half. We then took them upstairs . . . and booked them in the county jail." He thought that they had arrived there "between 10:00 and 11:00 P.M." "You may examine," Mr. Leavy informed the defendant.

Was Forbes absolutely sure about his times? Well, he didn't know whether "we took you to the county jail and booked you in and then detoured you to the show-up, or whether we took you right up to the show-up at that time and then booked you in the county jail afterwards." When did the show-up start? At 8:00 P.M. It must have lasted "at least an hour and a half to two hours" but he wasn't positive. Wasn't he able to state with any degree of certainty whether "you booked me first or whether you booked me after?" Chessman asked. Fricke exploded. "This has been asked several times," he growled. The defendant's neck reddened. "No further questions," he muttered angrily.

Forbes was the last witness Leavy used to rebut the defense's contention that any admissions Chessman may have made after his capture were bludgeoned out of him. The voir dire was over. While the judge was mulling over his decision on whether to permit the prosecution to introduce such statements, the cross-examination of the defendant, which had been interrupted for almost two days, was resumed. Leavy started out on safe ground by reverting back to the diagram of the Wanger house on Malibu Beach. When had Salembier given him this drawing? Sometime during his last month at Folsom. What did he know about Salembier? Well, he had worked with him in prison and he understood that he had once been Ludwig Bemelmans' secretary or butler. He knew that Salembier had been convicted of stealing but he had never learned any of the details of his crime.

Had he told Mr. Forbes all about this diagram? Yes, he had explained to the police officer that it was in connection with his novel, "that it just showed where this Mr. Wanger lived." Now, the diagram had six other houses marked on it;

didn't Mr. Bemelmans live in one of them? Yes, the sixth one. Isn't it possible that Salembier had told him that the floor plan he had drawn depicted his former employer's house and not that of Mr. Wanger? He did not.

Q. Were you going there to interest Mr. Wanger in your novel?

A. Yes, among other people. That is correct.

But he had never gotten around to visiting the producer.

Now, did he remember appearing in the show-up Forbes had mentioned? Yes, he did. Did he recall what had happened there that night? "I remember appearing in the show-up," he replied, "I remember these certain people I have subsequently seen in the courtroom at that time." Was he asked anything "about the use of a handkerchief for a mask?" He believed that he was told to put on a mask. He had been given a handkerchief by some officer who ordered him to put it on.

Q. Well, as a matter of fact . . . you made some statement to the effect you would put it on the way you wanted because you knew how it was when you used it, or words to that effect. Didn't you?

A. No, I didn't. I said I would put it on the way I wanted.

Leavy turned to Matthews. He was ready, he informed him, to take up the conversations between the defendant and Hubka, Goosen and Forbes. "Just a moment," the public defender said. "Has the court made a ruling about this matter of a free and voluntary statement?" Fricke looked up. "I have not approached the point," he told both lawyers, "where I have been required to rule on it." Matthews promptly gave him the opportunity. "We object," he said, "to any repetition of the questions by Mr. Leavy made to Mr. Chessman which we objected to on the ground there had been no foundation laid to show it was a free and voluntary statement." The judge immediately overruled the objection. Did His Honor's ruling cover both confession and admissions, Leavy wanted to know. "The free and voluntary rule does not apply to mere admissions," he was told.

The district attorney picked up a sheaf of papers and walked over to the witness chair. He started with the Redondo Beach job. Hadn't Mr. Chessman told Mr. Forbes that "I was there, but not David. I borrowed the gun from a friend"? The defendant didn't believe so. What about the statement that he had picked up Knowles at Hollywood and Vine just before he let another man off at a service station on Vermont? Yes, he had said that.

Q. Did you tell Mr. Forbes you had the .45 automatic on the seat between you; if anyone else had been with you, that is, besides David, you would have shot back? Did you tell him that?

A. I did not.

In fact, he hadn't said anything about a gun because there had been no gun.

After some witnesses had been brought in to look at him on January 24, hadn't Forbes said to him that he had been identified as the red spotlight bandit? Just the opposite. Forbes had admitted that "their witnesses refused to identify me." Come now, Mr. Chessman, Leavy murmured, Forbes reported to me that you told him, "Well, the witnesses have identified me. What more do you want. I wasn't on those two sex jobs, and I didn't work at night." Yes, he might have said something like that. And, the prosecutor continued, didn't the detective say to you then, "Explain the day jobs"? In effect, yes. Wasn't that followed by his admission that he had robbed a couple on Mulholland Drive near the Rose Bowl? Absolutely not.

No, he hadn't told Forbes that he had stolen the Ford in Pasadena. "Did he ask you where the red lens for this spotlight was?" Yes, about two hundred times. But you told him that you had used red cellophane, didn't you? He did not. And that you had thrown it away before you were caught?

Emphatically, no. After you were taken to Mary Meza's house, didn't Goosen say, "Why don't you clear up all the different jobs?" Every policeman in the Hollywood station had said the same thing to him. You're sure that you didn't tell someone that "Those kidnappings are a tough rap. I am allergic to the green room. I helped carry Farrington Hill, when he was gassed, out of that green room"? No, that was ridiculous.

Leavy paused for a minute and studied his notes. You told Forbes or Goosen, didn't you, that you hadn't hit Mr. Waisler on the head, that Knowles had done it? He had never made such a remark. "I told them I didn't know anything about the Redondo Beach job," he insisted. As for the attacks on the two women, he had informed Goosen that "I did not pull those two robberies. I am not a sex maniac." He had given the police the name of the man who was the real red light bandit. That was Terranova, I suppose, Leavy asked. Yes, it was. But he had not been referring to any specific crime when he had accused him.

Yes, he had given Forbes a description of Terranova. He had said that the man was about five foot ten, of medium build, with dark brown or black hair.

Q. As a matter of fact you stated, "Italian, 26, 5'8", fast talker," didn't you?

A. I remember mentioning about "talker," now, yes.

When Forbes had shown him a picture of a man named Tuzzolino, hadn't he answered, "I think that could be him, it looks like him. He hangs around Bradley's in Hollywood"? Yes, he had said that. "But I also said at this same time that I didn't think it was him. I wasn't sure, though. It could have been him. Because the picture was an old one, or something, and he didn't look like that right at the time."

Leavy was just getting warmed up. Did he remember his conversation with Forbes and Goosen after his interview with Dr. De River on the night of January 25? He did. The two officers had shown him a great many daily crime reports and asked him whether he had committed those jobs. He had told them that they were barking up the wrong tree. The district attorney pulled at his ear lobe. "When they showed you the Bartle or the Stone job or some report in reference to them," he demanded, "didn't you say to them in substance that you had committed those robberies?" No, he had never said anything like that.

What about an afternoon job he had pulled in the Mulholland Hills when he had taken a watch away from a man and then given it back because he was "a nice guy"? When Forbes and Goosen had asked him about that one, hadn't he said, "Did that son of a bitch report that job? He was a married man and out with a girl. He seemed to be a pretty good Joe, so I gave him back his watch"? That was not true. "Every robbery they accused me of they told me I got the merchandise. I was never credited with returning any of it."

Q. Forbes or Goosen did not tell you about that fellow, about such an incident?

A. Not as you have related it, no.

The Mary Meza kidnapping was next. Hadn't he told Goosen that he had kept the girl in his car for two hours? He wasn't sure. "At the last there, when they started to torture me," he explained, "I started to tell them anything they wanted me to tell them specifically during these times." At the word "torture," Leavy's eyebrows shot up an inch. Is this the same torture that he claimed Grant had inflicted upon him? That and the other things that had been done to him during his three days at the Hollywood station. What other things? "Constantly being nagged, constantly being threatened, constantly being cajoled," he said.

Q. It was not new for you to be questioned by police officers about robberies, was it?

A. No, and it was not new to me to be beaten.

When Goosen had talked to him about Regina Johnson, hadn't he asked him, "Why did you make Mrs. Johnson suck you off?" Definitely, no. And hadn't he answered the detective by saying, "All I did was pull robberies. I am not a sex fiend. I did not force any girl to suck me." Yes, he had said something like that but Goosen had never asked him "that specific question."

Leavy returned to Mary Meza. His notes indicated that the defendant had told Forbes that he had taken off all his clothes "except my shoes and socks." The police officers had then asked him, "Well, didn't you freeze? Wasn't it cold?" Chessman sat bolt upright in the witness chair. He never asked me that question, he shouted, "that is his fine graceful work that enters there." Leavy skipped over to the bench. "I move that answer be stricken out, if Your Honor please." It was stricken.

When the officers asked you why you hadn't raped Mary Alice, didn't you answer that "she seemed pretty young. I just took her home"? Never. "Didn't you tell Forbes and Goosen that you were not in the back seat?" Leavy asked. He didn't remember what his answers to their questions had been because they were "just fabrications."

Now, there came a time, didn't there, during your conversations with Mr. Goosen when he asked you, "Chessman, if you are convicted and then you are lucky and get a short sentence, what would you do when you got out? Would you use your intelligence to something worth while?" No, Goosen had never displayed "that much interest in my welfare." Was he positive that he hadn't replied, "I would commit more crimes, but I would be a lot smarter and not get caught"? No, sir, he had not.

Q. Did Mr. Forbes say to you, "Do you think crime would pay off in the long run? Why don't you get a job and apply your intelligence to this job? You could make something of yourself. Doctor De River said you are intelligent and have a high I.Q."? Did Mr. Forbes say anything like that to you?

A. No, he did not.

He had never told Forbes that "an ordinary job does not pay off fast enough, or enough. I have a mother who is ill and a father who is pretty old, and the bills are too much."

On Sunday night, January 24, hadn't his friend Knowles asked him, "Did you tell those fellows I was with you Friday night?" No, the circumstances surrounding this incident "were entirely different." And didn't you answer him, "You have nothing to worry about, Dave. I took the rap for everything"? Yes, he had told him that he was trying to clear him.

With one eye on the clock whose big hand was only ten minutes shy of four, Leavy raced through his last set of questions. Didn't he have a conversation with Goosen in which the detective had reminded him that Judge Drucker of the Adult Authority had been present when Chessman was booked at the Hollywood Station. He didn't remember "any reference to it." And didn't you then tell Mr. Goosen that "you thought he would shit green"? No, no. Judge Drucker had merely told him that he had followed the police cars to the Hollywood station that evening and that he thought he had made a big mistake "in letting you out." But that was about the extent of their conversation. Fricke's gavel brought an end to the day.

14

THE TRIAL—THE DEFENSE RESTS

(FRIDAY, MAY 14, 1948)

There was only one subject of conversation in Los Angeles on Friday. The creation of the State of Israel, with David Ben Gurion as its first premier, had fired the imagination of even a city that was long used to the flamboyant, the spectacular and the bizarre. For the first time since the trial had started, the courtroom was comparatively empty and, whether this was attributable to the news from the Middle East or the unseasonably hot weather, it epitomized the essential loneliness of a man on trial for his life.

Leavy, who had looked dead tired when court adjourned on Thursday, seemed to have regained much of his bounce. When Clerk Luskin handed him the People's exhibits, he extracted No. 37, the diagram of Walter Wanger's Malibu Beach house which Robert Salembier had drawn for Chessman in the basement of the warden's office at Folsom. At the time of its origin, Salembier was the secretary to Associate Warden Wilson, and the defendant was in charge of the prison's files and records.

The district attorney was interested in the circumstances that had led to the drawing of this diagram. As the defendant recalled it, he and Salembier had been working together in the basement for "a few months." The two men had become friendly when they learned that they were both aspiring writers and had the same literary agent. Salembier had been very much interested in the novel Chessman was writing and had even helped in its revision. "I didn't know what to do with it for sure . . . so he told me about his experience in Hollywood and the people he had worked for, and he included at that time Mr. Bemelmans, and told me perhaps I could interest him in something, and possibly get my book—"

Q. Interest him? Whom do you mean by that?

A. Mr. Wanger.

Q. He mentioned Mr. Wanger?

A. He did.

When he had expressed some doubt as to the extent of Salembier's acquaintance with Wanger, his fellow prisoner had "assured me that he knew him and told me several other people around there that he knew." It was after this conversation that Salembier had "drawn this little diagram for me and told me how to get there."

Q. That is what he made the diagram for, to tell you how to get there?

A. That is right.

But you knew, didn't you, that Walter Wanger was a Hollywood producer? Yes, he knew that. "It didn't occur to you," Leavy snapped, "that maybe you didn't need a map how to get there, and you might look it up in the phone book, or locate him through the motion picture industry in some way?" Of course, it did, but he had accepted the diagram "because this man wanted me to take it. I was willing to receive any help such as I could get with respect to my literary work."

Salembier had told him that the best place to meet people like Wanger was at their beach homes because an office appointment might be very difficult to get. Leavy took a long look at the diagram. I see, he observed, that your friend also drew some small squares next to the Wanger place. Do you know why he did that? "Just to show me how much he knew, I guess."

Q. You were not going to go down and check over No. 1, which was the Sterling Hayden property, and No. 2, that was where Doris Dudley lives, and No. 3 was occupied by the name Brice, you were not going to do that?

A. No, I was not.

He denied that he had ever told Forbes that the purpose of the diagram was to show him the highway landmarks so that he could find a particular house and that he had been heading in that direction on the morning that he had robbed Dr. Bartle.

Leavy picked up three photographs from the counsel table. He walked back to the witness chair and showed them to Chessman. Did they appear to be views of the Richfield service station where he had stopped to let Terranova use the men's room on the night of January 23? They looked like it, although he couldn't be sure that it was the same station. Take my pencil, the prosecutor urged, and show me just where the men's room is on those pictures. He thought it was "back here, in the back of this building." Joe had gotten out of the Ford near "the covered portion which says 'Lubrication.' "

He had driven into the gas station from the Hollywood Boulevard side. He wasn't quite sure where he had let Terranova off because "I kept moving as soon as I saw the police car starting to move." Then he thought that he had "come out on the Vermont side." By the time he and Leavy had agreed on his route through the station, the photographs were so cluttered with the X's the latter had inked in that Fricke ordered the thoroughly confused prosecutor to cross out the symbols that had proved false alarms. The impromptu art work was apparently too much for Mr. Leavy.

"I have no further questions," he informed the judge. With a smile, Chessman gave him back his pencil.

On redirect, Matthews decided to plug a few holes in the dike. First of all, did his "client" possess an Eisenhower jacket? No, he did not. How about a checkered overcoat? Again the answer was no. He also didn't own any leather jackets, "G. I. pants or khaki colored clothes." Secondly, did he have any information as to the times that Dr. Bartle and Mr. Stone were supposed to have been robbed. As far as the dentist was concerned, he had "never been told." He didn't even know the day, much less the hour, when Stone was held up.

Caryl, Matthews asked, do you remember when Mr. Leavy "indicated that the preliminary transcript showed that you asked a question of Mrs. Regina Johnson about the revolver, and whether the man who held it had taken the clip out of the revolver?" Yes, he did. "And he indicated, how did it happen that you had any information if you were not the man who committed the crime?" The defendant nodded. "Have you any explanation?" the lawyer asked. He did. "I had been hearing the details of these crimes, what had happened, and the significant factors, or *modus operandi*, for about three solid days."

It seemed that Forbes had introduced him to a Pasadena detective, a plain-clothes officer with "a pock-marked face," who had told him what Mrs. Johnson had said about the gun. "I asked him," he said earnestly, "how can you expose the bullets without removing the clip? How can you expose the bullets without taking them out of the clip there in the spring?" Like his Hollywood confrères, this man had also tried to talk him into confessing the crime. But he hadn't succeeded.

Leavy, who seemed reluctant to let the defendant go, was on his feet again. "You don't suppose," he wondered, "[that] any of your friends, Terranova, Tubby, the General, David

Knowles, any of your other associates had any such items of clothing as a leather jacket, a checkered overcoat, or G. I. pants, did they?" He wouldn't know about that. You just told Mr. Matthews, didn't you, that you didn't know "the hour of the Bartle robbery"? That was right. In fact, Messrs. Forbes and Hubka told you the details of each crime, didn't they? They did, but he didn't remember that the time of the Bartle holdup was ever mentioned.

Q. You did not question Doctor Bartle about the hour?

A. Not the exact hour, no; it did not occur to me.

Do you still maintain that you also don't have any idea "what hour . . . or day Mr. Stone was robbed?" Yes, sir. "It says January the twentieth, but I don't know if that meant the night of January 20 or the morning of January 21, or the night of the 19 and the morning of January 20."

Q. You did not ask Stone, "when you say midnight," whether it was midnight dating from January 19 to 20, or midnight dating from January 20 to 21, did you?

A. No. And neither do I recall the district attorney asking that question.

Getting back to Mrs. Johnson, did you see any details in the crime report which the officers showed you which would indicate "that the bandit who held her up in some way took the shells or the clip out to convince her the gun was real?" No, he had never said that he had seen that in the report. Then, how did you learn about it before the preliminary hearing? That was simple. "I claim sometime during this three day period, during this discussion with Forbes, Officer Hubka, Officer Goosen, two police officers from Pasadena, and the crime report, and being confronted with the victim on two occasions, that at sometime through there I heard some discussion about the gun and the bullets."

Leavy looked puzzled. I still don't understand, he said, why you felt it necessary to question Mrs. Johnson about the removal of the clip when she hadn't said anything about it on her direct examination. Chessman tried once more. "I wanted to know about it," he explained patiently, "because it is utterly ridiculous anybody could have shown bullets without the clip being removed. I had the idea it would give me a chance to exonerate myself." He had had enough experience with .45 automatics "to know how utterly ridiculous it was that bullets could have been removed by clicking something to show the bullets."

The prosecutor's nostrils quivered. So you've had a great deal of experience with guns, he mused. No, not very much.

Q. What do you call very much.

A. What do you call very much?

Q. I am asking you. I am not on trial.

A. Well, I don't know what you mean by very much.

Q. Well, I am asking you if you know what you mean.

A. Well, I have not had occasion to use a .45 or have a .45 automatic in my possession or ever know anybody for any considerable period that did own a .45 automatic.

His experience with .45s had been "strictly limited." Had he been just as ignorant of guns in 1943? Well, a revolver had been found in his apartment when he was arrested that year. But it had not been a .45. Leavy saw a chance to make a little rhetoric go a long way. I don't imagine, he said softly, that you had much use for guns between 1943 and 1947? Naturally, I was in prison, the defendant replied. Mr. Leavy chortled as he plumped down in his chair.

Matthews was up once more. How much did you weigh when you were arrested on January 23? He had weighed "about 194 or 195 pounds with my clothes." And when you were taken to the county jail three days later, how much did you weigh with your clothes on? 182 pounds. The deputy public defender turned to Fricke. "The defense rests, Your Honor." The judge made a note on his pad. "You may proceed with your rebuttal, Mr. Leavy," he announced. The dice had changed hands again.

The prosecutor's first rebuttal witnesses were the police officers who had interviewed Dr. Bartle and Gerald Stone shortly after the two men had been held up. According to Deputy Patrick W. Murphy's report, which he had dictated to a police stenographer at the Malibu substation early on the morning of January 18, Bartle had described his assailant as a man with "crooked teeth in front." Officer Lloyd A. Lundy's notes indicated that Stone had told him that the bandit might have been of Italian extraction.

Officer May was back once more. When Leavy showed him the three photographs of the gas station over which he had jousted with Chessman before the midmorning recess, the policeman identified them as pictures of the Richfield station through which he had followed a suspicious Ford coupé on Friday, January 23. As he remembered it, Chessman, who had been driving north on Vermont, had made a right turn into the station, steered around the pumps and, without stopping, emerged back on Vermont, but now heading south on the avenue. During this maneuver, he had seen nobody "get out of that car in the service station or any place."

Chessman, who had not bothered to ask more than a half-dozen questions of Murphy and Lundy, decided to hold the line against May. Painstakingly, he took the goodlooking police officer from the time he and Reardon had first noticed the gray coupé at "approximately 7:50" until it left the Richfield service station some two or three minutes later. At what point had he observed that there were only "two heads" in the Ford? When the car had turned into the gas station. Where had these two men been sitting? In the front seat.

Q. Was your visibility such that you could absolutely determine that there were only two occupants at that very time?

A. No, there could have been someone else on the floor.

As far as the interior of the car was concerned, he had only been able to see "about 75 per cent."

May was followed by Alfred Davis, the owner of a jewelry store on Hollywood Boulevard, who had been sitting in the courtroom on Tuesday when Leavy had asked him to stand up so that Chessman could take a look at him. The defendant, who had not included a visit to Mr. Davis' shop in the recital of his activities on January 17, had not remembered "ever seeing him" before. Mr. Leavy showed the portly witness People's Exhibit No. 34, a pawnbroker's "buy book." Yes, that was his book, all right. Everything but this signature, Caryl W. Chessman, was in his handwriting. He had written up this particular bill of sale at 2:00 P.M. on January 17.

Now, Mr. Davis, do you have some sort of a tremor in your right hand? Yes, he did. "I do scribble quite bad," he admitted, "but I never had occasion or reason to change anything in this book. No date I have made has been changed." On January 29, some police officers had come to his shop and put a hold on the items covered by this bill of sale. Leavy picked up two long sheets of paper. "What are these documents?" he wanted to know. Davis stated that they were purchase reports which had to be compiled daily and sent to the police department. At 2:00 P.M. on the seventeenth, they indicated that he had bought a stickpin, a watch, a chain and a pocket knife from a man who gave his name as Caryl W. Chessman.

The defendant had never taken his eyes off Davis' trembling hands while the pawnbroker was testifying. Do you remember, he asked him, some of the other purchases you made in January? "I don't remember those things," the jeweler replied, "I don't keep track of it at all." What about the people who sell you things, can you remember them? Not very well. "There are thousands of people who go by my store every day," he explained. "Many people come in the store. So it is very hard for me to remember people that come in. You know fellows like you come every day to buy or sell something." Outside of his records, he had "no personal recollection at all."

As for the purchase reports he sent to the police, he made carbon copies whenever he could find a piece of carbon paper in his place. "Some copies," he said, "you will find both copies are written up with ink. At that time probably I didn't have carbon paper enough, so I just started writing and I found it and put it in and wrote the copy."

Q. But where these two copies were made, they both would have been made up at the same time?

A. Those two copies were made at the same time, yes, sir.

The purchase reports and the bill of sale were the only records he kept.

Mr. Davis, when you make a sale, how do you ascertain the date? The pawnbroker looked at Chessman with amazement. Why, I look at the calendar like anyone else. Do you have a calendar? I should say so. And what type of calendar do you have? "I have a monthly, I have two months, three months; we have four months. Three months, four months, monthly calendar. I have maybe two or three calendars in that place."

Q. At the time you make a sale, do you consult your calendar?

A. Yes, I look at the calendar, and I look at the time.

He also always asked for the customer's name and address as well as some sort of identification, such as "a driver's license, or social security card, or sometimes a letter written to the person."

Mr. Davis had flown to Chicago shortly after buying the defendant's pieces. While he was out of town, the police had contacted his wife and examined his buy book and the jewelry. "They put a hold on them," he said, "they didn't take the book or the merchandise; they just didn't allow us to sell them until further orders." In fact, if you will take a look at the bill of sale, sir, you will see the words "Hold, January 29, 1948" written in red ink.

Chessman picked up the buy book and looked through it hurriedly. Did anyone else "ever fill this book in"? Well, once in a blue moon, Mrs. Davis might have purchased something and made an entry. In March of 1947, his brother had come out from the East to spend a few weeks with him and he had written up one purchase. "Otherwise, there is nobody else's writing in that except mine," he insisted.

Matthews, who had been studying the purchase reports, took over. "I assume, sir," he said, "at times the carbon is defective, isn't that right?" That was true—he wasn't in the habit of throwing away money on carbon paper. "Sometimes I use it for a great many sheets," he explained. The lawyer walked over to the witness chair. "What does this word mean here?" he asked. Davis peered at the long sheet of paper. The word is "gent's," he informed him. He had gone over it twice because "it might have been an old carbon." "I didn't buy carbon paper especially for this," he said, "so I paste two sheets together. Sometimes the writing is not exactly correct, so I usually write over. I have a habit of writing over like you noticed in 'gent's.' "

Juror King raised her hand. She asked Leavy whether "the number of the watch designates that watch?" The prosecutor shrugged his shoulders. "Ask the witness," he advised her. She repeated the question. "Yes, that is right," was the pawnbroker's answer. If that was so, why had he written the word "Gents" after the number? Well, that description was necessary so that the police could tell whether it was a woman's or a man's watch. Matthews, who was afraid that the jury was missing the point, intervened. "For your information, Mrs. King," he said, "it isn't if he sold these articles with this particular store; the question is whether it was sold on the seventeenth of January." "I'm glad to know it," she replied gratefully, "I wanted to know the importance of that."

Doris Dudley, the mother of eleven-year-old Butch Jenkins, one of Hollywood's corps of child-performers, had come to the movie capital in 1940 after a short but promising Broadway career. In 1936, she had received such excellent notices for her portrayal of Paula Frothingham in support of Ina Claire in "End of Summer" that R.K.O. had signed her to a long-term contract. According to critic Brooks Atkinson, she was "not only pretty but has become an actress who knows how to explore the interior of a part." In 1940, after a successful run as Cordelia Clark in "My Dear Children," the play that had brought John Barrymore back to the stage, she had moved to Los Angeles, but the slender brunette had not been able to garner better than bit parts. By the time of the trial, she had settled for the more prosaic but hardly less exacting rôle of a Hollywood mother.

Miss Dudley had telephoned Leavy on Thursday morning after she had read an article in the *Times* which stated that her house was "listed apparently on a drawing which was in Mr. Chessman's possession." Later that day, she had met the prosecutor in the courtroom where he had introduced her to Sergeants Forbes and Hubka. During the recess, the district attorney had shown her the Malibu Beach diagram and asked her whether she knew Robert Salembier. She did. "I remember the name from Mr. Ludwig Bemelmans, a very close friend of mine that lives in one of the houses on the shore," she testified. "Mr. Salembier was butler to Mr. Bemelmans."

The actress had sold her Malibu house in July of 1944, and moved to Santa Monica. When Leavy showed her the Salembier drawing, she identified the Number 2 square as her former residence.

Q. Do the houses run in just the order as they appear in this diagram?

A. No, they do not. There were many houses in between those. There were a great many people.

As far as she knew, all of the owners of the beach property were "people of means." She was "quite sure" that Walter Wanger had never lived there but she did remember a Dr. Wagner who had moved in shortly after she had left.

Bemelmans had been living there "for years" and she had visited his home "many, many times." In fact, she knew the floor plan of his house "intimately." Now, Miss Dudley, Leavy said, please take a look at the floor plan on this diagram; do you recognize it? She did—immediately. It was the floor plan of the Bemelmans place.

Q. Why did you recognize it immediately?

A. Because you have to enter it through the bathroom. It was an odd way. Either that, or walk all the way around the beach to enter through the beach. It was one house out there they asked you in through the bathroom.

To get to these homes, one had to take a little road that led from Roosevelt Highway to "a private cove, almost an all hidden cove." It was impossible to see the houses from the highway. "As you approach the little road that goes down to these homes, you can see the first couple; the rest are not visible. There is a grade that comes down there from the Roosevelt Highway, a little private road." The little road dead-ended on the beach.

Q. In other words, you cannot see these houses, the number, quite as well when you are up on the Roosevelt Highway.

A. No. I am sure you can not.

Mrs. Vamos was curious. She wanted to know why Miss Dudley had telephoned Leavy. The actress had done so because she had been frightened when she read in the *Times* that somebody had the plans of her house. "I have a small child," she told Mrs. Vamos, "so I was afraid of kidnapping. I didn't know whether it was another beach house, because we lived in two before this one." When she had spoken to the prosecutor, he had asked her to come to court. "That is why I came down. That was the only reason." The juror seemed satisfied.

After Gladys Lund, the principal clerk in the Record and Identification Bureau of the Los Angeles Police Department, had identified Davis' purchase report as having been received in her office on January 21, 1948, Colin Forbes walked up Department 43's middle aisle for the eighth time. Mrs. Lund had given him the pawnbroker's original purchase report several days ago, and he had picked up the carbon copy from "what we call the bum board—a list of copies of all business done by pawn shops in the Hollywood division only." January 29 was when he had obtained it.

That was the day he and Hubka had placed a hold on the jewelry that Davis had bought from Chessman. The handwriting in red ink was "all mine." He had released the hold on March 4.

Q. Did you ever discuss with Chessman those matters of those exhibits?

A. I never did discuss any of this stuff with Chessman.

He had brought the pawnbroker's buy book to Leavy's attention just before the district attorney had started to cross-examine the defendant.

Mr. Leavy handed two photographs to the witness. Did he know when they had been taken? He did, "last night about 7:45 P.M." They had been shot from the Roosevelt Highway "about a quarter of a mile north of Topanga Canyon facing the ocean, there is an empty lot that looks toward the ocean." The police photographer who took them had been "standing on the highway shooting towards the ocean."

Q. By highway, you mean the Roosevelt?

A. Yes. So all he could see is an empty lot. You cannot see any houses which are down below this bluff.

Then he and Sergeant Grant had walked down the little road that Miss Dudley had described, and visited some of the houses on Old Malibu Road.

Q. Tell me, as you drive along the main highway, can you see any of those houses down on Old Malibu Road, that would be a good landmark to find a location for turning off to the right, to turn off to get to the Palisades, to an old ranch house?

A. You can't see the houses down on the Old Malibu Road there, but as you turn off Roosevelt there you can see one or two houses, but after you get down the road you cannot see any.

Leavy had already released the detective when he came back for one more question. Had he ever heard the name Salembier "until the defendant mentioned it from the witness stand?" No, sir, he had not.

Sergeant Forbes, Chessman asked, where is Salembier ncw? He was in Chino State Prison. I suppose that you and Grant checked the floor plan of the Bemelmans house when you were out there last night? We did. "Does it agree with the plan that you had previously seen and taken from my pocket at the Hollywood station?" he inquired. No, it didn't agree. The answer kindled Leavy's curiosity. "How did you find out it does not agree?" he wanted to know. Ann Dvorak and her husband, the new owners of the house, had told them that the floor plan had been changed in 1946. The witness finally stepped down.

In January, Deputy Sheriff Howard Myers, who was assigned to the Photographic Laboratory, had been working in the "I" room on the tenth floor of the Hall of Justice. On Wednesday, Leavy had asked him to prepare a "quickie print" of a picture of the defendant he had taken on January 26 when Chessman had been booked at the county jail. How long would a print like this last? About thirty days.

Q. Regardless of the fact it is a quickie print and does not last, does it truly and fairly represent whatever the picture was before you made the negative?

A. Yes, it does.

Two days earlier, Manuel Fox had been unable to find either a swollen cheek or a puffed eye on Myers' photograph.

The three pictures of the Richfield Service station had been shot on May 11 by Frank Cooper, a policeman attached to the photographic section of the Scientific Investigation Division. He pointed out the location of the men's room which was the middle door on the Vermont Avenue side. The ladies' room was on the Hollywood Boulevard side. The best that Matthews could do with the witness was to extract the hardly edifying opinion that "you cannot see the women's toilet from the Vermont Avenue side."

It was a few minutes shy of 3:30. Leavy had Reardon waiting in the wings but, when he assured Fricke that his questioning of the police officer would take some time, the judge decided not to stand in the way of a long weekend. "I think we do not gain anything at all by starting with a witness at this time," he informed his grateful listeners in the jury box. "We will adjourn until 9:30 Monday morning."

15

THE TRIAL—THE REBUTTALS

(MONDAY, MAY 17, 1948)

There had evidently been a shift in prosecution strategy over the weekend, because the first witness called by Mr. Leavy on Monday morning was Walter Wanger and not young Reardon. The silver-haired motion picture producer, who was to have his own brush with the law some two years later,* was dressed in a light tan suit with a brown tie whose subdued hues contrasted strongly with the red, white and blue monstrosity that emblazoned Fricke's neck. Wanger proved to be a remarkably concise witness who answered all but five of Leavy's nineteen questions with "Yes, sir" or "No, sir."

Like Miss Dudley, he had called the district attorney's office when he saw his name mentioned in the newspapers in connection with some property on Old Malibu Road. He had never owned a beach home in Malibu or anywhere else for that matter. He did know Ludwig Bemelmans, who had worked with him on several of his productions, but he had never visited the writer's home. He believed that Bemelmans

---

* On December 13, 1951, Wanger shot Hollywood agent Jennings Lang for what he considered the latter's unwarranted attentions to his actress-wife Joan Bennett. The producer subsequently pleaded guilty to assault with a deadly weapon, and served three months and nine days in the Los Angeles County Honor Farm.

had once come to his house for a story conference. He was not familiar with Robert Salembier or any of Bemelmans' other servants. He conducted his business in a Hollywood office under the name Walter Wanger Productions. Yes, it was in the Los Angeles telephone book.

Officer Reardon was next. Over the weekend, he had studied Cooper's three photographs of the Richfield station. Like May, he was positive that they portrayed the service station through which Chessman had driven on the night of January 23. He, too, had seen only two passengers in the Ford. "As we went by them," he explained, "I could see there was one person behind the wheel, then after we made the U-turn to come up behind this other car I could see there were two people inside of his car, one on the right and one on the left." He couldn't have been mistaken because his headlights were shining directly on the other vehicle's rear.

16-T had followed the gray coupé into the service station, around the pumps, and out again onto Vermont Avenue. The two policemen were "possibly ten feet or a little closer all the way through that station until we hit the Vermont side again where the car pulled away from us."

Q. Did that car which Chessman was driving stop at any place on that service station lot?
A. On that service station lot? It did not.

It hadn't stopped "from the time we first saw it until it came to a stop on Shatto Place."

Q. Were you watching when you first spotted the car to see whether anyone would get out, if they got out?
A. We were watching the car to expect any unusual movements, such as a possible friend to meet the car or anybody getting out, or anything like that.

Nobody had left the Ford until Chessman and Knowles jumped out after the collison with the police car on Shatto Place. "Cross examine," Leavy told the defendant.

Officer Reardon, how close to the Ford were you and your

partner when you entered the gas station? We were "so close to the car that I was watching out for a sudden stop so I could stop and avoid running into the back end of this car." I suppose you had an unobstructed view of "the entire front side of the car, did you?" No, the patrolman admitted. "I could see through the rear window, and I could also see the right side of the car as it made its right turn." The witness illustrated with his hands. "I could see the complete right front side at an angle, and I could see the occupants through the rear window."

Q. If you were bumper to bumper to this car at all times from the gas pumps on, how were you able to view the people in the front there?

A. I didn't say bumper to bumper. I said about 10 feet from the car.

No further questions.

Leland V. Jones, the lanky chief of the Scientific Investigation Division, was back on view. Leavy pointed to Mrs. Howell, who was sitting in the audience. "Did you take hair from her head," he demanded, "and put it in an envelope." Yes, he had done that last Tuesday morning. He had mounted two of Mrs. Howell's hairs on slides and compared them with those of Mary Alice Meza as well as the hairs Hubka and Forbes had found in the Ford. None of the Pasadena housewife's hair was "analogous in appearance" to either of the earlier samples. He had also examined one of Mr. Howell's hairs but it showed "no similarity" to any of the others.

But he had to admit, when Chessman took over, that "hair identification is not completely definite anyway." No, he hadn't taken a scale count even though it "could be a factor." Was there anything in the structure of Mrs. Howell's hair that "definitely and positively ruled out that hair as being similar" to those that the officers had found in the Ford? No, he could not say that. But one of Mrs. Howell's hairs was "in the process of being gray. So I do not think that there is any similarity between that and any other hairs at all. It was by itself."

After Mrs. Howell testified that she had pulled a few more hairs from her head and given them to an investigator for the defense named Matthew Solomon a week ago Saturday, Leavy called Paul L. Corrigan, a process server assigned to Judge Fricke's court. He had been trying to find Ann Plaskowitz, Dr. Bartle's passenger, since early April. When he went to her rooming house at 1022 South Gramercy, Mrs. Swope, her landlady, had informed him that she had gone to Arabia. He had also checked with the Federal Reserve Bank where she had been employed, but had been told that she had left her job and gone to work for the Standard Oil Company in the Middle East. He had contacted her mother in Westfield, Massachusetts, who had told him that her daughter "had gone to Arabia, and would be there two years."

He had also looked for Esther Panasuk. Gerald Stone had told him that he had met the girl, who was a Pan American airline hostess, on a flight from Los Angeles to Manila. Miss Panasuk lived in San Francisco, but Corrigan had not been able to locate her family in that city. "She is a popular woman," he said, "and I tried several fellows that might know her. I found two or three that said she was an airline hostess in the airline service, knew she had not come back." He had learned from a letter that Gerald Stone recently received from his mother that the girl was "still . . . in Manila flying between Manila and Guam."

After Wilbur Callahan and Arthur Pauff had testified on Monday and Tuesday of the preceding week, Leavy had asked George Howell to take his car to a garage and have the speedometer removed. The accountant didn't remember the exact day on which he had complied with this request, but he thought that "it was last week." After a mechanic had removed the speedometer, Howell had turned on his dashboard lights. All the "other instruments illuminated red." That included the clock as well as the long panel which contained the gas, oil, water and ammeter gauges. Leavy handed the spotlight to the witness. "Did you at any time," he inquired, "with the pincers from your car or from any other place, apply them to this nut, this Exhibit 9, or to any other nut which was then on a bolt holding a clamp at the bottom of the rim support?" Howell shook his head. "No," he replied.

Colin Forbes, a familiar figure, was back on the stand. He had arrived at the Hollywood Police Station at 8:00 A.M. on January 24. He had taken Chessman and Knowles from their cells into the station lobby where Otis Phillips, the *Herald* photographer, had snapped a picture of Goosen and the two suspects. Later that morning, he had had a long conversation with the defendant upstairs in the Detective Bureau. Leavy nodded. Tell us in your own words, Sergeant, what you and Chessman talked about that day.

At first, the prisoner had denied that he had committed the Redondo Beach robbery, or any of the "petting party holdups." When Forbes asked him whether he had ever considered the possibility that he might have been caught or killed during those robberies, he had said: "That doesn't bother me. I have taken guns away from the police before." Tell us all about that, Forbes had urged him. Well, he and two friends had disarmed two Montrose deputies, stolen their car, and pulled some jobs with it. "It was easy," he had said, "because we had the police radio on. We could tell exactly where the police cars were from calls sent out to them." They had ditched the car when headquarters started using a code which they couldn't understand.

Once, he had been involved in a running gun battle on Roosevelt Highway. He had been driving a stolen Packard when the highway patrol had begun to chase him. After "his buddy took a bullet wound in the heel," he had left the Packard at a Santa Monica barbecue stand and stolen the

car of one of its customers. "I was thinking," he had told
Forbes, "of writing the Packard people about using this
chase as an ad for the Packard Company." Another time, in
Downey, he and two friends had disarmed a suspicious
policeman who had stopped their car, and shot a man who
had come to the cop's rescue. "He said then that some damn
girl that he knew turned them over to the Glendale police
and snitched on them. That is how he was caught."

Q. What was his attitude all along as you were talking
to him?

A. Very egotistical.

Finally, they had got to talking about the Redondo Beach
job. "Chessman, you're smart enough to know you can't beat
us on this particular job," Forbes had told him. "You are
in a stolen car, your car has got all the clothes and the man's
wallet; you have got a gun, it is just the right time from the
time of the Redondo job to the time you were caught; you
tried to get away from the police. You can't deny you pulled
that job." The logic of this had apparently not escaped the
defendant. "Well," he had said, "you got me on that job."
But Knowles had not been in it with him; he had picked
him up at Hollywood and Vine after the robbery. "Knowles
is a pretty good fellow," he had observed. "He did his time
and he had been going straight."

He had bought the gun from some fellow at the Cinema
Bowling Alley, and a friend had lent him the car. "He said
that he had another fellow in the car that he had met out
in Hollywood . . . that he let this fellow out in the oil station
prior to the officer's stopping." During the chase down Vermont, the gun had been in the front seat between the two
men, but Knowles had been too frightened to use it. "Anybody with some guts . . . probably would have shot back and
got away from the police," he had complained to Forbes. He
had thrown the gun away when he had jumped out of the
Ford on Shatto Place.

The interview had been interrupted for a few minutes

while the defendant was taken downstairs to let some witnesses look at him. When he had been brought back to the
second floor, he seemed resigned. "Well, your witnesses have
identified me," he had informed the detective. "What more
do you want? I am not on the sex jobs, and I didn't work at
night." Forbes had appeared appropriately sympathetic. Forget about those jobs, he had told him, and just tell us about
the ones that you did pull. Well, there was one involving a
couple on Mulholland Drive and another near the Rose
Bowl. The witness paused for a moment. "I then told Chessman that Rose Bowl job, Floyd Ballew, was at night time,
so if he admits doing that job at night time that he must
have pulled the other robberies at night."

It was then that the defendant had opened up. The gun
he had used was "a loaded .45 automatic" and he had stolen
the car "in Pasadena." He had found a box of groceries in
the Ford's back seat which he had thrown away. Later, he
had "put on other plates" but he couldn't remember where
he had picked them up. When Forbes asked him, "Where is
the red spotlight lens, that glass?", he had replied that he
had used cellophane which he had thrown away. Leavy
broke in.

Q. Up to that time, did you know it was cellophane
that had been used?

A. No.

After Mary Meza had identified the suspect as the man
who had assaulted her, the detectives had taken him to a
restaurant across the street from the Hollywood station. A
T-bone steak had evidently been no more persuasive than
the grilling, because Chessman had refused to own up to the
sex crimes. 'Kidnapping is a tough rap," he had explained
to the police officers, "I have an allergy to the green room."
He had seen one man executed in the San Quentin gas
chamber and he wasn't going to confess to anything that
might put him in there.

Goosen had then asked him, "Did you hit Waisler on the

head, or who hit him on the head?" He had blamed this on Knowles who, he said, "was back in the room with the two victims." The detective suddenly returned to the attacks on the two women. "How about those jobs where the girls were assaulted?" he had asked the defendant. No, he wasn't responsible for those jobs, he wasn't "a sex maniac." He thought that "it was a guy named Terranova who was pulling some spotlight jobs." He had described Terranova as "an Italian, 5 foot 8, 35 years old, curly hair, a fast talker." When Forbes had showed him a picture of one Nick Tuzzolino, Chessman had said, "Yes, I think that could be him. It looks like him. He hangs around Bradley's in Hollywood." Leavy handed him Tuzzolino's picture.

Q. Did you know the fellow in this photograph?

A. I do.

Q. Have you ever handled him in minor police offenses?

A. Minor cases. He has no prior conviction.

The next day—Sunday—Dr. De River had interviewed the prisoner. When the psychiatrist had left, Forbes again pleaded with Chessman to "clear up all the jobs." The two men had looked through the daily occurrence sheets and the defendant admitted that he had pulled the Stone and Bartle robberies. When Forbes asked him about another holdup which had occurred "on January 20 . . . around 3 P.M. up in the Mulholland Hills," and had been reported orally by a married man who had been parked with a girl, the suspect had become very angry and shouted, "Did that son of a bitch make a report? I returned his watch. He was a pretty good Joe. He was a married man, didn't cause any trouble, and I thought, what the heck."

Mary Meza had been in his car "about two hours." As for Mrs. Johnson, he had pulled that job, too, but there had been no sex involved. When Forbes had asked him, "Why did you make Mrs. Johnson suck you off?" he had answered angrily, "I did not force any girl to suck me off." Mary Alice had taken off all her clothes except her shoes and stockings but he hadn't raped her because "she seemed pretty young." Instead, he had taken her home. No, they had never gotten into the back seat. "I asked him," Forbes said, "if he knew Mary and Mrs. Johnson were menstruating, and he said he didn't know it, that he was told by them that they were." When the officer had asked the defendant if his conscience felt better now, he had replied, "What do you think?"

Leavy picked up the Malibu Beach diagram. Had he shown this drawing to Chessman? Yes, he had. He had asked him, "What was this map for?" It seems that he was going to visit "some friend up in the hills at the ranch that shows there up in the upper right hand corner." The house on the chart was "a landmark that showed so he would know where to turn off the road to go up into the hills." He had run into Dr. Bartle while he was on his way to the ranch. When Forbes asked him why he was going to the ranch so early in the morning, he had replied that "there were a lot of people went up there, got up early to go horseback riding in the early morning hours." Chessman had said nothing to him about Bemelmans, Wanger or Salembier.

Later that day, Goosen and Hubka had taken Knowles into Chessman's cell. Knowles had asked Forbes if the defendant had said anything about the former's participation in the Redondo holdup. "I took the rap for everything," Chessman had reassured him, "there is nothing for you to worry about." The meeting had ended with the defendant telling the detectives that he thought that Judge Drucker, the man who had paroled him, "would shit green" when he found out about his arrest.

Did you ever tell this defendant, Leavy asked, that you knew that he didn't commit any of these crimes, but you wanted him to confess to them anyway so that you could clear them up? Forbes thought for a moment. "There was something to that effect," he said, "when we were thumbing through the crime sheets, anything that we thought might fit the description of Chessman, the same *modus operandi,* he would say, 'Well, you have to clear them up. If you want to clear your books, just mark them off. I'll take credit for them.' "

Q. No. Did you ever tell him that you wanted him to do that?

A. No. In fact, Mr. Goosen and I told him that it would be useless and silly for him to take credit for some of the robberies because that would still leave the original robbery as far as he and I were concerned; all we wanted was the jobs he committed.

He had checked the .45 automatic with the gun files at City Hall, the Police Record Bureau, the Sheriff's office and the Crime Investigation Identification Bureau at Sacramento, and "it was not registered." "You may cross-examine," said Mr. Leavy.

Chessman stood up. There was another conversation on January 26, wasn't there? Yes, there was. You told Hubka and myself about some fellow named Abbott who "probably would have been convicted of murder if it hadn't been for some officers finding another man with the gun that actually killed the fellow." Wasn't that man's name Jetton? Yes, that was the name. He remembered one more conversation at the show-up that night. When Officer Rawson asked you to cover your face with a handkerchief, "you made the remark, in front of people in the show-up room and officers, that you were there, you knew how you wore it; so he gave it to you and you fixed it on your face the way you wanted to."

Forbes had seen various people identify the defendant during the show-up. He remembered that Mrs. Tarro and Mr. McCulloch had "pointed you out." But other victims had identified him at the Hollywood Police Station before he had been taken downtown. When Jarnigan Lea and Mrs. Johnson had seen him there, the latter had cried, "It's you! What did you do those things to me for?"

Q. Do you recall whether I did or did not ask you,

when you confronted me with the fact that I was
the red spotlight bandit, I asked you to bring the
victims over?

A. Yes, you made several remarks, "Bring on your
victims." But it was useless. We had already contacted victims that we were trying to bring in. They
were coming.

Sergeant, when you first talked to Dr. Bartle, didn't you tell
him, "We have your red spotlight bandit. Do you want to
come over and identify him?" No, sir. We told the victims
only that "we had a suspect in custody we wanted them to
look at."

Chessman shifted gears abruptly. Officer Forbes, isn't it
your practice to have a confessed suspect sign a written statement? Yes, that was standard operating procedure. Then
why didn't you ask me to do so? Forbes smiled tolerantly.
"I thought it would be useless to ask you to sign a statement," he said. What about notes, did you take notes of
what I said? No, I did not. Isn't it common practice when
you're questioning a suspect to take notes? Well, it all depends on the suspect in question. Some prisoners won't tell
you anything if they know you're writing it all down.

Now, about this red cellophane. You said I told you that
I threw it away? Yes, you did. Did I also say where I threw
it away? No, you didn't, because I never asked you about
that. Chessman's mouth fell open. "You didn't ask me where
I threw it away?" he asked incredulously. No, I did not.

Q. Was the red spotlight an important factor in this
case?

A. It was important to us.

The defendant leaned over and grasped the vial which
contained the nut from Leavy's desk. "When did you first
learn about the monumental significance of this little nut
with relation to this crime?" The prosecutor started to object but Fricke had anticipated him. "Reframe your ques-

tion, Mr. Chessman," he ordered. He would be happy to. When had Forbes first heard that "that little nut had been found in my right front pocket?" He had seen it on the arrest report when he had come to work on January 24. When he had questioned his prisoner about it, "you said that you didn't know anything about that nut or that paper clip around a nut." "Why in the world," the defendant had asked him, "would I want to carry a nut with a paper clip around it in my pocket?" That was about the extent of their conversation about the nut.

Had there been any more conversations about crimes? One that he recalled. The married gentleman who had been reluctant to report a robbery in the Mulholland Hills had finally been persuaded to take a look at the defendant. Forbes had brought him to Chessman's cell and said, "Well, here's your bandit. Here's the man that held you up." But the man had been unable to identify him. "He sure doesn't look like it to me," he had replied. Yet, the man had asked the defendant, "What did you do with my watch?" and the former had answered with a laugh, "Well, I gave it back to you." But there was no doubt about the fact that "he would not identify you."

Forbes had not bothered to go to the Cinema Bowling Alley to check on the gun. "I don't believe you bought it from anybody at the Cinema Bowling Alley," he told Chessman. "I believe you got the gun elsewhere." No, he had never had a forensic chemist check the automatic for blood stains, or analyze the defendant's hair "to determine if any . . . were in the back seat of that car." Just before the noon recess, Chessman asked the policeman whether he had found a wrist watch among the property which had been turned over to Sergeant Alley. "No," was the answer, "I checked your personal booking slip. On not one of those reports could I find a watch booked to you or credited to you. However, there was a pair of horn-rimmed glasses booked to

you that was not in your property now in the Sheriff's office.
There is no receipt for those glasses there."

After lunch, Fricke noticed that Al Matthews was not in
his seat at the counsel table. Did the defendant want to wait
for him? Chessman nodded. "If the Court please, I would
rather wait a few minutes, and if he is not here we can proceed." The judge said, "All right," and had just started to
busy himself with some papers on the bench when Matthews
burst into the courtroom. "If Your Honor please," he apologized, "I am sorry I am late. I tried to be here. Blame the
Board of Supervisors. That elevator service." Fricke understood completely. "We didn't wish to have the public defender's office out of the building and moved way down the
street," he complained.

After each conversation with the defendant, Forbes had
gone back to his office and made notes of their substance.
He knew that Sergeant Goosen had taken notes during the
discussions which were "similar" to his own. From these
records, he had filed all the charges against Chessman.
Hadn't he inquired about the robbery of the Firestone
bookie? No, that had never been discussed. But he had
talked to some of the other officers about "the fact that you
were suspected of the attempted holdup of some bookies."

Now, was I asked what type of slacks Mary Alice Meza
wore that night? Yes, sir, Forbes agreed, I asked you that
question myself. "I know you told me just the opposite of
what she had on that particular night," he added.

Q. You didn't answer my question. The question was,
did some officer in your presence while questioning
me ask me what type of slacks was Mary Alice Meza
wearing that night?

A. Yes.

Q. Do you remember what my answer was?

A. Well, your answer was that she was not wearing
slacks, your answer was she was wearing a skirt. She

was wearing slacks. It was just the opposite of what she had on.

He was sure of that. The fact that Miss Meza had testified on May 6 that she had been wearing a black skirt at the time had long since been forgotten.

Chessman turned to his literary career. Had there been any talk "about writing during the course of this three day period?" Yes, there had been. You told me that you had helped Ernest Booth, a fellow convict, write a novel. The detective was certain that there had been no conversation about the defendant's own books or about A. & S. Lyons, Inc., his agent.

Q. Did I or did I not tell you I had hoped to be a writer?

A. No.

Had there been any attempt to analyze the spotlight in order to see "if there had ever been any cellophane used on it, or whether there were any particles of red glass?" No, this had never been done. Was anyone instructed to check the light for fingerprints? No, because the witness had realized that "many people handled that spotlight after your arrest." The car had been dusted, however, but only illegible smears had been found. No prints of either Mary Meza or Regina Johnson had been discovered.

Leavy bounced up. Sergeant Forbes, he boomed, do you have Goosen's memorandum book with you? He did. The prosecutor handed the notes to Matthews. "I know they are not admissible in evidence here," he advised him, "but I want the record to show they are available to this defendant at this time if he wants them." Matthews looked dumbfounded. "Wants what?" he demanded. Why, Sergeant Goosen's record of his conversations with your client—didn't you ask me for them out in the corridor some time ago? Matthews scratched his head. I guess I did, he admitted.

While the public defender was glancing at Goosen's notes,

Leavy decided to repair some fences with Forbes. Every time a person touches something, he doesn't necessarily leave fingerprints, does he? That was true. If the person were wearing gloves, there would be none and sometimes oil on the finger tips would smudge a print. Fricke interrupted with a quasi-rhetorical question. "If the surface happened to be moist," he asked, "and you put your hand on it and dust the surface, it does not leave a print?" The policeman was quick to agree with him.

THE COURT: What percentage do you find prints that you could recognize?

A. Oh, I say about three per cent, ones that I have handled.

Leavy took Forbes through a brief survey of the communications system used by the Los Angeles Police Department. From a teletype machine at any of the fifteen local divisions, messages could be sent to the City Hall monitor who would relay them to some fifty-eight stations in California and outside the state. Fricke was duly impressed. "It is rather remarkable," he observed. "It is like a telephone, only instead of sending voice, it sends words." Forbes nodded his head. That's absolutely correct, Your Honor.

At 9:15 A.M. on January 25, the witness had sent a teletype message to all the stations in the Los Angeles area, calling their attention to the fact that Knowles and Chessman would appear in a show-up at the Hall of Justice the next evening. A full description of both men, the gun, the car, and the spotlight had been included in the report. He had also stated that Chessman had admitted pulling certain jobs in some of the divisions and "called their particular attention to the show-up."

The district attorney asked Matthews to let him have Goosen's notebook back for a few moments. After studying it briefly, he asked Forbes whether Chessman had told him about any other crimes. Yes, he had become quite loquacious, once he had started to talk. "He gave us one job above Linda

Vista, up in Pasadena . . . around 11 A.M., fourteenth, fifteenth or sixteenth." The detective read from his notes.
"Victim and girl in bushes. Victim approximately 50 years,
girl 35. Took money from wallet and purse. About $109.
Used car and plastic gun. Also had handkerchief." Then
there was one near the Rose Bowl on the evening of January 19 when he had stolen "about $30" from another couple.
At that time, he had worn glasses, a handkerchief and a hat,
and used a plastic gun. On either the eighteenth or nineteenth, with the same paraphernalia, he had rolled an "old
man and young woman" who had been quite drunk. His
take had been $150.

The next day, he had ambushed a man and woman in a
Cadillac on an old road near Las Flores Canyon, netting
some $225. On January 20, he had waylaid a couple in the
Mulholland Hills and picked up $40 and a Longine watch.
"That is the report job," Forbes explained, "where the fellow was married and didn't make a regular report, and he
wanted his watch back." The only one of these holdups that
had been officially reported was the one that had taken place
near the Rose Bowl.

Forbes looked annoyed when Chessman announced that
he had a few more questions. When had he made "this
alleged confession on the sex crimes?" Some time after three
o'clock Sunday afternoon. What time had the teletype message been sent? At 9:15 that morning.

Q. Does that teletype say I admitted my guilt?

A. It does.

THE DEFENDANT: No further questions.

On January 26, the show-up on the ninth floor of the Hall
of Justice had included some sixty suspects. They had been
paraded in groups of ten or twelve along the raised platform
that stood at one end of the room. Officer T. V. Rawson,
who had conducted the show-up that night, had shone a light
on each prisoner and asked him three or four questions so

that he could be seen and heard by the victims who were sitting in front of the catwalk.

Chessman's number was 49. When he had appeared on the platform, someone in the audience had asked Rawson to "hold him out." The show-up chief had commandeered a handkerchief from a bystander and "arranged it" around the defendant's face. He heard somebody instruct him to "pull his hat down," and, when he started to do so, Chessman "stated I had it wrong . . . he took the handkerchief and arranged it around his face, and pulled his hat down while the people in the audience looked out for any possible identification."

After a brief scuffle over the admissibility of several of the People's exhibits, Leavy was down to his last four rebuttal witnesses. He started off with Regina Johnson's husband Harry, who confirmed Rawson's version of the show-up. He had heard Chessman tell the police officer not to bother adjusting the handkerchief on his face. "I know how I wore it," he had insisted. Detective Goosen identified his notebook in which he had entered the defendant's statements after the latter had told him to "get your pencil and paper." Goosen added one new fillip. Chessman had told him that he had parked the Ford "a few blocks away from home," but he hadn't investigated the truth of that statement.

Jarnigan Lea was back once more. Had he studied astrology in the Navy? The witness raised his eyebrows. Not astrology, Mr. Leavy, nautical astronomy. The prosecutor handed the ex-submariner Defendant's Exhibit I, a letter from Charles H. Cleminshaw, Associate Director of the Griffith Observatory, about the position of the moon on January 19, the date of the attack on Mrs. Johnson. Yes, he had seen this letter before. It stated that the moon had been at the first quarter phase when he and Mrs. Johnson had parked above the Rose Bowl. There had been no trees or other obstructions "between us and the moon." Its beams, together with the bandit's "little pen-flashlight reflection from the glass in the car," had made it very easy for him to see his face and torso.

But there was still another source of light, he told Chessman when Leavy let him go. The lamps from the Sacred Heart Academy had also illuminated the scene. And all of this had given him "ample opportunity to see this person, is that correct?" It certainly did, Lea retorted. As he testified, the witness's eyes were fixed on the defendant's even smile. Suddenly remembering that he had sworn at the preliminary hearing that the "tough-looking egg" who had robbed him had "crooked teeth," he blurted, "I never told the police that you had crooked teeth." Chessman chuckled softly. You also told Judge Guerin that you were certain that the bandit had been wearing a light gray hat, didn't you? Yes, but "I probably meant dark brown hat."

As Lea left the stand, Mrs. Vamos asked Mr. Leavy why Exhibit I also mentioned the moon's position on January 17. Well, that was the night that Mrs. Tarro had seen Chessman crawling out of her bedroom window. He hadn't bothered to question her about it because "I don't believe Mrs. Tarro knows . . . anything about astrology." Fricke, ever the perfectionist, thought that the record should indicate that he meant "astronomy" and not "astrology." "That shows how much I know about it," Leavy laughed, "I know the moon when I see it." The judge seemed lost in thought. "There is still some question astronomically," he mused, "as to whether when we look up in the sky we actually see the moon or merely a shadow." The prosecutor covered his embarrassment by barking, "Mrs. Johnson, come forward."

Mrs. Johnson was, if anything, more subdued than she had been when she had first mounted the witness stand on the trial's first day. It was even difficult for Leavy, who was standing only a few feet away from her, to hear her answers to his questions and he was constantly exhorting her to raise her voice. When she first saw the defendant, he had not been masked. She remembered that he had been wearing a white handkerchief around his neck, but he had not pulled it up to cover his face until Mr. Lea had taken out his wallet.

Q. Did you get a look at this defendant Chessman before the defendant pulled the mask up at that time?

A. I did.

When she was sitting in his car she had seen the headlights of another automobile approaching from the direction of the Sacred Heart Academy. "I told Mr. Chessman," she said, "he had better pull his handkerchief down, it might be noticed, and if they would see us that way it might show up." He had agreed with her "and he reached and pulled the handkerchief down." As she was leaving his car to return to Lea's, he had shouted at her, "Oh, take this." He had then handed her Lea's keys. "He was looking straight at me," she asserted.

Q. Did you get another look at his face unmasked then?

A. I did.

After Matthews said that he was willing to accept Leavy's statement that daylight saving time had gone into effect at 2:01 A.M. on March 14, the latter informed Fricke that "the People rest, if Your Honor please." Chessman had some more witnesses but, since one of them had to be brought in from another county, the judge decided to adjourn early. As the delighted jurors filed out of the courtroom, an extra was on the streets announcing a report from Israel that the Jews had succeeded in breaking the Arab ring around Jerusalem.

16

THE TRIAL—THE LAST DAYS

(TUESDAY, MAY 18, 1948—
FRIDAY, MAY 21, 1948)

The next morning, two deputies escorted a slim, dapper man dressed in prison gray to the stand. He gave his name as Rene Robert Salembier, present address: Chino State Prison. "Jeeves with a record," as Matthews referred to him, had met Chessman at Folsom. Just before the latter was paroled in December of 1947, Salembier had drawn the Malibu Beach diagram for him. As he recalled it, "Chessman was preparing to go out on parole. He was writing a novel which I was very interested in . . . and I had at one time been employed by a writer in Hollywood. I felt that an introduction to this man would possibly further Chessman's literary aspirations." He had planned to write a letter of introduction to Bemelmans but this "could not be done because the institution would not let it go out."

Accordingly, he had given his fellow prisoner the floor plan of his ex-employer's house because "I felt this man . . . his living and his house personified one of the characters that Chessman was trying to portray in his novel." His friend's novel was going to be a satire of life in Hollywood and he had enjoyed reading the part that had already been written. When Matthews showed him a manuscript entitled

245

"Dust Thou Art," he recognized it at once as the book's prologue. He was convinced that Chessman's novel was at least equal to a similar satire which Bemelmans had just written.

Leavy started out with a rush. When Salembier had prepared the diagram, hadn't there been some discussion that a few of the houses listed on it might be a good landmark for someone driving north on Roosevelt Highway? No, nothing like that had ever come up. But now that the prosecutor had mentioned it, "for this alley they are a landmark there, an indication to turn left. You turn left off Roosevelt to go into them going north." Yes, he was sure that you could see some of the houses from the highway.

He had left Bemelmans' employ in April of 1945 to begin serving a sentence for robbery. He had started working for the writer as a butler, but he had been promoted to his secretary. He "assumed" that Sterling Hayden, Fannie Brice, Doris Dudley and the other people who lived on Old Malibu Road were all well off. He didn't believe that Doris Dudley had still been living there in 1945; he had put her name on one of the diagram's squares because "I was trying to indicate where this house was." Chessman had never been there before and he had wanted to make it as easy as he could for him to find Bemelmans' place.

Bemelmans' address had been 18708 Old Malibu Road. If that was so, Leavy inquired, why had he put that designation on the "number four house that you have listed as Wanger?" Well, that was the house he thought Bemelmans had been renting in 1945. "As a matter of fact," he said, "I paid some bills, some rent bills on it at the time."

Q. In 1947 when you drew this diagram for Chessman, you believed Bemelmans was living in this house listed as number 4, where it says "Wanger"?

A. That is correct. I think there are other houses in there, to be frank with you. I think there may be a few houses in there.

No, he didn't know that the floor plan of 18708 had been changed since he had gone to prison.

Now, these homes on Malibu Road, they were resort houses, weren't they? Well, there was a beach nearby, Topanga Beach. Leavy's tone was sharp. That isn't what I mean, he snapped. You knew, didn't you, that during the winter the owners of these beach houses spent very little time in them? That isn't true, the witness retorted. "They are mostly occupied throughout the year. I would say many of them live quite continuously in them."

Q. You knew that many of these houses, around January, people may be away from their homes part of the time, didn't you?

A. I would venture to say there was probably always someone in those houses, or homes.

If Leavy was trying to paint a picture of a midweek caper in the uninhabited lairs of the rich, he was meeting stubborn resistance. It was clearly time to try another road.

If the purpose of the diagram was to direct Chessman to Mr. Bemelmans, why had Fannie Brice's home been included? Well, his friend had been interested in all aspects of life in the movie colony. He had "wanted to know whether they were the people connected in the motion pictures, weren't people perhaps to whom he would sell the novel about motion pictures that he was writing with respect to motion pictures." Leavy hung on grimly. "Didn't Chessman question you with particularity as to exactly what these people were doing, what their contacts were in the motion pictures or writing world?" Yes, that was substantially correct.

Bemelmans was a wealthy man in his own right, wasn't he? He supposed that he was. Did it ever occur to you that, instead of going to the trouble of drawing a diagram, you could have told Chessman to locate your ex-boss in the telephone directory? That would have done no good because Bemelmans' telephone was an unlisted one. Then why not give our literary neophyte the number itself? "It would not be available," Salembier explained, "to anyone just calling the operator. She would say there is no phone for the number given for Bemelmans' home."

No, he had not told Chessman that Walter Wanger lived on Old Malibu Road. Three minutes later, he thought that he "probably did." "I'm not sure," he said, "but I think I did because you see Wanger, as I told you before, I was under the impression that Sir Charles Mendl owned the house and Bemelmans rented it from them. I know he was renting from somebody." If this sounded like double-talk, you couldn't tell it from the bland expression on Leavy's face.

The diagram had been the result of a casual conversation between the two prisoners when they were working together on the records of parole violators. After he had drawn the sketch, he had no recollection of having given it to Chessman. But he was sure that the defendant's interest in the people on Old Malibu Road had been legitimate. "You don't give information to people in prison," he pointed out, "unless you are sure it is bona fide."

Q. You did not know for sure what Chessman had in his mind?

A. I am not a soothsayer. I believed the man was going out and try to make good. I would never have given it to him otherwise.

As the deputies bustled Salembier out of the courtroom, he just had time to shout "Good luck, Chess!" before the doors of Department 43 closed behind him.

Little Dr. De River, looking as if he resented the entire judicial process, was back for a brief return visit. Chessman merely wanted to know if the psychiatrist could remember if he had admitted any sex crimes to him. "As I recalled," the witness answered curtly, "when we touched on that subject you said you would not talk about it. There was no discussion of any crimes you committed whatsoever." When several of the jurors complained that they could not "hear the words," Leavy ordered Mr. Perry to read the diminutive doctor's answer aloud. That was all for De River, who scurried out of the courtroom as fast as his short legs would carry him.

The last rebuttal witness for the defense was a Pasadena policeman by the name of Fred C. Buzzard, who, on January 18, had interviewed Floyd Ballew and Elaine Bushaw. He had brought with him the report he had made after his conversation with the couple. He read the bandit's description aloud: "John Doe. Male. Age 35. Approximately 5 foot 7 inches. 150 pounds, ruddy complexion, plain glasses, pointed chin. Wore brown leather jacket and brown hat. No description of pants. Suspect driving a 1946 Ford sedan, gray or cream in color, with red spotlight on driver's side of car. Weapon used was .32, .38 blue steel automatic pistol."

Leavy was all politeness. It frequently happens, Officer, does it not, that what information you obtain from the victims initially may not check out accurately? That is very true. Sometimes, they even forget certain things until they get a chance to look at the suspect, don't they. Buzzard agreed completely. In fact, some things that happened during the commission of this crime, such as the bandit's slapping Miss Bushaw's face, are not even in your report. Yes, that was so.

Q. That is one of those things you can always elicit later from the witness when he testifies in court, is that right?

A. Yes, sir.

Chessman returned to the stand briefly to deny emphatically that he had ever told Forbes or anybody else that he had assaulted either Regina Johnson or Mary Meza. "That is all for the defense," Matthews told the bench. "The People rest," said Mr. Leavy. If counsel wished, the judge intoned, we can take a short recess before the arguments began. Counsel wished, and Fricke granted a ten-minute adjournment. Leavy took advantage of the respite to put the prosecution's exhibits in numerical order.

The ten minutes had stretched to sixteen before Fricke returned to the bench. After emitting a throaty grunt that might have passed for an apology, he told Leavy to get on with the business at hand. The district attorney opened on a homey note. He had chosen "you folks because I believed you were the right ones." Don't be fooled or misled, he warned them, because we've all had a few laughs during the trial. With a "spouting ego" like the defendant's, it's difficult to avoid some levity. But to him, it was a deadly serious matter and he hoped that they, too, would regard it as such.

After Mrs. Vamos had inquired and been enlightened as to the rôles played by the various attorneys, Leavy pressed on. He had prepared a chart of the dates, times and places of all the crimes which he tacked onto the courtroom blackboard. This was, he informed his twelve listeners, "a little eye-appeal to assist you with respect to the words I will use here in my argument." As the Chinese say, he misquoted, "one look is worth 10,000 words." They would not be able to take the chart into the jury room but he had prepared a typewritten chronological list of all the crimes, which would be made available to them later.

He was asking for the death penalty. That was the least punishment this fellow Chessman had earned. Just take a look at his background, he exhorted them. He was convicted of robbery and felonious assault in 1941 and sent to prison. Two years later, he escaped and was immediately arrested for another robbery for which he was sentenced by Judge Still to five years to life at Folsom. On December 8, 1947, he was paroled and here he was back on trial again. "I am not quarreling with parole," he assured the jury, "some fellows should be paroled. But not Chessman."

He was convinced that the defendant had put on an act for the benefit of Judge Drucker's parole board. If he had really intended to go straight, why would he have had Salembier's diagram in his pocket when he walked out of Folsom? He had been out of circulation for four years and, if he was going to renew his life of crime, he needed a starting point. That talk about asking Bemelmans for help with his novel was just so much poppycock. He had told Hubka and Forbes quite another story when they were questioning him about the Bartle holdup. He was using the diagram "as a landmark . . . where he would turn off to go down there to a ranch and visit a friend." He was going to do a little early morning horseback riding and he had only pulled the Bartle job because it didn't take him out of his way.

Now, ladies and gentlemen, let's look at the evidence. First, there is that holdup of Carl Hoelscher's store in Pasadena on January 3, just twenty-seven days after our friend here was paroled. You heard Don McCullough, Mr. Hoelscher's clerk, identify Chessman as the man who had rifled the cash register that day. Then, ten days later, he finds Mrs. Howell's Ford with the keys in it, parked only six miles away from his home. It was just the kind of car he needed for what he had in mind because it had a spotlight.

After the Tarro burglary attempt on the seventeenth, he had really started using Rose Howell's car in earnest. He had knocked off Dr. Bartle at 4:35 A.M. the next morning, and Floyd Ballew that evening. Ann Plaskowitz and the Bushaw girl had gotten off lucky. Leavy waggled his head. "It strikes me," he said, "as downright depraved, perverted how a man can become sexually excited as this defendant did during the course of kidnappings and robberies. Think of that, will you, when you get into the jury room."

Elaine Bushaw got a good look at the man who had slapped her. Why, he had been standing right under a street light and she certainly didn't seem like the kind of a girl who would identify a man who wasn't there. He turned and pointed a stubby finger at the defendant. "I say," he insisted, "Chessman has got a face that you would, I am sure, have never seen one just like it; protruding chin, nose, manner of his speech, his size." Granted that all of the victims were not able to pick out every feature accurately, but don't be fooled by that. They saw him at different times of the day, they were understandably excited, but they all said he was definitely the man.

The Lea-Johnson episode had taken place the next evening. You heard Mr. Lea, a man with remarkable powers of observation, point to the defendant and say, "That is the man." And you saw "poor Mrs. Johnson," a polio victim, forced to commit an act of sexual perversion that she will never forget. "I have heard many things in the courtroom," he orated, "I have seen human emotions twisted and torn from the witness stand thousands and thousands of times . . . but I have never seen the mental anguish that Mrs. Johnson undoubtedly experienced from what she told down here from this stand." At this dramatic point, Fricke decided to adjourn for lunch.

The prosecutor roared back after the noon recess. Keep in mind, he pleaded, that we don't ask for the death penalty in every case. "I do not think you folks think we are a lot of witch burners up here," he said. But here, where this pervert kidnapped this woman while he was engaged in a robbery, the law says that "the death penalty is one of the proper punishments . . . in my judgment there is only one proper punishment, and that is the death penalty."

His next crime was the holdup of Gerald Stone and Esther Panasuk on Mulholland Drive on January 20. Mr. Leavy smiled indulgently. Everybody has parked somewhere during his life, he owned. Today the young people spooned in cars; his folks did it in a horse and buggy. That fact of life is just what a fellow like Chessman counted on. But this time, he wasn't relying only on his ability to get away fast. He was wearing a mask. "Apparently after the Bartle and

Ballew and Bushaw robberies, he was taking a little more precaution," he speculated.

Two nights later, it was Mary Meza's turn. "Isn't it horrible," Leavy asked rhetorically, "to have a young girl introduced to her sex life by this fiend here?" But Mary had more to tell than just a story of rape and perversion. She was the only witness who saw the defendant "do something to the spotlight." If he recalled her testimony, she said that "he had a flashlight over there in the area where the spotlight was." What else could he have been doing but removing the red cellophane that had covered the lens? When you tie this in with the little nut that was found in his pocket when he was captured two days later, then you know exactly what he was doing.

Now, how had Chessman tried to discredit Mary's testimony? By showing that she had been wrong when she swore that "there were two places where they were illuminated by a red light" on the Ford's dashboard. But Chessman knew that the speedometer had been removed before the girl entered his car and he gambled that "it was not that car, because that did not have two places that illuminated red." That was why Leavy had asked Mr. Howell to take out the speedometer and check the panel's lighting. You heard him testify that, even with it removed, there were several places that "showed red" when the lights were turned on.

The district attorney pointed to the last crime on his chart. Even when Reardon and May caught him with the loot on his back seat, the defendant refused to admit that he had pulled the Redondo Beach job. "I thought he would have the good sense to admit Waisler and Lescher were kidnapped for the purpose of robbery," he remarked. Despite the fact that Mr. Lescher's wallet, filled with his identification cards, was found in the Ford coupé, our friend insists that he had nothing whatever to do with that holdup. It was this mysterious fellow Terranova who might have pulled that caper, but not our fearless parolee who obligingly drives

hot cars for comparative strangers "without any consideration, without any pay."

Then, when he spots Reardon and May behind him on
Vermont, he turns into a gas station to see whether they are
really following him. The moment the police car pulled into
the station too, he knew that the officers were after him.
When they finally brought him to bay on Shatto Place, he
drops his gun and runs for his life. He claims that Knowles
lost his guts. He wasn't so brave himself when the chips were
down. He wants you to believe that the only reason he was
caught was because he was creased with a bullet. He got that
wound on his head when Phillips hit him with his flashlight.
But a bullet wound is more glamorous and "he wants to
have all the glamor he can put into his case, because he is
a show-off, aside from being depraved."

As for the defendant's claim that he was beaten by Detective Grant, he sneered, that is ridiculous. Officer Snyder was
with him all the time and he didn't see anything of the sort.
Neither did any of the other policemen or newspapermen
who were swarming all over the Hollywood station that
night. But you don't have to believe them. Just look at the
picture that Mr. Phillips, the *Herald* Photographer, took
the next morning. "If you can see anything in that picture,"
he asserted, "that shows the defendant was assaulted, I'll put
in with you." The suspect had confessed simply because he
couldn't help bragging about the successful escapades he had
pulled.

Leavy was almost through. There was only the matter of
the alibis. Maybe Chessman's grandmother was buried at
noon on January 3, but the Hoelscher robbery did not take
place until seven that evening. Even if you accept Mrs. Cora
Fleming's recollection that Chessman was still there when
she left Larga Avenue "after dark," on the third, the records
show that the sun set at 4:56 that day. There was plenty of
time to drive the six miles to Pasadena and hold up the

haberdashery. As far as Winona Phillips was concerned, if you can believe a woman who bases her remembrance of a certain date on a new plot idea which did not come to her until three days later, then you're welcome to it. "We just hope," he observed, "that the novel she is writing is a bit more coherent than her testimony."

Chessman told you that he was home all day on January 17, the day of the Tarro escapade, except for trips to the druggist and the grocery store. But he'd forgotten all about his visit to Mr. Davis' pawnshop. If he wants us to believe that he was in Bradley's with Helen Denny and Ollie Treon on the night of January 20, that's fine. He is not charged with any crime committed on that date. "He made the unhappy mistake of thinking that the Stone crime had been committed on the night of the twentieth . . . when we know from the police reports that it was committed on the night of the nineteenth, just past midnight the following morning." As for the Terranova story, "it is not worth while paying any attention to."

The district attorney wound up with a flourish. If you don't send this man to the gas chamber, society may have him back on its hands again. You know that life imprisonment does not mean what it says. Even habitual criminals, who used to be sent to prison for life after their fourth offense, are now eligible for parole because the state legislature recently changed the law that applies to them. So if you send Chessman back to prison on the kidnapping charges, the fact that the statute now reads "without possibility of parole," doesn't mean that it won't be altered in the future. "I told you when I started my argument, as far as I was concerned, in the proper administration of justice there was only one proper penalty." He paused for a moment to let his words sink in. "I still am saying the same thing when he comes with his argument. That is the only proper penalty." Send him, he begged, where he can never again ruin the lives of a Mary Meza or a Regina Johnson—to the little green room he fears so much.

As Chessman stood up, Fricke wanted to get one thing straight with Matthews. "I am only going to allow one counsel to address the jury," he told him. "I am not going to permit you to argue, and then the defendant." When the lawyer started to protest, the judge was adamant. "Only one counsel for the prosecution. I am only going to allow one on the other side," he repeated. But, in all fairness to the defendant, if he thought that Matthews should have a chance, he would give it to him. Then he turned to Chessman. "You are limited in your argument to the argument of the evidence here in the court," he pointed out. "You are not permitted to make any explanation you have in regard to any matter which has not been shown by some evidence somewhere in the record. You understand?" The defendant indicated that he did.

He started with a little analogy. When he was a boy, he and a friend had each owned a Model T Ford. The engine in his friend's car had been specially adjusted so that it was capable of much greater speed than his own. One day, the police were chasing his pal who was rocketing along at eighty miles an hour. The latter escaped by careening around a corner and the cops gave Chessman a ticket for speeding. "The only thing that really established my innocence," he said, "was the fact that when they looked under the hood of this automobile it was strictly stock. It could not go 30 miles an hour downhill."

He looked straight at Foreman Harte. You know that I have not been an angel. I have been a thief, I have been in trouble with the police, I have violated many sections of the penal code. But I have never been guilty of any sexual crimes. In fact, I have robbed men rather than women and I have never stolen from anybody in a car. This is the first time in my life that I have been accused of attacking women

1948 police identification photographs of Charles Saverine Terranova, who was accused by Chessman of being the real "red light
bandit."

United Press International Photo

Caryl Chessman standing before the prosecution's chart which lists
the various crimes of which he was accused. Chessman used this
chart for his summing up to the jury on May 19, 1948.

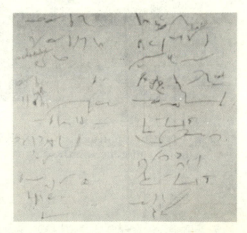

Four samples of Ernest R. Perry's shorthand notebooks from which Stanley Fraser completed the Chessman trial manuscript.

Brad Williams Photos

Caryl W. Chessman as he answered reporters' questions during his last press conference on the day before his execution.

or raiding lovers' lanes. "If you honestly, after you have deliberated, feel that I am the person who committed these crimes," he challenged, "why, I think the defense had better state right now that they are asking the death penalty, too!"

He wanted to set the record straight at the outset. "I am not on trial for being an egomaniac; I am not on trial for being a wise guy; I am not on trial for being a thief except as regarding specific crimes; I am not on trial because I do not fraternize with policemen; I am not on trial because I had a diagram of some silly little piece about a producer named Wanger." He was only charged with the crimes that Mr. Leavy had listed on his chart. "The question you must decide is whether I am or am not guilty, and the answer as far as I am concerned is an answer that is not based on the question of being a wise guy; it is not based on being an egomaniac; it is not based on any forced theatrics, mere dramatics, histrionics." He paused for a long moment. "I am not guilty," he reiterated.

Now, let's take a long look at the evidence against me. Donald McCullough said I was 5 foot 10, weighed about 150 pounds and had a mustache. Mary Meza swore that I was smaller than the average man, while none of the other witnesses had me weighing more than 160 pounds. He pulled himself up to his full height. Look at me, Ladies and Gentlemen, I don't think any of you could visualize me as weighing only 150 pounds or being shorter than the average man. I weigh 190 pounds and I am six feet tall.

Mr. Leavy claims that there was plenty of time after the sun set on January third, the day of my grandmother's funeral, for me to drive over to Pasadena and hold up a clothing store at seven that night. If that was so, then how does he explain away Mrs. Adair's testimony that she spoke to me at home at that very hour? Mr. McCullough testified that the bandit touched the cash register, yet there was no attempt by the police to dust it for fingerprints. If I was there, that would have clinched it for once and for all.

Lastly, if my face is as unique as the district attorney says it is, why didn't young McCullough report that I had a broken nose instead of a non-existent mustache?

Mrs. Howell's car was stolen on January 13. If I stole it, then I could not have been working with Winona Phillips on her novel at the same time. Mr. Leavy has tried to discredit her by showing that she was somewhat confused as to just how she knew I was visiting her on the nineteenth, but he never referred to what she said about the thirteenth. The parole officer had verified his recollection of where he had spent that morning; why should he be any less truthful about the afternoon?

On the night of January the seventeenth, I was supposed to have tried to break into Mrs. Tarro's home, a house that was less than two blocks away from my own. Mr. Leavy has called me a criminal genius, a man with a high I.Q. Is it reasonable that I would think of burglarizing a house in a neighborhood where I was well known? Why, one of my best friends lives next door to Mrs. Tarro and I frequently visited him. And what would I be looking for in Mrs. Tarro's house? What would I try to get?

In his excitement, he began to shout. Then, after escaping from Mrs. Tarro, I'm supposed to have gotten up before dawn, driven north to Santa Monica, and robbed some dentist at 4:35 A.M. Here I am, a two-time loser, with a face that nobody can forget, risking a lifetime in the penitentiary, for a fifteen-dollar holdup. "It hardly seems reasonable to me. Fifteen dollars!" As soon as he paused a moment for breath, Fricke seized the opportunity to remind him that it was time to adjourn for the day.

When Chessman resumed his argument the next morning, it was apparent that the three-day growth of beard which he had been sporting on Tuesday had disappeared. He picked up where he had left off with the robbery of Dr. Bartle on Malibu Road. As he remembered Bartle's testimony, the dentist said that the bandit had walked over to his car and asked him for identification. Then he had returned to his own automobile to which Bartle had followed him, only to be confronted with the business end of a .45 automatic.

This must have given the victim "a reasonably good look" at the man who had robbed him. Bartle had later described him to the police as a man of stocky build who was approximately thirty years old, 5 foot 6 tall, and weighed 150 pounds. But Dr. Bartle, being a dentist, had also noticed that his assailant had "crooked teeth in front." Fricke came to life. "To the best of my knowledge," he recalled, "there is no evidence about that." With the observation that the bandit would have had "to open his mouth fully clear back to the tonsils for us to make reference to whatever he was intending to make reference to," Leavy seconded the motion. People's Exhibit 56, Deputy Murphy's report of the Bartle robbery had apparently been lost in the shuffle.

The next robbery was supposed to have taken place that same night near the Rose Bowl. This time, according to the victims, Floyd Ballew and Elaine Bushaw, the thief was thirty-five years old, 150 pounds, 5 foot 7 tall, and bespectacled. But now, the gun was "a .32 or .38 calibre automatic pistol." Furthermore, the bandit's car was suddenly a two- or four-door sedan and not the coupé which Dr. Bartle had seen. When Mr. Leavy had shown Miss Bushaw a hat that was found in the coupé, the girl had identified it as the one the robber had been wearing. Chessman picked up the hat from the prosecution table and pulled it down on his head. "It fits like a beanie," he said. "You can pull it down as tight as I can, still it is very obviously not my hat." Whose hat was it? Terranova's, of course.

Twenty-four hours later, he was supposed to be back in the coupé and attacking Mrs. Johnson in the Flintridge Hills. Even if you don't think that I was with Mrs. Phillips that night, he asked, how can you believe that I was the person described by the very observant Mr. Lea? The man the ex-sailor had seen was "between 5 foot 8 and 5 foot 10" and weighed about 160 pounds. Mrs. Johnson had said much the same thing, and she had a far better look at the bandit than did her companion. After all, she had walked alongside the man who had assaulted her. Under such circumstances, he was certain that "you would not miss a person's height, if you were asked to do it, by four inches."

Then on January 20, he was supposed to have held up Gerald Stone and his girl and stolen two dollars from them. But, at the preliminary hearing, Stone had refused to identify him. Unfortunately, he had no alibi for that night because he had been home in bed. But, from reading Stone's testimony before Judge Guerin, he had thought that the crime had taken place at midnight on the twentieth and he had asked everyone who had seen him in Bradley's that evening to come to court and testify for him. "If I had known what night it was," he reasoned, "I would have known where to say I was."

Two days later, Mary Meza had been attacked. He was sorry about that, but he couldn't be the man who had been responsible for the crime. The man who had assaulted her was, in her own words, "just a little bit taller than I am" and she was "5 foot 4 or 5." In fact, when he had questioned her during the trial, he had asked her, "Could the bandit possibly have been six feet tall?" and she had answered, "No." She had told the police that her assailant had a scar over his right eyebrow, a narrow nose with a hump, and a slight accent which might have been Italian. Like Mrs. Johnson, the girl testified that the man had told her that he was unfamiliar with Los Angeles because he came from New York.

This brings us to the robbery of the night of January 23 at Redondo Beach. "I admit, ladies and gentlemen," he said, "I have no alibi for this robbery as far as anyone to substantiate where I was or what I was doing." But you saw

Knowles try on that coat that was found in the Ford. It was much too large for him. And what kind of a gun was I supposed to have been using that night? A toy cap pistol. "Here is a vicious bandit portrayed to you by the prosecution, using a cap pistol." Yet on nickel and dime robberies, I show up with a .45 automatic in my hand. It just doesn't make sense.

As far as the car was concerned, would he have been so stupid as to have kept it after all the crimes he was supposed to have committed with it? The police swear that he said it was a lemon but "if I had stolen this car it is logical to assume I would have determined its potentialities with respect to speed." Finally, there wasn't a single witness to connect him with this Ford until he took it into Callahans' to have its front spring repaired. Forbes and Goosen didn't even bother to check if it had been parked near his house, as they testified he had told them.

Then there's the matter of the red cellophane and the little nut. If he was the spotlight bandit, where did he get rid of the cellophane? "It would have been the most important, most incriminating thing that could have been shown against me," he argued, "and yet the police were not even interested in knowing where I was supposed to have thrown it." As for the nut, Officer Cremins said it was still on the spotlight when he first inspected the car. Suddenly it shows up in my pocket. He pounded his fist on the counsel table. "Ladies and gentlemen, that little nut was not in my pocket! It originated from some other source in the first place." The police report says: "Found in defendant's right front trouser pocket: One nut with twisted wire." Yet every cop who was in the Hollywood station that night saw the nut all by itself. Where did the wire come from?

Forbes picked up a couple of hairs six days after the Ford coupé is impounded. Then Jones finds that they are "similar" to Mary Alice's. Isn't it remarkable that they never checked my hair—or Mrs. Johnson's? But even Mr. Jones

admits that "you cannot by just looking at a hair and comparing it, you cannot tell if it belongs to some person."
Furthermore, no pubic hairs were found in that car. "Was
it reasonable," he wondered, "that there would or would
not be pubic hairs in that car?"

While we're on the subject of Lieutenant Jones, the
chemist testified that the adhering debris on the little nut
resembled shavings found on a pair of pliers in the Ford's
glove compartment. "But at least, remember this," he
warned, "he did not make any actual scientific test to
determine if it was metallic substance, or merely the resemblance." This is just another example of the web of cir-
cumstance that Mr. Leavy was trying to weave around him.
"I do not think this should put a man in the gas chamber,"
he argued hopefully.

Nurse Thornton swore that he saw no marks, scars or
bruises on me when I was taken to the prison hospital. Yet
Dr. De River, who examined me two days earlier, said he
saw lacerations on my knees, a scab on my head and wounds
in my legs and gluteal region. But Mr. Thornton didn't see
anything. "All of a sudden when he found, when the district
attorney's office phoned, he had to take the stand, he called
me up about two hours before I was to come to court that
day and made another examination." The only thing he can
remember, after examining hundreds of men since he last
saw me is "the fact that I was bragging."

When his father had come to see him in jail, the defendant had told him that Officer Begay was present when Grant
was working him over. Yet, despite the fact that Mr. Leavy
had brought half the Los Angeles police force into the courtroom, "Officer Begay somehow didn't appear." As for those
bruises on his face that nobody saw, he had always claimed
that he was beaten from the neck down. Detective Grant
was much too smart to advertise his devotion to the third
degree. Of course, no one else had seen the incident. It had

all happened during that half-hour before Forbes, Hubka and the reporters had arrived at the station house.

Mr. Leavy had gone into ecstasies when he described the scientific efficiency of the Los Angeles police. Yet they had never shown his clothing to the victims or tested it for hairs or semen. They didn't even attempt to check the pistol. "A man gets hit on the head and he requires stitches. Surely there is going to be some signs left that a forensic chemist could determine." They didn't do any of these things because they didn't want to uncover any evidence that might have cleared him.

After lunch, he disposed of the question of his courage. If it was true that the automatic was in his hand when he left the car at Shatto Place, it wasn't any lack of guts that would have kept him from squeezing the trigger. He had been in gun fights before and he didn't lose his guts then. He had simply tried to get away, not because he was guilty of any crimes, but solely because he had violated his parole. If he was as depraved as Mr. Leavy said he was, he would have tried to kill anyone in his way.

He finished where he had started, with the story about his friend's Model T Ford. "The only way that I was able to establish my innocence and convince this officer that I was not guilty, they were able to lift the hood and look in the car. Fortunately, there they could do that. I wish there were some way, figuratively speaking, to lift up the hood of my mind and heart, look under there to see if I was capable . . . of doing these crimes, going 80 miles an hour in this respect, I mean." He was sure that once the jury had analyzed the evidence, it would find that "I am not the person who is guilty of these crimes, and most particularly, I am not the red spotlight bandit."

Leavy sprang up with the outraged air of a father who has just learned of his favorite daughter's seduction. He hadn't intended to say anything more, he assured the jurors, but the defendant had made so many misstatements that he felt it was his duty to clear some of them up. Of course, some of the witnesses were wrong by a few pounds or a couple of inches. But even the professional weight guessers at carnivals sometimes made mistakes. And isn't it natural to expect that a six-footer like Chessman, who might be afraid that he would be recognized some day, would deliberately slouch so that his victims would be confused as to just how tall he was?

All right, McCullough said that Chessman had a mustache. In the picture with Mr. Phillips took of the two suspects on January 24, it was clear that Knowles had a mustache then. "Just because McCullough sees two men in there he will be more apt to put a mustache in the crime report. Or maybe the officer put the mustache on the wrong man in the crime report. I don't know. Just that those things happen." But remember that the shoe clerk stood up in this courtroom, took a long look at this fellow, and swore, "I know it is you!"

Leavy picked up some photographs of the Howell car. He knew that some of the witnesses had called it a sedan while others had thought it was a coupé. But these weren't people leisurely studying cars in a dealer's window. They were terrified human beings who didn't know whether they would live to see another day. "I do not think these witnesses should be too severely criticized because they did not tab the automobile with particularity," he urged. "We do not charge this automobile committed these crimes, or that dashboard committed these crimes. Chessman was identified." But, personally, he was "satisfied that it was the same car."

We didn't give Lieutenant Jones any of Mrs. Johnson's hair because she had never been in the back seat of the car like Mary Meza. And Chessman is quite right when he says that we didn't test any of his hair. But he could have had it tested if he wanted to. Just the way he didn't call Officer Begay who he says was in the room when Grant was supposed to be beating him, he didn't offer any of his hair. Maybe he was afraid of the results.

You've heard him talk a great deal about his mother here. He couldn't be guilty of all these crimes, he told you, because a fellow with a sick mother just doesn't go in for that sort of thing. Well, his mother's welfare never stopped him before. It didn't prevent him from pulling jobs in 1941 and 1943. "If he was a real man, he would not even mention his mother in this trial. He is just attempting to do it in his soft-spoken way to have something more to hide behind and gamble with." As for Mrs. Chessman's testimony that Caryl was home when Mary Meza was raped, "I don't think this boy's mother knew what he was up to." And that goes for his father, Winona Phillips and the Greenes as well.

Leavy's voice had worn thin. Fricke signaled him to stop and adjourned until ten the next day.

There was an air of finality about Thursday morning. The reporters, who had been ignoring the trial for more than a week, were back in force as Leavy continued his harangue. His opening topic was the scar that Miss Meza said she had noticed over Chessman's right eyebrow. He offered several theories for the girl's seeing something that clearly did not exist. The most intriguing of these was the possibility that "the defendant used studio make-up to put a scar on him." But, in the main, he hammered at the idea that a frightened seventeen-year-old might have been confused by the reflections from the car's dashboard.

The prosecutor disposed of Terranova by stating flatly that he had never existed except in Chessman's imagination. As for the absence of tests for semen, he assured his listeners that "there is no expert, no one who could testify that particular semen is from a particular person." The best we could have shown you is that it is animal or human semen. Matthews interrupted to indicate that "semen is classified, Your Honor, it is just as with hair. It is like telling the twelve jurors classifications of semen are used as negative evidence." The judge was "willing to have the jury keep that in mind."

The missing piece of red cellophane was next. Mr. Chessman claims that the whole case against him is the result of a mammoth frame-up. If Forbes and Hubka were out to frame him, wouldn't it have been just as easy for them to pick up a piece of cellophane and claim that they found it with the little nut in his pocket when they searched him at the Hollywood police station? The simple fact of the matter is that "Chessman was not working a spotlight job that night." And if Cremins said that he saw the nut on the lens rim when he impounded the car, he had gotten "a wrong impression."

The district attorney had almost finished. He hoped that the jurors would not shy away from the death penalty if they honestly thought it was deserved. Sending the defendant back to prison would be worse than nothing; he would only be out again and they would have themselves to blame for the tragedy of another Mary Meza or Regina Johnson. "I hope when you come down here you can look me square in the eye and tell the defendant and tell me by your verdict that you have done your duty; and tell Chessman by this verdict that it is his last chance." This is what they would do in the cow counties; Los Angeles juries should do no differently. He thanked them for their attention and sat down.

It was time for Fricke's charge. Turning his chair so that he was facing the jury box, he began reading in his booming voice from a neat pile of typewritten papers on the bench in front of him. "It becomes my duty, as judge," he told his attentive listeners, "to instruct you concerning the law applicable to this case, and it is your duty to follow the law as I shall state it to you." After warning the panel against being influenced by "mere sentiment, conjecture, sympathy, passion, prejudice, public opinion, or public feeling," he proceeded to define each crime of which the defendant was

accused. As he neared the end of his fifty-one-page mono-
logue, he came to the subject of the four kidnapping counts.
"It will be your duty," he charged, "to determine whether
the person or persons subjected to such kidnapping suffered
bodily harm. The law provides that in such a case the defendant shall suffer death or shall be imprisoned for life,
without possibility of parole, at the discretion of the jury."
He paused for a moment before resuming. "But if such person or persons suffered no such harm, you will say nothing
about the matter of punishment in your verdict."

The jury retired at 11:55 A.M. At 10:55 the next morning,
it returned to the courtroom to ask whether "a person committed to prison for life without possibility of parole could
by any possibility be released from prison before he had
served his full life term." The judge stated that "there could
be no positive assurance that that person would not be free
again." Foreman Harte also wanted to know if the jury
could impose the death penalty if it found that the kidnappings were "without bodily injury." Fricke was just as suc-
cinct. "There being no bodily harm," he answered, "the
penalty could be a life sentence only."

The long Friday dragged on. At 12:30, the bailiff escorted the eleven women and their male foreman to lunch,
but the reporters who searched their faces could see no indication of an early verdict. Three times during the afternoon,
rumors swept the courtroom that a decision had been
reached but they proved to be false alarms. At six o'clock,
the jurors were taken across the street for supper but the
expressions on their faces were as unrevealing as ever.

Finally, at 7:30, word was sent to Fricke that a unanimous
decision had been reached. At 7:55, the jurors filed back into
Department 43. Their faces were grave. "Have you agreed
upon a verdict, Mr. Foreman?" the judge asked. "We have,"
replied Mr. Harte. He handed a sheaf of paper slips to the
bailiff who brought them to the bench. Fricke scanned them

quickly. "I find here, Mr. Foreman," he said, "with reference to Count X there are two signed verdicts. I will ask you to take another look at them and see which is the verdict of the jury." Harte looked at the two top slips. "The second one, Your Honor," he answered. The bailiff returned them to Fricke, who handed them to the clerk. The judge leaned back in his chair. "The clerk may read the verdicts as returned by the jury," he said.

Chessman's face was expressionless as Luskin began reading. "We, the jury . . . find the defendant guilty of robbery, a felony, as charged in Count 1 of the amended Information, and find it to be Robbery of the 1st degree." The verdict was the same for all the remaining seventeen counts except the attempted burglary of Mrs. Tarro's house. For the kidnappings of Mary Meza and Regina Johnson, "We . . . find that the person named suffered bodily harm and fix the punishment at death." It imposed "life imprisonment without possibility of parole," for the assault on Melvin Waisler.

After the verdicts were recorded, the court thanked the jurors and set June 11 for judgment and sentence. As the talesmen hurried out of the courtroom, the defendant stared into each one's face. Only Mrs. Vamos and Mrs. King returned his look. "All right, Chess, let's go," said one of the two deputies assigned to return him upstairs to the county jail. He arose woodenly and, without a word, walked slowly past the jury box and out of the rear of the courtroom. As an attendant began switching off the lights, Matthews was angrily sweeping papers into his briefcase.

17

THE LONG YEARS

(JUNE 25, 1948—MAY 2, 1960)

It was not until Friday, June 25, that Fricke got around to imposing sentence. At 9:45 that morning, Chessman was brought down to Department 43, where he met Al Matthews. The two men sat in the almost empty courtroom, chatting and smoking cigarettes, until the judge put in his appearance precisely at ten o'clock. It was a warm langorous summer day and through the west window one could see fleecy clouds floating in a blue early-summer sky.

When Fricke asked, in his basso profundo, whether there was any legal reason why judgment should not be pronounced, Chessman proffered one. "The defendant is absolutely innocent of these charges," he proclaimed. "That," replied the court, "is not a legal cause." He paused a moment to pick up a sheet of paper. "There being no legal cause," he read ponderously, "it is the judgment and sentence of this Court that you, the said Caryl Chessman, be delivered by the Sheriff of the County of Los Angeles, to the Warden of the State Prison of the State of California, at San Quentin, to be by him executed and put to death by administration of lethal gas in the manner provided by the laws of the State of California, the time and date hereafter to be fixed by order of this court within said State Prison."

For good measure, Fricke imposed fifteen sentences for the other convictions, ranging from five years to life imprisonment without possibility of parole.

With these formal details out of the way, the defendant asked for permission to say a few words. It was granted. He wanted to point out to His Honor that Ernest R. Perry, the official court reporter, had died of acute coronary thrombosis two days earlier, before he had transcribed more than a third of the trial testimony. Fricke took "judicial notice" that the elderly stenographer was indeed dead, but he didn't think that this "unfortunate occurrence" necessitated a new trial. When Leavy assured him that the district attorney's office would do everything in its power to help with the preparation of the transcript, Fricke ordered that "to the limit of human beings in their use of ingenuity, the entire record of this trial be prepared in as complete a manner as possible."

On July 2, Knowles and Chessman were handcuffed together and taken by car to the Glendale station where, with eight other convicts, they boarded a northbound prison train. Twelve hours later, when they reached Richmond, the prisoners were driven to the boat slip and ferried the three miles across San Pablo Bay to the creaky dock under the yellow turreted walls of San Quentin. After being checked in, the new inmates were separated and Chessman, now known officially as Convict No. 66565-A, was taken to the Distribution Department where he was issued blue jeans, a denim work shirt, a light jacket and soft slippers, the traditional garb of the condemned man. Then two guards escorted him across the yard to the North Block rotunda where he was whisked by elevator up five flights to Condemned Row. There he was placed in Cell 2455, a concrete and steel cubicle, $4\frac{1}{2}$ feet wide, $10\frac{1}{2}$ feet long and $7\frac{1}{2}$ feet high. The paunchy row officer who locked the door behind him offered a word of advice. "If you cooperate," he

said, "you will make it easy on yourself. Try to get along."
His prisoner nodded curtly.

In the middle of July, at Leavy's suggestion, Perry's shorthand notebooks were turned over to Stanley Fraser, a stenographer who had once shared an apartment with the dead
man in Seattle where they both had been employed as court
reporters. Fraser, who used the Graham Pitman system of
shorthand, which he claimed was "very close" to Perry's
Success method, studied his old roommate's notes for "two
weeks, maybe ten days." He then informed the County
Board of Supervisors that he thought he could make "an
accurate transcription" of the record. In the middle of September, despite the fact that the Los Angeles Superior Court
Reporters' Association had called Perry's notes "completely
undecipherable," Fraser was hired to translate them.

In February of 1949, the reporter sent a rough draft of
his transcription to Judge Fricke. On April 11, the completed record was filed with the judge and a copy sent
to the defendant at San Quentin. After perusing the transcript, Chessman indignantly wrote to Fricke and pointed out
what he claimed were more than two hundred mistakes.
After a three-day hearing in early June, at which Fraser was
the only witness, Fricke made some eighty corrections in
the latter's draft. On August 18, the judge conducted another hearing, at the conclusion of which he stated that he
was completely satisfied with Fraser's work. The defendant
was not present at either hearing although he had begged
Fricke to let him sit in.

On December 2, 1949, the Protestant chaplain at San
Quentin delivered a telegram to Cell 2455. Hallie Chessman had died of cancer during the night.

The following spring, Chessman asked the California Supreme Court to order Fricke to hold another hearing in connection with Fraser's transcript. On May 19, 1950, it denied
his motion. According to Associate Justice B. Rey Schauer,

"We have concluded that the transcript before us, with certain augmentations hereinafter described, will permit a just and fair disposition of the appeal on its merits." The "augmentations" he had in mind were the inclusion of Leavy's opening statement and the examination of the prospective jurors, both of which Fraser had omitted. Two of the seven justices, Jesse W. Carter and Douglas L. Edmonds, thought that the defendant should have a new trial because of Perry's death.

Three weeks later, the same court rejected a petition for a writ of habeas corpus which Chessman based on what he termed "a spurious, prejudicially incomplete and inaccurate transcript." The majority indicated that it was not impressed by the defendant's contention that he had been deprived of "federal Constitutional due process and the equal protection of the laws." On October 9, 1950, the United States Supreme Court refused to review the state court's decision.

It was not until the end of 1951 that the California Supreme Court decided Chessman's appeal on the merits. However, while that decision was pending, he went into the federal courts and asked unsuccessfully for a writ of habeas corpus. On December 18, 1951, Judge Schauer, writing for four other members of the state's highest court, found no merit in the defendant's thirty-five objections, and affirmed the convictions. "A reexamination of these arguments and the transcript," wrote Schauer, "leaves us convinced that the transcript permits a fair consideration and disposition of the appeal."

Judge Carter dissented violently. "A reading of the majority opinion," he said, "convinces me that many flagrant errors were committed during the trial which would ordinarily be held to be prejudicial and require the reversal of a judgment of conviction.* In fact, the only way I can ra-

* Although Mrs. Nana L. Bull and Mrs. Mary E. Graves, two of the Chessman jurors, said in 1958 that Fricke had exhibited no bias towards the de-

tionalize the majority opinion is that those concurring therein feel that a person charged with seventeen felonies of the character of those charged against the defendant and who represents himself, is not entitled to a trial in accordance with the rules applicable to the ordinary criminal case. I cannot subscribe to this doctrine."

Two months before Schauer's decision, Chessman had applied to Fricke for permission to open what would be tantamount to a full-scale law office in a neighboring Death Row cell. Specifically, he wanted to be able to correspond with all state and federal courts, to conduct "reasonably necessary legal research," to build up a law library, and to consult with "attorneys of his own choosing and with other responsible persons." Hearings on this motion did not begin until October 26 because, as a result of various infractions of prison rules ranging from helping another inmate prepare legal papers to disorderly conduct, the defendant was confined to the "quiet cell" at San Quentin. When the sessions concluded on March 7, 1952, Chessman was given everything he had asked for.

The defendant's execution, which had, after the affirmance of his conviction by the California Supreme Court, been scheduled for March 28, 1952, was stayed by Judge Carter on February 29 when the prisoner asked the United States Supreme Court to review Schauer's decision. In his brief, Chessman pointed out that the transcript was defective, that he had not been given sufficient time in which to prepare for trial, that his confession had been coerced, and that Leavy had been unfair in his presentation of the case against him. On March 31, the high court refused to inter-

---

fendant, a Los Angeles lawyer, whose name was withheld at his own request, later submitted an affidavit to Governor Edmund G. Brown in which he swore that, during the trial, he had heard the judge declare "that Chessman had an I.Q. of approximately 140, that he was a smart aleck who was too smart for his own good, that he had just made the mistake of dismissing his own attorney, and that he would see to it that Chessman would rue the day that he chose to defend himself."

fere and, after it announced on May 3, that it would not grant the defendant a rehearing, Fricke informed Warden Harley O. Teets that he had set June 27 as the day on which the "administration of lethal gas" would take place.

On June 9, the federal district court in San Francisco denied another habeas corpus petition. Chessman then appealed to the United States Court of Appeals for the Ninth Circuit. Because of the pendency of this appeal, a stay of his execution was granted by District Judge Albert Lee Stephens four days before it was scheduled to occur. When the Court of Appeals affirmed the lower tribunal's ruling on May 28, 1953, Chessman applied once more to Washington. In December, the Supreme Court found no reason to change its earlier decision and, on February 1, 1954, denied a petition for a rehearing. Fricke promptly rescheduled the execution for May 14. The same guard who informed the waiting man in Cell 2455 of the judge's action also told him that Serl Chessman had just died in Glendale.

On May 13, just sixteen hours before the effective date of the Death Warrant, a third stay was ordered by Judge Thomas F. Keating of the Marin County Superior Court, this time to give Chessman an opportunity to apply to the California Supreme Court for another writ of habeas corpus. When this move came a cropper, July 30 was set as D-Day. Fourteen days earlier, the defendant filed another petition with the court, claiming that he was illegally detained because of the "fraudulent conduct of the deputy district attorney of Los Angeles County." The seven justices declined to change their minds and, on July 21, 1954, turned down Chessman's plea. A week later, Judge Carter signed a stay of execution to permit him to try Washington once more.

On August 14, the defendant's petition was filed with the Clerk of the United States Supreme Court. Five days later, Attorney-General Edmund G. Brown asked the California court to vacate the stay on the ground that Carter didn't have the power to grant it. On October 7, Carter's stay was

upheld by his colleagues, although several of them made it clear that they hardly approved of it. At the end of the month, the Supreme Court sent the matter back to California, "without prejudice to an application for a writ of habeas corpus in an appropriate United States District Court."

Chessman wasted no time in taking advantage of this open invitation. On December 30, he was back in the San Francisco federal court with another petition. When it was denied by Judge Louis E. Goodman on January 4, 1955, a fifth execution date was set for January 14. However, seventy-two hours before doomsday, Chief Judge William Denman of the Ninth Circuit's Court of Appeals granted a certificate of probable cause of appeal and scheduled the matter for the consideration of his full bench. On the same day, he postponed the execution indefinitely.

On February 1, 1955, the Supreme Court of California decided to close Chessman's prison law office. It cancelled Fricke's 1951 order which had given him mail, library and consultation privileges. Judge Carter was appalled by his associates' action. "The rights sought by petitioner and granted by the trial court," he wrote, "are the rights which must be accorded to all prisoners if the concept of 'equal justice under law' is to have any significance whatever."

Two months later, the Court of Appeals, sitting *en banc*, affirmed Goodman's denial of the writ. Another death warrant—the sixth—dated July 15, was sent to San Quentin. But it was to have no better fate than its predecessors because the filing with the Supreme Court of the defendant's appeal from the Ninth Circuit's ruling resulted in a further stay, this time by Associate Justice Tom Clark, on July 5. In October, five of the nine justices in Washington decided that Chessman's petition should not have been dismissed by the San Francisco court without a hearing on his charges that the transcript had been fraudulently prepared. The case was remanded for "proceedings not inconsistent with this opinion."

After seven days of hearings in January of 1956, Goodman concluded that there had been no fraud and adhered to his original denial of the writ of habeas corpus. The Ninth Circuit again affirmed and Chessman filed his seventh petition with the Supreme Court. On June 10, 1957, Mr. Justice Harlan, with the caustic observation that "this case presents a sorry chapter in the annals of delays in the administration of criminal justice," ordered California to either conduct a full-scale investigation of Chessman's charges that the transcript had been fraudulently prepared or release him. "Judge Goodman," he said, "considered that our order of October 17, 1955, restricted the inquiry before him to the issue of whether the settlement of the state court record had been tainted by fraud, and that the accuracy of the record as such was not an issue in this proceeding. The petitioner has never had his day in court upon the controversial issues of law and fact involved in the settlement of the record upon which his conviction was affirmed."

On August 14, Chessman appeared in Judge Goodman's court. Acting under the Supreme Court's mandate, Goodman gave California until December 1, 1957, to settle the final transcript of the record. The defendant, whose books and typewriter had been commandeered by Teet's successor, Warden Fred R. Dickson, then asked the California Supreme Court to give him an assist in his preparation for the hearing. It immediately vacated all its previous judgments and sent the case back to Department 43 "for further proceedings not inconsistent with the opinion of the United States Supreme Court." The speed of its action so impressed Dickson that he promptly returned Chessman's portable and some of his papers.

On September 17, by order of Superior Court Judge Louis H. Burke, the defendant was returned to the High Power Tank in the Los Angeles County Jail where he was "to be allowed to confer freely and privately with his counsel, witnesses, investigators and other responsible persons connected with the preparation of this matter on any day between . . . 9:00 A.M. and 3:00 P.M., . . . 3:30 P.M. and 5:00 P.M. and . . . 6:00 P.M. and 9:00 P.M." Because Judge Fricke was undergoing surgery for cancer of the throat, the hearing on Fraser's transcript was adjourned to November 25. When Fricke returned from the hospital, he wrote a letter insisting that another judge be assigned to the case. On November 13, Judge Walter R. Evans, a Mono County import who was then sitting in Department 67, was named as a substitute. No sooner had Judge Evans been assigned than he was asked to order Dickson to release an unpublished novel entitled *The Kid Was a Killer,* a fictional sequel to Chessman's 1954 best seller, *Cell 2455, Death Row.* Evans ordered the book released and it was finally turned over to the defendant in court on December third.

The transcript hearing opened on November 25. A slightly grayer and newly bespectacled Leavy, assisted by Clifford Crail, another deputy district attorney, who was later to prosecute Dr. R. Bernard Finch and Carole Tregoff for the murder of the physician's wife, produced twelve witnesses to support the People's contention that Fraser had accurately transcribed Perry's notes. Chessman countered with forty-three people in his attempt to prove that the stenographer had worked hand and glove with the prosecutor to produce a fraudulent and prejudicial record. In the main, he contended that Fraser, who, it appeared, was Leavy's uncle-in-law, was a habitual drunkard with a long police record who had made wholesale alterations in Mr. Perry's notes.

Fraser was Leavy's first—and most important—witness. After swearing that the disputed transcript was "a true and accurate transcription of the original notes," the reporter admitted that there were literally hundreds of symbols which he hadn't translated "because I couldn't read them at the time." When Chessman asked him to state how many words there were in one untranscribed section, he said that "I don't know how many words are in there because I couldn't read it with sufficient accuracy to make it significant enough to me to put into the record."

Q. So that you felt that the wisest course under those circumstances was to omit it completely, is that correct?

A. Yes.

He had made "no assumption" as to the relative importance of the omitted material.

Upon occasion, he had added words where sentences were incomplete in Mr. Perry's notes. When a literal reading of the dead man's shorthand didn't "make sense," he had taken the liberty of changing the context. Perry, he said, had been such a "poor penman," that the witness was frequently forced to confer with Mr. Leavy as well as with some prosecution witnesses in order to decipher certain testimony. Over the years, he had received "approximately $10,000" from the Board of Supervisors for his work. No, he had "never made a close study; only a casual examination of his [Perry's] notes." In the thirties, he remembered, he had looked over the dead man's shoulder "while he was dictating in the dictaphone, on a number of occasions."

The People buttressed Fraser's testimony with that of Bessie Lill, a court reporter since 1929. Early in September, she had compared a carbon copy of the Fraser transcript with photostats of Perry's notes. She was convinced that Fraser had constructed a "fair rendition" of the Perry notes. But, on cross-examination, she told Chessman that she had found almost two thousand of what she called "emendations" in Fraser's work. According to Mrs. Lill, a reporter had the right to "clarify the meaning" in order to make the transcript read more "intelligibly."

On September 16, 1948, Harry R. Person, Chairman of the Executive Committee of the Los Angeles Superior Court

Reporter's Association, had written to the Board of Supervisors. In his letter, he had stated that his organization had "serious doubts that any reporter will be able to furnish a usable transcript" of Mr. Perry's notes. Association members who had "examined and studied Mr. Perry's notes . . . have reached the conclusion that many portions of the same will be found completely undecipherable because, toward the latter part of each court session, Mr. Perry's notes show his illness." When Crail asked Person whether he agreed with his September 16 letter, he stated that he did not. He had signed it only because he had been outvoted by the other two members of the Executive Committee. However, when Chessman asked him to read a photostatic copy of a page of the Perry notes, he was unable to do so.

After Leavy and Fricke had testified in support of the Fraser transcript, Chessman called Frank Hanna, the former head of New York's Success Shorthand School, who had sixty-five years of stenographic experience behind him. According to Mr. Hanna, Perry had used "basically a Ben Pitman system, using a few Graham expedients and also some outlines from the so-called Success shorthand system." His study of the dead reporter's notes had convinced him that his "style of writing, aggravated by his evident disability and reporting idiosyncracies, is such that the task of another reporter attempting to decipher his notes is rendered difficult in some places and impossible in others, if the goal is an accurate transcription and if guesswork is not liberally employed and if license to edit freely is not permitted." Fraser's transcription had been "freely edited" and contained "hundreds of places where . . . the meaning placed upon particular outlines is not justified." It was his "firm conviction that these notes are not decipherable with accuracy or certainty, and in many instances that they are not decipherable at all, as evidenced by the fact that many hundreds of outlines have been left untranscribed." Mrs. Molly Kalin, a stenographer since 1938, shared Hanna's opinion.

The defendant took the stand and pointed out the errors which he claimed permeated Fraser's work. He was followed by Dr. James H. Cryst, who had been the stenographer's physician from 1947 to 1953. According to Cryst, his patient "had frequent alcoholic drinking bouts during many of which he would call me up and talk to me in an alcoholic state." Dr. Louis F. X. Wilhelm, a dermatologist who had also treated the reporter, testified that "he was a great partaker of wine." So much so that he suffered from a "toxic dermatitis . . . caused by the use of this wine." Mrs. Eva Hoffman, who owned a liquor store next door to Fraser's apartment house, claimed that she had often seen him hopelessly inebriated. In fact, he had been arrested twelve times since 1940 for varying degrees of drunkenness.

After forty-two days and some five thousand pages of testimony, the hearings adjourned on February 14, 1958, two weeks after Fricke's sudden death in St. Vincent's Hospital. At month's end, Judge Evans had made up his mind. "This Court is of the opinion," he wrote, "that the shorthand notes of Mr. Perry were decipherable and that Mr. Fraser was competent and qualified to transcribe those notes fairly and in a substantially accurate manner." He attached some eighty-nine pages of corrections as an exhibit to his opinion, and indicated that "when the transcript corrections have been made, the Court will certify the transcript." He was quick to point out that the corrections he had made "individually or collectively in no way change the substance and nature of either the People's case or the defendant's defense."

Complications developed immediately. The typists who had been employed by the Court to make the necessary changes reported back to Evans that some ninety of his suggested alterations would produce "unintelligibility or manifest incorrections." The judge told them that some of his corrections could be ignored, while others could be modified so that they would make sense. While the record was being prepared, Chessman was returned to his cell at San Quentin.

On May 1, Evans certified the completed reporter's transcript and a copy was sent to the defendant. Two months later, the Supreme Court received an impassioned plea from Cell 2455, asking it to order the lower court "to explicitly grant petitioner an opportunity to be heard in person or by counsel in opposition to its action with respect to its ninety changes." On October 2, Evans was directed to schedule a hearing and, eight days later, Chessman was returned to the Los Angeles County Jail to await the court's pleasure.

The hearing began on November 24 and lasted for two days. The defendant called Evans as a witness and questioned him about the ninety changes. The judge testified that "I did my best to go over them and determine whether they were typographical in my opinion, or what they were, and ordered their insertion at the place that I deemed proper under the situation. We attempted first to check the transcript to see if we could determine that there had been a typographical error and have the correction made as it should have been made. Where we couldn't determine that, of course, there was nothing else we could do than just order the change deleted."

When Chessman insisted on asking specific questions, Evans refused to answer them. His stand precipitated an immediate defense motion for either "the assignment of another judge" or permission for the defendant to apply to the California Supreme Court for a ruling as to whether Evans could decline to testify and still preside at the hearing. The judge-witness promptly denied the request and Chessman refused to proceed any further. Evans then ordered him to take the stand himself and indicate for the record what questions he had in mind. "It is my position," Chessman retorted, "that the Court is without jurisdiction. I do not choose to answer." That was enough for His Honor who promptly disallowed all objections to the ninety corrections.

On December 12, the day that the certified record was filed with the Supreme Court in San Francisco, the defendant was returned to Death Row.

The State's highest court announced its decision on July 7, 1959. In its opinion, it concluded "that the corrected reporter's transcript is substantially accurate and sufficiently complete in every respect to permit a fair review of the appeal from the judgments of conviction and we reject defendant's arguments that our acceptance of such transcript denies him constitutional rights." It also found no merit in Chessman's claim that, on some twenty-odd substantive grounds, he was entitled to a new trial, and affirmed "the judgments and order appealed from." Four weeks later, it turned down his request for a rehearing.

A week after Evans had refused to disturb the disputed ninety changes in the corrected transcript, the Marin County grand jury indicted Prentice-Hall, Inc., the defendant's publisher, Joseph Longstreth, his literary agent, and George T. Davis, one of his attorneys, for conspiring to smuggle the manuscript of *The Face of Justice,* another Chessman book, out of San Quentin. On October 31, 1959, the District Court of Appeals decided that the evidence against the three defendants was, in the main, hearsay and did not support the charges. In dismissing the indictments, Justice Matthew O. Tobriner sharply criticized the prosecution. "An odor of totalitarianism infects the concept that any product of the prisoner's mind automatically becomes the property of the state," he said. Two months later, the California Supreme Court agreed with him.

In early September, 1959, a row guard handed a curt note to the man in Cell 2455. "Dear Sir," it read, "On this date I received Death Warrant in your case issued August 10, 1959, by the Honorable Herbert V. Walker, Judge of the Superior Court of the State of California, in and for the County of

THE LONG YEARS / 283

Los Angeles, fixing date for Friday, October 23, 1959. Fred R. Dickson, Warden." But on October 21, in Washington, Associate Justice William O. Douglas granted a stay of execution "pending the timely filing and consideration of a petition for certiorari." Within two weeks, a 224-page brief was on its way eastward. When the Supreme Court announced on December 14 that it would not disturb the convictions, Chessman immediately asked for a rehearing. This was denied on January 11, 1960, and a new execution date of February 19 was set.

Two weeks later, after an all-day session, Judge Goodman refused to reconsider the accuracy of Fraser's transcript, but suggested that several of Chessman's contentions, particularly his claim that his eleven and one half years on death row constituted cruel and unusual punishment, "may well be asserted to the Governor and the Supreme Court under their clemency powers." On February 8, 1960, Chief Judge Richard H. Chambers of the United States Court of Appeals, after reprimanding Goodman for attempting to throw the condemned man "a life line," upheld his decision. On the fifteenth, the Court of Appeals denied Chessman's application for a stay of execution and, two days later, the Supreme Court of California, by a 4 to 3 vote, refused to recommend executive clemency. Since the state constitution provided that no commutation of a second felony offender's sentence was possible without the "written recommendation of a majority of the judges of the Supreme Court," Governor Brown announced that "I have no power to grant clemency . . . and the question is closed."

But, on February 18, barely ten hours before the defendant was scheduled to die, the Governor received a telegram from the State Department, informing him that the Uruguayan Government was very much concerned that Chessman's execution might set off riots in that country when President Eisenhower visited it in March. The former Attorney General promptly granted a sixty-day reprieve and called a special session of the California legislature to consider the abolition of capital punishment. On March 10, after a sixteen-hour marathon hearing, the Senate Judiciary Committee voted 8 to 7 to kill the proposal which had, by then, been watered down to a three-and-a-half year moratorium rather than an outright abolition. Eight days earlier, Superior Judge Clement D. Nye had signed Death Warrant No. 9.

On April 25, a strange press conference took place in George T. Davis' San Francisco office. Two writers, Milton Machlin and William R. Woodfield, Jr., revealed that they had informed Cecil Poole, the Governor's clemency secretary, that Chessman's 1948 claim that a "Joe Terranova" was the real red light bandit merited further consideration. At the time of the defendant's trial, they asserted, a man named Charles Saverine Terranova was in the Los Angeles County Jail under a twenty-two-count indictment for kidnapping, burglary, possession of a sub-machine gun and other assorted felonies.

According to Machlin and Woodfield, Terranova, who was twenty-eight in 1948, sported the same kind of a scar above his right eyebrow that Mary Alice Meza had included in her description of the man who had assaulted her, and was much closer to the "about five feet four or five" height she had attributed to him. Furthermore, Terranova, who was a swarthy man of Italian descent, possessed the type of protruding teeth that had attracted the attention of Dr. Bartle and several other witnesses. Chessman, the writers pointed out, wore dentures as a result of a reformatory fist fight and his teeth were even and straight.

But Mr. Poole, Machlin said, had given him short shrift. "I don't think much of your stuff," the clemency secretary had told him. When reporters questioned Leavy about the possibility that Terranova, who was then a fugitive from several forgery and bad check charges, might have committed the crimes of which Chessman had been convicted, the deputy district attorney said that "I think this is an attempt to make somebody buy a fish story." He reiterated the position he had taken in his summation to the jury that "Joe Terranova is a fiction."

He pointed out that Terranova had been in the County Jail with Chessman all during the trial. "Do you think that if Charles Terranova was 'Joe Terranova,'" he asked, "he would not have been produced in court?" In addition, since both men had been confined in San Quentin from 1948 to 1955, "Chessman must have known that, if Charles was 'Joe,'" he stated. "Obviously, he didn't know it because there was no Joe." The Governor apparently shared the prosecutor's low opinion of the Machlin-Woodfield hypothesis.

Four days later, Attorney-General Stanley Mosk revealed that a twenty-nine-year-old ex-convict with an uneasy conscience had confessed to him that he and eight associates had committed "red light" robberies in many of the areas in which Chessman's crimes took place. "But," said Mosk, "every one of the group has denied they were armed, that they ever committed forcible rape, or that they ever used a red light in the course of their operations." A week of intensive investigation had convinced him that "there is nothing that justifies the delay of Chessman's execution on Monday. I cannot in good faith recommend a reprieve at this time."

In San Quentin, Warden Dickson made a notation on his desk calendar: "Chessman execution—Monday, May 2, 10 A.M." Time, it seemed, had finally run out.

18

THE POSTLUDE

(MONDAY, MAY 2, 1960)

On Sunday afternoon, the dark-haired prisoner in Cell 2455 was taken to the sergeant's office at the east end of Death Row. There he changed into a new pair of blue jeans, a clean denim work shirt and fresh socks. Then he was taken by elevator to the ground floor where he was placed in the first of two brightly lit, green-carpeted holding cells. In the tiny cubicle, there were only an unlidded toilet, a shelf and a mattress.

When the sun rose on Monday morning, the sleepless man had just finished the last of the seven letters he had written through the long spring night. Shortly before eight o'clock, he handed the envelopes to the turnkey who brought him his breakfast tray and asked him to give them to the warden who had promised to see that they were delivered. Several chaplains stopped by before nine to ask whether they could be of any help. The prisoner thanked them all graciously, but said that, as an agnostic, he had no need of spiritual guidance. They wished him luck and said goodbye.

Across the bay, in San Francisco, it was a cold, clear day. At 8:05, the seven justices of the California Supreme Court began their deliberation on a petition for a writ of habeas corpus which George T. Davis, the condemned man's attorney-in-chief, had filed with them on Saturday afternoon. An hour later, by a 4 to 3 vote, they decided to deny the application. At 9:25, Davis begged them to grant a brief stay of execution so that he would have time to appeal once more to the United States Supreme Court. At 9:50, the stay was denied.

Five minutes later, Davis and Rosalie S. Asher, another defense lawyer, arrived breathless in the chambers of United States District Judge Louis E. Goodman. They again pleaded for just enough time to prepare the necessary papers for another appeal to the Supreme Court. While the federal judge was listening to them, it was announced in Washington that Justice William O. Douglas had refused to intervene. Goodman agreed to stay the execution for an hour and ordered a clerk to ask Celeste Hickey, his secretary, to telephone his decision to Warden Dickson. It was then 10:03. In her nervousness, Miss Hickey dialed the wrong number.

While the two lawyers were rushing to Judge Goodman's office, the man in the holding cell put on the clean white shirt which had been given to him by the guard who had brought his breakfast. At precisely ten o'clock, the cell door was unlocked and a four-man crew escorted him the thirteen steps that led to a riveted bulkhead door which opened outward into the corridor. Behind this door was an octagonal steel capsule-like chamber with apple-green walls and a domed ceiling. To the rear of the two perforated straight-backed metal chairs which faced the door were five thick glass windows. The square panes were set in five of the chamber's seven sides which projected into an observation room crowded with sixty witnesses. On benches below each window sat five guards facing the spectators. Oddly enough, one of the spectators, a Los Angeles police officer was Regina Johnson's new husband. In the spring of 1950, nearly two years after the Chessman trial, Harry Johnson had died of cancer in Alta Vista Hospital.

The four deputies accompanied the impassive prisoner into the steel chamber where they quickly strapped him into the right-hand chair. With a piece of adhesive tape, the end of an electric stethescope was attached to his chest. The clock read 10:02. One of the guards said a few comforting words to the silent figure in the chair and then the four men left the chamber. The last one out carefully shut the steel door behind him and twirled its spoked wheel until he was satisfied that the tiny cell was hermetically sealed. He then turned to Warden Dickson, who was stationed behind the only one of the chamber's windows which was hidden by venetian blinds, and said, "It's all set, sir."

It was exactly 10:03:15. Almost imperceptibly, Dickson nodded to a man in a dark business suit standing beside him. There was a slight click as the trigger released the cyanide pellets into the bucket of sulphuric acid solution under the chair in which the man sat motionless. As the invisible fumes swirled up toward his nostrils, he turned his head to the right where the witnesses were pressed up against the heavy glass windows. He was trying to say something but the hushed observers could not hear his words through the sound-proof glass. Eleanor Garner Black, a reporter for the *Los Angeles Examiner,* read his lips. "Tell Rosalie I said good-bye. It's all right," she repeated in a choked whisper. She then made a circle with her thumb and forefinger to indicate that she had understood. He just had time to smile once before his head fell forward on his chest.

Suddenly, the heavy silence in the room was broken by the shrill ring of a telephone bell. Associate Warden Louis Nelson picked up the receiver. Miss Hickey, who had finally gotten through, was on the other end. "Hold up the execution," she said, "Judge Goodman has granted a one-hour reprieve." Solemnly, the prison official informed her that it was too late. As he hung up, he looked at his watch. The hands stood at 10:04. Ten miles away, in the judge's anteroom, Rosalie Asher sobbed uncontrollably.

At 10:12, the physician who was listening intently at the free end of the stethescope, indicated to Dickson that he could hear no heartbeat. The warden signalled with his hand and a guard started the blowers which would clear the lethal gas out of the chamber in a little more than an hour. That afternoon, a hearse from the Harry M. Williams Funeral Home in nearby San Rafael backed up to the prison morgue and received the body. The next day, it was cremated in Mount Tamalpais Cemetery, according to the instructions which had eight times before been given to Mr. Williams by the dead man. The case of California versus Caryl Whittier Chessman was at long last unalterably closed.

CHRONOLOGY

May 27, 1921	Carol Whittier Chessman born, St. Joseph, Michigan.
November, 1921	Chessman family moves to Glendale.
July 15, 1937	Sentenced to Preston Industrial School for vehicle theft and burglary.
April, 1938	Released from Preston.
May 6, 1938	Arrested in Glendale for vehicle theft and forgery.
May 7, 1938	Recommitted to Preston.
June, 1939	Paroled from Preston.
October 13, 1939	Arrested for car theft; sentenced to Los Angeles County Jail and assigned to Road Camp No. 7.
June 30, 1940	Paroled from county jail.
April 28, 1941	Convicted of robbery and assault with a deadly weapon.
May 7, 1941	Sentenced to San Quentin State Prison for auto theft, assaulting a police officer and robbery.
May 27, 1943	Transferred to California Institution for Men at Chino, California.
October, 1943	Escaped from Chino.
November, 1943	Arrested in Glendale.
December 21, 1943	Convicted of robbery.
January 18, 1944	Sentenced to five years to life at San Quentin on recommitment.
August 6, 1945	Sent to maximum-security Folsom State Prison.
December 8, 1947	Paroled from Folsom.
January 3, 1948	Carl Hoelscher's Pasadena haberdashery hold-up.
January 13, 1948	Rose K. Howell's Ford coupé stolen in Pasadena.
January 17, 1948	Attempted burglary of Tarro home in Glendale.
January 18, 1948	Dr. Thomas B. Bartle held up at 4:35 A.M. near Malibu Beach.
January 18, 1948	Floyd E. Ballew and Elaine Bushaw robbed near Rose Bowl at 7:30 P.M.
January 19, 1948	Regina Johnson attacked in Flintridge Hills.

January 20, 1948   Gerald Stone and Esther Panasuk held up on Mulholland Drive.

January 22, 1948   Mary Alice Meza kidnapped.

January 23, 1948   Robbery at Town Clothiers in Redondo Beach.

January 23, 1948   Chessman and Knowles captured after a five-mile chase down Vermont Avenue; both men booked at Hollywood Police Station.

January 26, 1948   Transferred to Los Angeles County Jail.

February 18, 1948   Original informations filed in Los Angeles Superior Court.

February 20, 1948   Arraigned with Knowles. Morris Lavine appears as counsel.

February 27, 1948   Amended informations filed in Los Angeles Superior Court.

March 5, 1948   Arraigned on amended informations. V. L. Ferguson appears as counsel.

March 9, 1948   V. L. Ferguson relieved as counsel. Time to plead adjourned to March 12.

March 12, 1948   Public Defender relieved. Not guilty plea filed.

March 18, 1948   Refused services of Deputy Public Defender Al Matthews.

March-June, 1948   Visited in jail by Attorney William Roy Ives.

April 26, 1948   Motion for separate trial granted.

April 29, 1948   Refused services of Public Defender as counsel and offer of Al Matthews to act as legal advisor.

April 30, 1948   Accepted Al Matthews as legal advisor. Trial begins in Department 43, Superior Court of Los Angeles, before Judge Charles W. Fricke.

May 3, 1948   Jury of eleven women and one man impanneled.

May 21, 1948   Found guilty by jury of 17 out of 18 counts.

June 23, 1948   Court Reporter Ernest W. Perry dies after transcribing one-third of record.

June 25, 1948   Sentenced to death by Judge Fricke on two kidnapping counts, five years to life on others.

July 2, 1948   Notice of Appeal filed with Clerk, Superior Court.

July, August, 1948   Visited in jail by Rosalie S. Asher, Sacramento attorney, at request of Al Matthews.

July, 1948   Perry's notes turned over to Stanley Fraser.

September 7, 1948   Fraser employed by Los Angeles County Board of Supervisors to transcribe Perry's notes.

October 16, 1948   Letter to Board of Supervisors from Executive Committee of the Los Angeles Superior Court Reporters' Association calling Perry's notes "completely undecipherable."

November 1, 1948   Petition for writ of prohibition attacking preparation of transcript filed with California Supreme Court.

November 22, 1948   Writ of prohibition denied.

February, 1949   Rough draft of transcript sent by Fraser to Judge Fricke.

April 11, 1949   Fraser certifies portion of transcript prepared by him; copy sent to Chessman at San Quentin.

May 10, 1949   Defendant's motion attacking transcript filed with Clerk, Superior Court.

June 3, 1949   Judge Fricke certifies transcript after three-day *ex parte* hearing.

June 10, 1949   Record on appeal filed with Clerk, California Supreme Court.

June 15, 1949   Clerk writes to defendant asking him either to name an attorney to argue his appeal or make a request for the court to appoint one.

June 30, 1949   Defendant's motion to "impeach, correct, and certify record" filed.

August 15, 1949   Clerk writes again to defendant to ask if the court should appoint an attorney to argue his appeal.

August 18, 1949   After another *ex parte* hearing, Fricke again approves transcript.

September 21, 1949   Rosalie S. Asher appointed counsel to defendant.

September 23, 1949   Rosalie S. Asher's appointment as counsel terminated at defendant's request.

December 2, 1949   Hallie Chessman dies of cancer in Glendale.

March 17, 1950   United States District Judge Louis E. Goodman denies writ of habeas corpus.

May 12, 1950   Petition for writ of habeas corpus attacking transcript filed with California Supreme Court.

May 19, 1950   Writ of habeas corpus denied; appeal from order of certification dismissed; transcript augmented in two respects.

June 12, 1950   Petitions for rehearing and habeas corpus denied.

October 9, 1950   United States Supreme Court denies certiorari.

December 4, 1950   Writ of habeas corpus denied by federal court.

February 27, 1951   Federal Court of Appeals affirms denial of writ of habeas corpus.

April 6, 1951	Petition for writ of habeas corpus filed with California Supreme Court.
May 14, 1951	Certiorari denied by United States Supreme Court.
December 18, 1951	Convictions affirmed by California Supreme Court. Execution scheduled for March 28, 1952.
January 15, 1952	Petitions for rehearing and habeas corpus denied.
February 29, 1952	Stay of execution granted by Judge Jesse W. Carter.
March 7, 1952	Fricke orders warden of San Quentin to give defendant certain privileges.
March 31, 1952	United States Supreme Court denies writ of certiorari.
April 28, 1952	Petition for rehearing denied by United States Supreme Court.
June 9, 1952	Writ of habeas corpus refused by Judge Goodman. Execution scheduled for June 27, 1952.
June 23, 1952	Stay of execution granted by United States District Judge Albert Lee Stephens.
May 28, 1953	Judge Goodman's refusal upheld by federal Court of Appeals.
December 14, 1953	United States Supreme Court denies writ of certiorari.
February 1, 1954	Rehearing denied by Supreme Court; execution scheduled for May 14, 1954.
May 4, 1954	Berwyn A. Rice retained as counsel.
May 13, 1954	Rice asks Marin County Superior Court to issue writ of habeas corpus because of faulty transcript; Judge Carter signs stay of execution.
May 24, 1954	Writ of habeas denied.
July 16, 1954	Petition for writ of habeas corpus filed with California Supreme Court.
July 21, 1954	Writ of habeas corpus denied. Execution scheduled for July 30, 1954.
July 28, 1954	Fourth stay of execution signed by Judge Carter.
August 14, 1954	Petition for writ of certiorari filed with Clerk of United States Supreme Court.
August 19, 1954	Judge Carter's stay upheld by Supreme Court of California.
October 25, 1954	United States Supreme Court denies writ for certiorari "without prejudice to an application for a writ of habeas corpus in an appropriate United States District Court."

December 30, 1954	Petition for writ of habeas corpus filed with Federal District Court.
January 4, 1955	Judge Goodman dismisses writ of habeas corpus; execution scheduled for January 14, 1955.
January 11, 1955	Chief Judge William Denman of Court of Appeals grants certificate of probable cause; stay of execution ordered.
February 1, 1955	Defendant's privileges cancelled by California Supreme Court.
April 7, 1955	Court of Appeals affirms Goodman's denial of writ.
May 6, 1955	Rehearing denied; execution scheduled for July 15, 1955.
July 5, 1955	Stay of execution granted by Associate Justice Tom Clark pending appeal from Goodman's ruling.
October 17, 1955	United States Supreme Court remands case to Judge Goodman for hearing on disputed transcript.
December 8, 1955	Motion to transfer defendant to custody of United States Marshal.
December 22, 1955	Custody motion denied by Judge Goodman.
December 29, 1955	Motion to disqualify Judge Goodman on ground of "personal bias or prejudice."
December 30, 1955	Judge Goodman refuses to disqualify himself.
January 4, 1956	Defendant's motion for transfer to Alcatraz Prison during hearings denied by Goodman.
January 7, 1956	Motion to join California as a party in transcript hearings denied.
January 9, 1956	Defendant's request for free photostatic copies of Perry's notes denied.
January 10, 1956	Motion for defendant to proceed *in forma pauperis* granted.
January 16, 1956	Defendant's motion for an adjournment of transcript hearings denied but court reporter ordered to furnish him daily record of proceedings without charge.
January 16-25, 1956	Hearings before Judge Goodman in San Francisco federal court.
January 31, 1956	Goodman decides that there is no evidence of fraud in the preparation of the transcript.
October 18, 1956	Goodman's ruling upheld by Court of Appeals.
April 8, 1957	United States Supreme Court grants certiorari.
June 10, 1957	Case remanded for full hearing on preparation of transcript.

August 14, 1957	Judge Goodman gives California until December 1, 1957 to commence transcript hearing.
August 29, 1957	California Supreme Court vacates its judgments of May 19, 1950 and December 18, 1951.
September 10, 1957	Defendant ordered transferred from San Quentin to Los Angeles County Jail.
September 23 to November 22, 1957	Preliminary hearings in connection with defendant's preparation for resettlement proceedings.
November 25, 1957 to February 14, 1958	Resettlement hearings before Judge Walter R. Evans in Superior Court.
February 28, 1958	Judge Evans approves transcript with corrections.
April 2, 1958	Defendant's "Motion for Hearing and Discharge from Custody" denied by Judge Goodman.
May 1, 1958	Evans certifies transcript.
May 13, 1958	Certified transcript sent to defendant at San Quentin.
June 16, 1958	Objections to transcript filed in Superior Court by defendant.
June 19, 1958	Corrected transcript filed in California Supreme Court. Defendant informed by Clerk that his opening brief must be filed within thirty days.
July 2, 1958	Defendant files petition for mandate attacking ninety changes in transcript.
July 14, 1958	Defendant asks for permission to file opening brief by August 19, 1958.
July 16, 1958	Clerk refuses to grant extension of time until notified of the name and address of the defense attorney who would argue appeal.
July 19, 1958	Defendant informs clerk that he intended to file his opening brief himself but that he hoped to have Rosalie Asher or A. L. Wirin argue the appeal.
August 7, 1958	Extension of time to August 19, 1958 to file defense brief granted.
August 18, 1958	Time to file defense brief extended to September 3, 1958.
September 2, 1958	Defendant's opening brief attacking conviction and resettlement procedure filed.
October 2, 1958	Hearing ordered to consider ninety changes in transcript.

October 10, 1958	California granted until October 27, 1958 to file reply brief.
October 11, to November 14, 1958	Preliminary hearings in Superior Court.
November 10, 1958	California granted until ten days after filing of the re-settled record to file its brief.
November 24, 25, 1958	Settlement hearings in Superior Court.
December 2, 1958	Chessman's publisher, literary agent and attorney indicted for book-smuggling.
December 10, 1958	Defendant's motion for mandate and prohibition denied by California Supreme Court.
December 12, 1958	Judge Evans certifies transcript again.
December 18, 1958	Certified transcript received by California Supreme Court.
December 31, 1958	California's time to file reply brief extended to January 9, 1959.
January 12 ,1959	California's reply brief filed.
January 20, 1959	Defendant given until February 10 to file closing brief and supplementary brief as to the re-settlement.
February 9, 1959	Defendant's supplementary opening brief filed.
March 13, 1959	California's supplementary brief filed.
April 7, 1959	Defendant granted until May 5, 1959 to file closing brief.
April 26, 1959	Defendant's motion to file petition for habeas corpus with United States Supreme Court denied.
May 4, 1959	Defendant's closing brief filed.
May 13, 1959	Oral argument waived by both sides.
July 7, 1959	Convictions affirmed by California Supreme Court.
August 10, 1959	Execution scheduled by Judge Herbert V. Walker for October 24, 1959.
October 15, 1959	Executive clemency hearing before Governor Edmund G. Brown.
October 19, 1959	Governor refuses to grant clemency.
October 21, 1959	Stay of execution granted by Mr. Justice William O. Douglas "pending the timely filing and consideration of a petition for certiorari."
October 31, 1959	Book-smuggling indictments dismissed by District Court of Appeals.

December 14, 1959	Writ of certiorari denied by United States Supreme Court.
December 23, 1959	Dismissal of book-smuggling indictments upheld by California Supreme Court.
January 11, 1960	Rehearing denied; execution scheduled for February 19, 1960.
January 28, 1960	Hearing before Judge Goodman in United States District Court.
January 29, 1960	Goodman refuses to pass on accuracy of Fraser's transcript.
February 8, 1960	Chief Judge Richard H. Chambers of the United States Court of Appeals affirms Goodman's decision.
February 15, 1960	United States Court of Appeals denies stay of execution.
February 17, 1960	United States Supreme Court denies defendant's motion to file original writ of habeas corpus.
February 18, 1960	California Supreme Court refuses to recommend executive clemency.
February 18, 1960	Governor Edmund G. Brown grants sixty-day reprieve and recommends abolition of capital punishment to state legislature.
March 2, 1960	Judge Clement D. Nye signs Death Warrant for May 2, 1960.
March 9, 1960	California Supreme Court refuses to annul Death Warrant.
March 10, 1960	Senate Judiciary Committee votes against submitting governor's proposal to full legislature.
April 25, 1960	Application for stay of execution denied by Mr. Justice Douglas.
April 29, 1960	California Supreme Court again refuses to recommend executive clemency.
May 2, 1960	California Supreme Court denies petition for habeas corpus, at 9:05 A.M.; at 10:03 Judge Goodman indicates that he would grant one-hour reprieve if not too late.
May 2, 1960	Defendant executed at San Quentin at 10:03:15 A.M.

INDEX

INDEX

301